BALKYMOR

THE TALIPES EFFECT

All inquiries should be addressed to:

Book Domain LLC.
543 E Louise Dr Phoenix, Az 85050

Ordering Information:
Amount Deals. Special rebates are accessible on the amount bought by corporations, associations, and others. For points of interest, contact the distributor at the address above.

Printed in the United States of America.

ISBN-13	Paperback	978-1-964100-69-2
	eBook	978-1-964100-68-5

BALKYMOR

THE TALIPES EFFECT

JIM CURRIE

A STORY LOOSELY BASED
ABOUT A YOUNG SCOTS LAD
BORN WITH A CLUB FOOT.
INSPIRED BY THE FOUR WOMEN IN HIS LIFE
DOREEN, MY WIFE DOLLY, MY MOTHER “MA”
ELAINE, MY DAUGHTER
KELLY, MY GRAND DAUGHTER
“MY HOPE IS CONSTANT IN THEE”

A doer not a dreamer, tis better to die trying than to live to an old age dreaming.
Elaine Currie, Oct 7, 1983

If you go through life worrying about all the bad things that could happen, you could convince yourself that doing nothing is best.
Unknown Author

CONTENTS

BALKYMOR 1 1

SCOTLAND 1933-1960 1

BALKYMOR 2 8

BALKYMOR 3 12

BALKYMOR 4 21

BALKYMOR 5 26

BALKYMOR 6 34

BALKYMOR 7 39

BALKYMOR 8 59

BALKYMOR 9 76

CANADA, 1960-1983 76

GOING HOME OCTOBER 1982 (SCOTLAND CHAPTER) 120

BALKYMOR 10 138

THE SAUDI ARABIA ADVENTURE, 1983-1988 138

THE CYPRUS 25TH ANNIVERSARY TRIP,

NOVEMBER 1984 175

ADDENDUM 1 240
OCTOBER 29, 1998 240
EPILOGUE 247
ADDENDUM 2 248
KELLY LYNN CURRIE 252
ABOUT JIM CURRIE 253

March 27/1997

Years of positive confidence in dealing with what life had to offer evaporated in a few minutes as I sat in a wheelchair with tubes supplying vital fluids to my recovering body from a full knee joint replacement while holding my first granddaughter Kelly in my arms. The tears began to flow with a mixture of absolute joy and despair as my hands caressed her 2 tiny malformed feet and my own discomfort was quickly forgotten as I thought of what the coming weeks, months and possibly years would bring to this beautiful child and her parents.

It seemed like just yesterday when our first grandchild (Jake) was born and the first question on all of our lips was "Are his feet ok?", "Yes" replied the doctor and we were overcome with relief. Somehow with Kelly this question had not seemed necessary, genetics maybe after all hadn't been a real concern "we thought". This was not to be the case as we discovered some time later.

After the initial outburst of emotion, for some reason I felt calm and peaceful as I looked into her puffy little eyes and then she cried for her mum. The nurses wheeled me back down the hospital corridor to the elevator still with some tears in my eyes where I would return to the recovery room floor with my own thoughts of **"where this all started almost 60 years ago."**

BALKYMOR 1

SCOTLAND 1933-1960

Rumblings of discontent rattled throughout Europe in the 1930s following the Great Depression, the British government and many other European countries were concerned about where the German economy and the people lead by the emerging Adolph Hitler were heading with their philosophies of life, but somehow the lads from Borrowstouness (Bo'ness) in Scotland seemed unaware of what was developing as they had more pressing local issues to deal with. The primary issue was to find a job and earn a living in either the Kinneil Colliery or the "woodyard" which was located near the town harbour. The other important issues to most of the young men at this time of their lives was to make one of the local football teams, preferably Bo'ness Corinthians, or to find a pretty young girl at the area dances held most Saturday nights. The visit to the dancing only came after the traditional gambling behind the coal bings which seemed to be everywhere in West Lothian and a few pints at the local pub to provide the courage to face the "lassies".

One such young lad "Geordie Currie" had left school at 12 years old, as many young men before him had done to earn some money and contribute to the family income which was never enough to feed and clothe the kids. The family included several brothers and sisters from a mixture of relationships which to this day are still unclear. It seems that when we look back that most of the families from this area and in this era had more than one marriage or arrangement of living and it was of little concern as long as the families were fed, clothed and had a place to sleep.

Geordie was a simple uncomplicated man with very little formal education but gifted with above average common sense and a good sense of humour who enjoyed soccer, drinking smoking, dancing and gambling. A spirited young man who seemed to let the world happen to him and also enjoyed moaning and complaining as well as having a good argument which often landed him in trouble as he became a bit obnoxous while under the "influence". Geordie and his brothers were fiercely loyal to each other and never far removed from a good scrap.

My Dads mum Granny Currie, Mary Ann Brogan, born 1880 daughter of Irish parents John Brogan and Bridget Cramer was the catalyst for the family that found itself in the "Derry Close", Bo'ness living in a small council house on the second floor of a two-storey building which had a wee balcony overlooking the courtyard where all the bairns played. We found out years later when such things became important that Granny Currie had more than one partner, which may have accounted for the different features within the brothers and sisters.

Auld Jock was the "man of the house" during Geordie's formative years, a crusty old chap who seems to have given everyone a hard time with his authoritative nature and little regard for the finer things in life. The mystery to all the family members was how Granny Currie had ever got involved with Auld Jock in the first place. Turns out that he was brother to her deceased husband.

Geordie was a product of the first marriage for Granny Currie as were 3 other brothers and 2 sisters, the 2 other brothers we can only assume were Auld Jocks kids.

Geordie followed his z older brothers into the woodyard after weeks of lining up each morning hoping to get employment and finally being selected by the day foreman who had been convinced it might be in his best interest to hire "our wee brother" can't imagine what other alternatives he had been offered, apparently the Currie boys had developed a reputation by this time.

The close-knit family included James the oldest son who was quite refined, good natured and a young gentleman who had decided at a very early age that Bo'ness wasn't for him and set about working towards this goal, which he achieved some years later. John or "Jock" as he was called was the youngest of the 3 brothers from Granny Currie's first marriage was not only Geordie's wee brother but also his best pal too and their lives followed similar paths with each looking out for the other in the early days, Jock could hold his own in most situations but wasn't as aggressive as his elder brother was.

Mary the elder sister was the same cut of cloth as James but didn't have the same desire to leave her hometown and eventually married one Davie McLardy a fun loving man who was in the merchant navy and loved the sea almost as much as he loved his wife, Davie always had many stories to tell of his travels and adventures which were often told with tongue in cheek and with a mischievous smile which made it difficult to determine the truth from figments of his imagination.

Bridget, Bunny and young James (the Trawlerman) completed the family, they all seemed to resemble Auld Jock in one way or another (looks, behavior, manners) but it was assumed Bridget was a product of the first marriage. Bunny and young James were rough and tumble characters who enjoyed a fight most Saturday nights and were always there for any of the family who may end up in trouble. Bunny's claim to fame was while shaking hands he would somehow take the person's thumb and bend it back to submission, for some reason this gave him great satisfaction?

The whole Currie family loved the game of football (fitbae) and were staunch supporters of the local junior team, Bo'ness Utd and also any team that the kids were involved in during their formative years. Bo'ness Utd always seemed to have a very competitive team in spite of a limited budget and had success in winning league championships as well as lifting the Scottish Cup on more than one occasion. One such occasion was when my dad decided to take me on the supporter's bus "special from man of war street to Hampden Park to see Bo'ness Utd play Shawfield in the Scottish Junior Cup final, we won 2-1, it was particularly memorable because I went with one welly boot and a leather boot on my club foot (took some kidding about that) but of course we had won the cup and had a great day. While the Currie family from Bo'ness was trying to make ends meet and the individual members were pursuing their individual goals (known as living your life in these days) a young woman called Dolly Fell, the daughter of Elizabeth Fraser Fell and her second husband Wullie had finished school and was also trying to earn a living at whatever was available. The family lived in #4 Upper Bow Edinburgh, close to the Lawnmarket (the Lawnie to the locals) which leads to the historic Edinburgh Castle.

Dolly who had a very good relationship with her family but in particular with her younger sister named Jean and an older brother Alec who adored her and was responsible for the nickname "Dolly" because in his opinion that was what she looked like when she was born.

Two other brothers and sisters were the result of the first marriage to William Burns who was a saddler from Moffat in the borders. The brothers were named Wullie and John and the sisters were Lily and Mary and the family seemed to work well together in the early years.

Dolly was successful in finding employment in the Edinburgh rubber mill where the pay was relatively good, but the work was demanding and the hours long, Dolly however was up to the challenge and with her friendly outgoing attitude soon made many good friends at "the mill". With growing confidence and now earning a living Dolly was encouraged to start getting out and about, this of course meant dancing and the odd lager at the local pub. Dancing became a favourite pastime with Dolly and her friends and soon they started going to the dances out of town to places such as Balerno, Broxburn, Queensferry, Dalkeith and even as far afield as Bo'ness on occasion.

Saturday nights were the highlight of the week and all the lassies looked forward to the dancing since most of the young men were in good spirits after playing football, gambling and having a few pints at their local pub.

It was somewhere around the fall of 1933 at a dance in the Carriden Hall in Bo'ness on a Saturday night where Geordie's team "the Corinthians" which included his brother Bunny were celebrating an important victory over one of the local rival teams that Geordie first met Dolly. It would be so romantic to say it was love at first sight, but such was not the case. Geordie who had enjoyed a few pints caught sight of this very attractive new face at the dancing and although Dolly accepted his invitation to dance, found him to be a little bit loud and offensive for her taste, his confident arrogant attitude fueled by several pints helped her decide one dance on this particular night was as much as she could handle. However, Geordie was smitten and made a right nuisance of himself for the rest of the night. His invitation to accompany Dolly home was graciously declined but could have proved embarrassing if he had found out this nice-looking girl who he had taken a fancy too was from Edinburgh, some zo miles away.

Dolly had some interesting stories to tell her friends at "the mill" the following week and seemed pleased at the response of her mates who informed her that Geordie was one of the better-known football players on the Corinthians and she decided maybe she would try the dancing in Bo'ness one more time. Meanwhile Geordie had been bragging to his "Ma" about this lovely lass who had caught his eye at the dancing and was sort of fabricating his own version of what had happened, but unfortunately for him his brothers, Bunny and Jock were listening and gave "Ma" their version of Geordie's night out. Needless to say, Geordie got his blessings but also some encouragement to pursue this young lass who had caught his eye.

It was a coincidence that a very important football match was to be played the next weekend and Bunny and Jock knew that Geordie had an auld enemy on the opposing team that was more concerned about kicking lumps out of Geordie than winning the game, so they had agreed to set up a meeting after the game at the crown royal pub. The purpose of the meeting was for the two auld enemies to try and settle their differences one way or another. Auld Jock, the father figure at the time was aware of what was developing and looked forward to the weekend with great anticipation, Granny Currie was not to know as she would just get upset.

Saturday arrived and the game was played in great spirit with Geordie and Jock Purves at each other's throats for most of the game with warnings to both from the referee on numerous occasions. The match ended in a 1-1 draw and as the players walked off the field Geordie took a swing at Jock Purves but Bunny and John were able to keep them apart with the promise of settling this later after a few pints.

Meanwhile, oblivious to what was developing, the mill girls from Edinburgh were on their way to Bo'ness for a night of fun and dancing, they thought.

At the pub after the game Bunny, Jock and two of Jock Purves pals were making the arrangements for the lads to settle this issue once and for all. The plan was to let them have a few pints then take them to the large lavatory where they could go "at it" with the doors held closed by "their respective friends". Dolly and her pals were in the pub and were somewhat disappointed at the lack of attention they were receiving, not knowing of course about what was happening. Geordie decided to talk to Dolly, bought her a drink and said, "I will see you later at the dance" Dolly replied "We'll see".

Bunny and Jock ushered the two combatants towards the lavatory "arena" and were told to settle their differences and the others would watch for the local police and warn them if problems arose. The way the story was told afterwards is that Geordie and Jock knocked lumps off each other in a fierce fight which was only interrupted by the police arriving and all their "friends" having deserted their posts leaving them both at it. Geordie and Jock Purves became the very best of friends after this event and showed up later at the dance all bruised and battered but happy to have been freed by the police with just a warning about future behaviour. Their "friends" were all anxious to buy drinks and make up. Dolly was upset at the sight of this young man dancing with her with swollen lips and mouth and some minor cuts, but she was quite chuffed to be dancing with this chap who seemed to have so many friends. Geordie introduced Dolly to his brothers and teammates and the two danced and talked for the rest of what had been an eventful night. Dolly went home with her friends that night having enjoyed the evening but not sure of how she really felt.

BALKYMOR 2

Life in Bo'ness and the Upper Bow in Edinburgh went on as usual except that Dolly and Geordie were now seeing each other on a regular basis, Saturday nights at the dancing and the occasional night out at the pictures. The distance between the two homes seemed to shrink as their relationship grew. They spent a lot of time-sharing stories about their respective families. Dolly's relatives seemed to be migrating to "the Lawnie" when council houses became available and by a weird coincidence Geordie's younger brother Jock ended up in Riddles Court years later. Geordie's brother James had moved to Glasgow, Bunny was now working in Kinneil Colliery, young James was off to the trawlers, Mary and Bridget had been courted and wooed by two local lads and were now married.

It became obvious to both families that Dolly and Geordie would get married in the not to distant future in spite of Geordie continuing with his gambling, drinking and soccer interests, Dolly was excited about her rough-cut diamond and was convinced that when they got married "it would be different". Geordie had met most of Dolly's family and established a fairly sound relationship with her brothers and sisters but Granny Fell was a different kettle of fish. She was not impressed with this brash confident young man from out of town and was less impressed when she discovered his bad habits (by her definition).

On July 12/1935 Dolly and Geordie got married, Jean was the bridesmaid and Alex fell was the fill in best man for Geordie's younger brother Jock who had become incapacitated! The two flower girls were Christine Stupart, Geordie's niece and Isa Burns, Dolly's niece. From all accounts the wedding was a huge success but unfortunately Dolly was to experience the first of many disappointments in her young life due to excessive drinking by Geordie.

In spite of a rather fragile start to their marriage they set about obtaining a small council house that became available in Bo'ness at 7 Balkymor Terrace much to the delight of Geordie and his friends and family and dismay of Granny Fell and her family because Dolly had to give up her job at "the mill". A whole new way of life was about to begin for Dolly.

Dolly and Geordie were very much in love and enjoyed each other's company for the most part, but Geordie continued on with his work, football, gambling, drinking, smoking as though he was still single much to Dolly's dismay. She shared her feelings with Grannie Fell who really didn't have much to say except to remind her "that I warned you". Grannie Fell did advise her daughter to get a wee job until the bairns come along. Dolly got a wee job and tried to get involved as much as possible with Geordie and his brothers and pals with limited success but the extra money coming in gave her a bit of independence and she started to buy things for their house. Saturday nights were still a lot of fun and Dolly became a favourite at the local pub as she was outgoing and willing to take her turn and sing when requested, seems that ladies singing in the pubs was a bit unusual in Bo'ness.

Geordie's Ma was very fond of Dolly as were his brothers and sisters, everyone waited anxiously for the first baby to come along but according to Bunny "they must be doing something wrong" and Geordie was the subject of some good-natured kidding for at least two years while other folks seemed to be having babies without really trying.

The wee house in Balkymor Terrace was starting to look quite nice by the standards in these times, what with two incomes and nae bairns, yes, the Currie's were doing away just nicely. Wouldn't you know it but in the spring of 1937 as the prospect of a war in Europe was looming Dolly gave birth to the biggest baby girl born in Bo'ness since they started keeping records, Elisabeth Fraser Fell Currie 13lbs 4Ozs was born and the families rejoiced as Dolly slowly recovered from the difficult birth.

Needless to say, Geordie was fair chuffed and did his share of bragging to his brothers and mates, a good few pints were scoffed on the night the baby was born. Geordie now had some additional responsibilities and the work at the woodyard was becoming just a means to an end, not very satisfying but the possibility of getting drafted into the army was becoming a reality as the situation in Europe was deteriorating by the month. The baby was nicknamed "Betty" and became the focus for Dolly and George as they went about everyday life in Bo'ness, Geordie's interests were changing as they do when a family comes along but he still enjoyed his soccer and pint after the games.

Dolly spent lots of time with the baby and enjoyed her trips to Edinburgh to visit her family, sometimes with Geordie, other times on her own. By now several members of her family had moved into council houses near "the Lawnie" close to Grannie Fell's house which made it convenient for visiting the stork paid a second visit to Dolly and I was born on November 12/1938, James Currie (named after Geordie's elder brother) but to be known as "Jim" weighing in at 11lbs 8ozs, considered a good weight but a featherweight compared to my "big sister" Betty.

Geordie's delight in having a wee laddie, with thoughts of him playing fitbae in the future were short lived when it became apparent that something was not quite right with my wee "laddies left foot".

A visit to the Doctor after six weeks of anxiety for my parents confirmed the worst, I had been born with a congenital deformity in my left foot (Talipes) more commonly known as a "clubfoot" which would require immediate attention if it was to be functional at all. The Doctor informed my parents that this would require many visits to the specialists in the Princess Margaret Rose Hospital and the Sick Childrens Hospital in Edinburgh for frequent remedial surgery.

Obviously, this was going to have a huge impact on Dolly and Geordie's life and would also have a huge impact on Betty who was one and a half years old and used to lots of attention by now. Dolly had decided that she was responsible for my problem, and nobody could convince her otherwise, including Geordie, the doctors, or any members of either family. This would have a huge effect on everyone over the years to come, Dolly seemed to dedicate her life to "that poor wee laddie".

"That poor wee laddie" as Ma called me wasn't much aware of what was going on in the early years of life but while Ma was shuttling back and forth to the hospitals in Edinburgh, Betty was shuttled between Granny Currie, Granny Fell, my dad and occasionally an aunt or Uncle who would help out. Dad was doing his best to work as much as possible to pay for additional expenses, look after the house and spend time with Betty with the knowledge that the war was looming and he could be called up at any time. The future didn't look too promising.

BALKYMOR 3

My earliest recollections of Balkymor as our small house in Bo'ness became known as, are sketchy to say the least, I remember a very small living area with some chairs and a kitchen table, the kitchen had a tiny hand basin with a small working area to the left. Two very small recesses hidden by curtains served as "the bedrooms" and unfortunately the lavatory was outside in a common hallway.

I have a recollection of the horse and cart which plodded up the slight incline to the houses delivering St Cuthberts milk to those who could afford it, the horse would stop just outside our door and the milkman would put a piece of wood called a chock behind the wheels of the cart to stop it from rolling back. The milkman always came and picked me up to go see "the horsey" which had a mind of its own and would move forward when it thought the milk and rolls were delivered, I was already getting special attention due to what people were apparently calling my handicap.

By now it was the early 1940s and Dad was off to the Royal Artillery to train as a gunner, later to be assigned to the Merchant Navy on ships plying the north Atlantic. Ma was still travelling with me on the bus as often as was necessary to the hospitals in Edinburgh for my surgery or therapy and Granny Fell was trying to get our family to move back to Edinburgh since Geordie was away all the time. Betty was getting close to starting school, and this was another reason the move to Edinburgh seemed to make sense to Granny Fell.

When Geordie was home on leave Dolly raised the issue with great trepidation and got the response she had anticipated "she is just an interfering auld bugger" said Geordie as he stormed out the house on his way to the pub where such matters were usually discussed with the locals. This time the locals had a surprise for Geordie as they all came to the conclusion that all things considered it might be the thing to do, what with Dolly having to carry the laddie into Edinburgh so often.

Granny Currie had a wee chat with Geordie and was able to convince him that it would be best for Dolly and the two bairns to pack up and leave Balkymor and move to the upper bow in Edinburgh and live with Granny Fell since it appeared it was going to be a long war in Europe, and he could be gone for very long periods of time. Dolly and her young family moved during Geordie's home leave, this was to be the beginning of a very turbulent time in our lives. The war years (1939-1945) were filled with all kinds of wee stories and also some significant events and I can only comment on those events that seemed important to me at the time and as they related to our family and friends.

My Uncle Wullie Burns was made exempt from active service in the forces due to being hearing impaired (rather crudely defined as deaf in these days) and had decided to set up a chimney sweep/bricklayer/odd job business in the Lawnmarket working out of an old storeroom in Riddles Court. He had acquired an old two-wheel cart which he used to carry the tools of the trade and pulled behind him as he went about trying to establish a business for himself in the area. By an interesting coincidence my Uncle John Burns was also exempt from active service as he was considered essential services personnel in the Custom and Excise department, you can only imagine the stick that the two "Burns boys" took from all the other family members and friends who were drafted into active service.

Uncle Davy Mclardy in Bo'ness had been in the Merchant Navy for years and made the decision to stay with this assignment while my Uncle Jock Stupart had serious health problems and was allowed to continue work at the Shell Refinery in nearby Grangemouth. My Dad, and Uncle's, James Currie, Bunny Currie, Jimmy Currie (the Trawler man), Davy Gibb and Alex Fell went into the army while young Jock Currie opted for the Navy, the men accepted their lot in life and left their women and kids behind in tears not really sure when or if they would see each other again. Such is the reality of any war where the choices of the man in the street are very limited.

The business that Uncle Wullie had set up prospered right from the get-go, he became very busy cleaning chimneys, repairing brickwork and any general maintenance work in the area. He had decided that when the war was over God willing, he would ask the other male members of the associated families to get involved and expand the business. In the meantime, he was providing very well for his immediate family, wife Isa, daughter Isa, and his mother-in-Law Granny Redpath who was blind and had been bedridden for several years.

Uncle Wullie was a happy soul who enjoyed life and was always looking out for others, so needless to say while my dad was away at the war, he made sure my ma, Betty and I were looked after. I remember on one occasion he wanted to take me to Hampden Park to see Scotland playing in a really important International football match and we were actually going down the steps at a place called the Mound which leads you to the railway station where all the football specials leave from when my Ma came running after us, she was crying and had decided I really should not go as she would only worry about me.

Uncle Wullie couldn't convince her I would be okay, so I didn't get to go. Another incident I recall about Uncle Wullie was when he was looking out his window onto the Lawnmarket he saw a man being attacked by two young thugs and rushed down to help out, the two young men turned on my uncle, he ended up with a broken jaw. He spent the next six weeks with his jaw wired shut and drinking soup through a straw. So much for being a Good Samaritan, he used to say, but he remained a compassionate human being.

My Dad "Geordie" although conscripted in the Royal Artillery was being trained as an ack-ack gunner and would serve most of his time on the merchant ships which had been fitted with guns. He had some great stories to tell about his ships being attacked and shooting down some "Gerry planes" but the credibility of his stories was always in question by his brothers and in-laws but he took the kidding in good spirit when he came home on leave.

One of his favourite stories I recall included how he suffered his most serious injury during the "war", damaging a cartilage in his right knee while playing football for his company team during a match in England. He spent six months assigned to a very pleasant English home recuperating wearing the traditional "blue" pyjamas which all" wounded" personnel wore while being treated royally by the staff.

Another story he often shared with anyone who would listen was the night he was on duty on one of the merchant ships which was under attack, and he personally shot down one of the German planes. According to my dad he had managed to retrieve and smuggle a piece of the plane which he brought home for my sister and I. We were suitably impressed and bragged about our dad to our friends but alas the rest of the family didn't buy Dad's version of the story.

Meanwhile my dad's best pal and younger brother Jock was in the Navy but unfortunately the ships he was being assigned to always seemed to be in trouble and often were sunk, but he seemed to survive whatever happened and undaunted he would be re-assigned and head back into the action. His claim to fame was being assigned to the HMS Hood in the Mediterranean and somewhere near Malta it was also sunk but not before causing great destruction to the German Navy boats in the area. When the crew of the HMS Hood finally made it back to Britain on leave, they were welcomed as heroes by the press and friends and family. Unfortunately, some didn't make it back home and the medals that were struck for their efforts did little to console their families. The special medal was awarded to all the crew members for their efforts against the German dictator.

My Ma, sister Betty and I were settling in quite well at Granny Fell's house in Edinburgh at #4 Upper Bow close to other family members, Ma had got a job at Ross's Garage near Morningside and was kept very busy looking after all of us while putting in 40 to 50 hours a week at work, on top of this I was in and out of hospitals as the Doctors were trying to correct my club foot and of course my Ma was asked to ensure my foot was getting all the necessary daily therapy and massaging as was prescribed by Professor Stirling and Doctor Aird, the specialists at the Sick Childrens.

Hospital near the meadows. The walk to the hospital through the meadows was about 2 miles long and my Ma carried me all the way there and back as often as was necessary, no wonder she ended up with a bad back many years later.

Granny Fell was a great help to Ma in her own way but she seemed to change dramatically when Dad was home on leave, their relationship had never improved from the early days and of course when Dad was on leave "he needed" time with the men for a pint and to watch football games that continued on through the war years. The situation was so bad that on more than one occasion we were asked as a family to leave the house.

By now Auntie Jean and Uncle Davie lived on the same floor next door to Granny Fell in #4 Upper Bow but on the occasions, we were thrown out they couldn't put us up as they barely had enough room for themselves. Any way as Auntie Jean put it, we don't want to fall out with Granny Fell. So back we would go to Granny Currie's and Auld Jock's in Bo'ness where different problems would await our family.

Auld Jock didn't like having "greetin faced" bairns to deal with and after a few weeks we were in trouble again. He liked to have his few nips and pints on a daily basis and come home to a quiet house which of course wasn't possible with Geordie and Dolly's bairns around. This caused no end of trouble for the good natured and kind Granny Currie. The silence was deafening when he got home, we could hear the wall clock tick and Auld Jock pealing in the sink while Ma kept all of us as quiet as she could in the small back bedroom.

It seems to me we were like a rubber ball bouncing back and forth from Bo'ness to the Lawnie in Edinburgh for about 3 or 4 years while Dad was in the army which I am sure disrupted my sister Betty's schooling, but she always seemed to do well in class and was always in the top 3 in the class.

All this disruption had a serious effect on my Ma's health, and it was only when Dad was away on service that Granny Fell would have us back at the Upper Bow as she realized "Dolly" had her hands full and was showing early signs of a nervous breakdown.

We had moved to Edinburgh again and Betty got enrolled back into Castlehill School and she was doing well, Ma had got her job back at Ross's Garage and things seemed to be going well, with

Dad away at the war. I was making progress with what had become known as my gammy leg and Granny Fell was happy to have someone helping to pay the bills. Ma always seemed to manage a special treat for dinner on a Friday and we will aways remember the mouthwatering "spare ribs" that came from a butcher's shop up at Morningside near Ross's Garage. The other treats we had came from "Davie the butchers" who had his shop round the corner from us on the Lawnmarket, he always gave Ma special cuts of meat and good stock for Granny Fell to make soup. He was a really nice man who enjoyed having Betty and me around while he was working.

Granny Fell was doing her best but from what I remember she wasn't what I would call a "happy granny" but maybe under the circumstances that was understandable as she would often comment to my Ma "how come all the other families seem to be managing on their own?" Poor Ma she had no answer to that, but she resolved to pursue her "ain house" through the local council in Edinburgh. She gave forth the argument that she had a wee laddie who needed special care and his own room, but it would be some time before this would happen.

Living at Granny Fell's house with Dad away at the war was quite comfortable and we had many memorable moments, usually Betty and I would be put to bed around 7pm and of course neither one of us was very tired at that cruel time to go to bed we thought! But we had some good blethers about the day and fun annoying each other to the constant chant from the small living room, "you had better be quiet or I will skelp your bums", which was more just a veiled threat than anything serious.

One night after Betty and I had quietened down I was at the back of the 3/4 bed I shared with my Ma and Betty and I started picking at what was left of the wallpaper, no sensible reason but I was just doing it. Dozens of wee bugs and fleas started coming out from under the wallpaper and I was so scared I would get a row for picking at the wallpaper I couldn't tell Betty who was lying next to me half sleeping till I couldn't stand it anymore and I started crying. I was probably about four or five years old at this time. When Betty did turn around to see what was wrong with me, she saw all these wee beasties crawling all over the bed and let out an almighty scream. Granny and Ma came running through to the bedroom and almost had a fit when they see what had happened. Granny went to the nearest phone booth and called the city council right away and the housing inspector came as soon as he could. We had to move out for a few days living with relatives wherever there was space available until the house was fumigated and declared ok by the health department.

Although Ma tried to convince me it wasn't my fault I have never attempted to pick at wallpaper since.

I was able to crawl about in my early days and now had a small caliper attached to the first pair of boots I wore to try and keep my left foot straight after the first few operations, I also wore a metal cast bandaged to my foot for sleeping at night.

Occasionally when the wailing sirens went off (a sound that stays with you forever) we had to be wrapped up and taken to the "shelters" that had been built under Johnstone Terrace and I can remember asking my Ma "what was all the noise about" but she didn't tell me about the German planes that were trying to hit strategic targets close to Edinburgh, she just replied "oh wheesht and go back to sleep". As if we could sleep in the wooden bunks underground and everyone scared to death and breathless with excitement, some even messed their underwear, and I must confess to being one of them. Suddenly the "all clear" would sound and we would all make our way back to the house. Once again though with me having a metal cast on my foot, poor auld Ma had to carry me there and back. Betty and Granny helped in any way they could.

How they managed to keep smiling with the wailing sirens, the bombing, shortages of everything from food to clothes is way beyond me.

Granny Fell always loved cats much to my Dad's dismay but she said her "Tibby" (a big Persian cat) kept all the mice away from the house and it seems there was lots around in the "Auld" toon. Ma often related the story to our relatives in later years after Tibby had died and was buried in (Grannies Green") that Dad who did not like cats, was sitting in front of the fire one night he was home on leave and a big mouse ran up his trouser leg. Seems Dad was running around daft trying to get rid of the mouse and was yelling at Granny Fell "where the hell is Tibby when we need her?", Granny quietly replied "call yourself a soldier".

BALKYMOR 4

In 1943 having spent a fair bit of time in a wheelchair while recovering from corrective surgery I become well known as the wee laddie whose wheelchair was chained to the gate at Tollbooth St Johns Church. My Ma had decided it would be good for me to be out in the fresh air as much as possible and she would take the wheelchair down first, set it up chained to the gate then come back upstairs to the house and then carry me down all wrapped up according to the weather that day. The bus drivers got to know me and would wave to me as they drove past going on their different routes, the neighbors basically adopted me and spoiled me rotten with sweeties and the like. This wasn't so bad after all, I was becoming a bit of a celebrity it seemed. The kids in the neighbourhood would stop and talk to me on their way to wherever and people in general would give me a few minutes of their time. I didn't realize till years later how important talking and listening to people would become in my life ahead. Mrs. Robinson on the second floor at #1 Upper Bow was one of my favourites, she always had Smiths Crisps with the wee blue bag of salt, or McGowans Highland Toffee and lemonade of some sort readily available for me. What a nice old lady she was and even as I got older, she would always be at the window and throw down some sweeties.

Betty was attending Castlehill School and doing well, Ma enrolled me in that school in September of 1943. I was once again very fortunate as my first teacher was a Miss Abernethy who happened to be a spinster and because I was handicapped, she decided I would be her "pet". Schoolwork turned out to be something I really enjoyed and for some reason I always did very well in most subjects. So, because I was the teacher's "pet", and I was doing so well with most subjects I soon became the target for the troublemakers that are in all schools. It turned out I had a hidden ally in the class by the name of Norman Hanlon ("Boko") who even at this very early age had become a gang leader of the Valdor gang who hung out near Tollcross at the "Valdor Café".

"Boko" decided I needed looking after and became my minder all the way through primary school, the message was out, don't mess with Jim Currie or you will have to answer to "Boko". You know to this day I can honestly say we hardly spoke two words in all these years but he was always there for me?

One particular incident comes to mind, I was in the playground with some friends when a bully who was in my class was giving me a hard time (Frankie Pullar from the High Street) for some reason he hit me on the head with an empty HP sauce bottle and it left a bump. That night at home Ma was bone combing my hair for lice and she kept hitting the bump and I would withdraw from her until finally I had to tell her what had happened, she was mad and took me to see the Headmaster the next day. Frankie Pullar claimed I was annoying him, so he had hit me with a "kipper", both Ma and the Headmaster laughed and reprimanded Frankie. When "Boko" got wind of this he gave Frankie such a beating I was never under threat again. I learned years later that "Boko" had evolved to a life of crime around Tollcross area and spent lots of time in Saughton Prison as the result of gang fights and petty thieving. Despite all this I believe there was some good in "Boko" somewhere!

The Historical surroundings we lived in at the Upper Bow, the Castle, Royal Mile, Greyfriars Bobby, Deacon Brodie's Tavern, Holyrood Palace, Gladstones Land, Ramsay Gardens, The Witches Well, St Giles Cathedral, Riddles Court, James Court, the Bridge's, Art Gallery, the Museum (the list could go on and on) were all secondary to every day existence, it was only years later we would realize how important all this was to our Scottish history.

Castlehill School had its own claim to fame with a section of the school called Cannonball House (now a whisky heritage centre originally built in the 16th century) during one of the many battles during the siege of 1745 a cannon had been fired from the Castle and became imbedded in the building which now housed the school or so the story goes, another explanation is that the ball marked the level to which the water could rise by gravity from the city's first piped water system coming from Comiston Springs to the Castle Hill reservoir which is still in use to this day.

By this time, I was able to get around one way or another between remedial operations, when strong enough I would discard the wheelchair, use crutches or walking sticks while using the caliper attached to my left boot and shuffle around, I was happy just to be up and about. When Dad came home, I was always quite chuffed to show him what I could do. Occasionally he would roll a football to me, and I would do my damdest to get it back to him. My love and passion for fitbae was inside and real and I think Dad knew this. He decided while he was home on leave to take me to Easter Road to see the Hibs play his team Glasgow Celtic. Celtic won 4-1 but I fell in love with the Hibs much to Dad's dismay. My most vivid memories of this first time at a match were first of all waiting outside a pub with a bag of my favourite Smiths Crisps and a Fanta drink and secondly him lifting me over the turnstile so I didn't have to pay to get in. My final instructions on the way home were "now son don't be telling your Ma I went for a pint okay".

Granny Fell could always tell when Dad had a couple of pints, and it didn't seem to matter how hard he tried when home on leave they were still at odds most of the time much to my Ma's dismay. Other than this strained relationship life was going on all around us, the war seemed to be moving toward some conclusion according to the family discussions I heard, and the men were now talking about what they would do when they were demobbed. Uncle Wullie Burns was still hoping to expand his wee business but my Dad said "famIly and business interests should be kept separate" and I think my Ma agreed with him.

During this period of time I was fortunate enough to be included with the Crippled Childrens Society on bus trips out of town on weekends, on one such trip to Rosewell a small village south of Edinburgh out in the country I fell off a swing and broke my arm, the poor nurse who was responsible for us felt just awful but as my Ma explained to her I was now becoming a bit too adventurous for my own good, "how did Ma know I was doing things on the swing I wasn't supposed to be doing?"

Consistent with my occasional mobility opportunities and my adventurous spirit my sister Betty took me and a couple of school pals down to Princess Street gardens on a Saturday morning to see the puppet show and, on the way, home I was climbing on the hand rail at the Mound (a steep incline) and wouldn't you know it I slipped and got my arm punctured by the spike on the railings. Betty was beside herself with fear thinking about what Ma would say, was dripping blood and bawling my eyes out "cause I didn't want to go to hospital ever again" when a man and woman who just happened to be passing took us all home, picked up Ma and off to the hospital we went. Several stitches and a couple of hours later we were back home again and Ma and Granny Fell were discussing "what are we going to do about that laddie?"

At Castlehill School, although I couldn't play football at this particular time because of my foot I was a staunch supporter of the "Canaries" the school team, they didn't win many games, but it was fun to watch. The teacher who coached the team was a Doctor Low who had a wooden leg but loved sports and proved to be a huge inspiration to me a few years later when he became my teacher, he said "you will play for this team one day Jim", my Ma thought he was daft, but time would prove him correct. School work seemed to be a breeze and I really wanted to be more active so I got involved in a game in the playground called Heading Tennis which didn't require a lot of leg activity, basically it was a very small football pitch with goals identified by coats and you would throw a ball in the air and try to head a goal at the other end, it a was a lot of fun and I won the odd match. The other activity I became involved in was keepy uppy, standing close to a wall you would head the ball against the wall and the objective was to keep the ball bouncing off the wall without it touching the ground for longer than anybody else. By the time I was eleven years old I had the school record of 227 and Doctor Low said, "when you do start playing football you should be good in the air".

Needless to say, I was starting to annoy my Ma by constantly asking "when do you think I can start playing football" she was noncommittal but her response often would be wait till you can walk properly.

Some of the boys who I became really friendly with during this time included Alex Lauder, Jimmy Small, Alec Guild, Bobby Gibson Wullie Russell, Joe Maringhi, Sandy Cornelius, John Middlemas, Donald Urquhart, Alfie Douglas and Donald Reid.

BALKYMOR 5

Somehow or other we had made it to November 1945, Betty was eight and a half years old, I was nearly seven and all around us people were happy and excited, the war was over. I remember all the neighbors out on the Lawnmarket, singing, dancing and drinking whatever was available (including Uncle John Burns whisky from the custom and excise warehouse, which had been delivered each week to Granny Fells for discounted prices). Betty and I were thrilled to bits because now Dad would be home, Ma wouldn't have to work, and we could find a house of our own hopefully. The challenges of rehabilitation were not even a consideration in the euphoria of the moment.

Granny Fell reminded Ma to go see City Council about a house almost before the hangovers of the end of war parties had subsided, Council promised to give us serious consideration but nothing at the moment! Dad came home in his demob suit with whatever money he had due him, which wasn't much, and a note to go to the dole and sign on for work. The Second World War was over, but another war was about to come to the boil at #4 Upper Bow. Ma and Dad, Betty and I were all sleeping in the back bedroom, Granny Fell had reluctantly moved to the small bed settee in the living room, she wasn't happy, Ma and Dad weren't happy, and Betty and I could feel the tension building.

Dad couldn't find work in Edinburgh (no specific skills) and had started drinking and going to football matches again, Ma had to give up her job at Ross's Garage because the "men" were home, Granny was grumpy and somehow or other with Betty and I in the bedroom and Ma insistent that she didn't want any more bairns she fell pregnant.

It was all becoming too much for Ma so she asked Dad to go to Bo'ness for a few days and see if he could find a job either in Bo'ness or nearby Grangemouth at the petrochemical plants, so off he went with additional instructions to see if Granny Currie could put us up for a few weeks. Within two days he had got himself a job in a chemical plant close to Bo'ness and Granny Currie said she would look after our family until we got settled. Granny Fell was very upset with Ma for leaving but she explained it was for the best so off we went to Bo'ness. We had two suitcases, the clothes on our backs, some money Ma had managed to save from her wee job and Dad with his demob suit and "nae money tae speak off" and Auld Jock waiting in the wings still not knowing he was having Dolly and Geordie and the bairns coming to stay.

The trip to Bo'ness was quite uneventful, a corporation bus to St. Andrews Square, an SMT bus to Grange pans in Bo'ness with a stop at Queensferry and within an hour we were there, what now we all were thinking.

Betty and I were quickly enrolled in the Grange School, Dad got started in the chemical plant working shifts almost immediately which he hadn't expected, Ma was looking around for a wee cleaning job but didn't have much luck and Granny Currie tried to make sure that Auld Jock was looked after as much as possible. He spent most of his time in the Crown Royal Pub and occasionally enjoyed my dad's company at a football match on the weekends. Unfortunately, conflict was never far away in the Derry Close where we were staying again. Auntie Mary and Auntie Bridget lived close by and visited us quite often so there were always more people in the house than Auld Jock was used to so Granny Currie got blamed for that among other things.

Dad settled in very quickly at work, he enjoyed having a regular pay coming in, going to the football matches again, his pint and of course Dolly and the bairns were "there" for him, or so he thought. Ma was struggling with being pregnant, staying with in-laws, looking after Betty and occasional trips to the Edinburgh hospitals with me and trying to make ends meet plus still pursuing a Council house anywhere for us.

On July 13, 1946, my wee brother Alan was born, so now there were 5 of us staying with Granny Currie and Auld Jock, he did not like having a "bairn" in his house and "Geordie better do something about this". Between 1946 and 1949 we must have moved back and forth between the two Grannies' houses at least three times while waiting on the list for housing. I was becoming quite active now as my foot and left leg were getting stronger, but I was still getting therapy which meant Ma had to get me to the hospital wherever we stayed. What was really a pleasant surprise for my parents was the fact that Betty and I continued to do exceptionally well at school despite all the domestic upheavals.

My Dad continued to work at the chemical plant, but his breathing and general health were being affected so the Doctor advised him to look for another job. He steadfastly refused to consider working with Uncle Wullie in Edinburgh but to his credit eventually found a job with the Gas Board down at Granton so the latest move to Granny Fells worked out for him, then lo and behold my Ma got a call from the City Council in Edinburgh. A single end had become available in #1 Upper Bow with two front windows overlooking Johnstone Terrace. Granny Fell was delighted and told Ma to take it sight unseen which we did. It turned out to be very small with a living room, one bedroom, a lavatory and a tiny kitchen area. When Ma and Dad went to get the keys, they got a nice surprise because #1 Upper Bow was actually two single ends with a common corridor and Council had been contacted by the Children's Aid Society that I needed my own room, and we were getting the use of both single ends for at least two years.

Their pleasure was short lived though because the place was very damp and in disrepair, but family and friends rallied around, and it wasn't long before we moved in to our first house which had been nicely decorated for us.

Life was good, we had our own house finally, Dad had a steady job, most of my Uncles were working, Ma was slowly getting over the pregnancy and enjoying the "bairn", Betty and I were back at Castlehill School and doing well, I had a skinny left leg and a small left foot "but" I could now walk and sort of run even with orthopedic boots on.

One disappointment some of our relatives in Bo'ness often talked about after we moved back to Edinburgh was the "possibility" that had I continued to be first in the class at the Grange School till I finished Primary school, I could have been the school "Champion" and ridden a horse in the Bo'ness Fair parade which is held each July. This obviously was very important to the locals and quite an honour we were informed. Later in life I couldn't even consider this as a missed opportunity, but it was nice to know that my relatives had even thought about it.

Both Grannies were now glad we just visited once in a while and we were all slowly recovering from the turmoil of the Second World War, the team I had adopted (Hibs) were playing great football with a forward line that was to become known as "the famous five" (Smith, Johnstone, Reilly Turnbull and Ormond).

Much to my Dad's dismay however, him being an ardent Celtic fan, the "Hibs" would win the Scottish Football League in 1948/1951/1952 and the Famous Five would be selected to represent the Scottish team on more than one occasion. My passion for football was growing by the day and I continued to enjoy the wee games I played in the closes and at school with some of my early pals, Alex Lauder Donald Reid, James Lindsay, Sammy King, James Small and Bobby Gibson. They were all very considerate about my lack of mobility and tried to include me where possible. George Anderson was another young boy who hung around with us at the time, he had also been born with a club foot but unfortunately, he didn't have the dedicated Mother that I was blessed with and spent all his life on crutches, watching as we played football, sad really but a constant reminder to me of how fortunate I had been.

Dad was really enjoying his job with the Scottish Gas Board and although his official position was a labourer, he had become mates with Wullie Swan who was by trade a fitter (a good friend of my Uncle Davie Gibb who also was a fitter to trade), Wullie thought the world of my Dad and they worked well together for many years, also becoming close friends away from work.

Ma was really starting to enjoy her three bairns now, she had her "ain house", Geordie was working and providing for us, Granny Fell was as crabby as ever but still had a few days where she enjoyed her family without getting too close. Most of the aunts and Uncles visited back and forth to share what was happening in their lives and of course there was the odd party where a singalong would eventually occur as the men slowly came under the influence of the "carry oots". Uncle John continued to provide bottles of whisky each week at discounted prices to those who were interested, needless to say my dad was always interested, as a result of these weekly visits Uncle John became very fond of me, I had always made a fuss of the fact that he cycled everywhere and during his visits allowed me to sit on the saddle of his bike at the bottom of the stair at #1.

Some of my friends had acquired bikes and I was in complete awe of them as they mastered the skill of cycling around the neighbourhood, little did I know that my Uncle John had bought a secondhand bike and was fixing it up for me. I don't remember the exact date or time, but he had come to the door as usual with his delivery of whisky for Dad and he said to me "C'mon down the stairs I've got a surprise for you". At the foot of the stairs was a beautifully painted blue bike with white trim and butterfly handlebars, he looked at me and said "This is for you son" as Ma and Dad watched from the door. I can honestly say that that moment was without a doubt the happiest moment up to this point in my young life, I didn't sleep for days after due to the excitement I felt. Cycling was to become an important part of my teenage life, I discovered later.

Betty had continued to do well at school and in sports in general in spite of the attention that seemed to come my way, in retrospect she had lots to deal with but handled it as well as she could. In 1949 she graduated from Castlehill School in the top three of her class and decided to go to James Clarks School taking a commercial course suited to her strengths with a view to becoming a secretary.

In 1949 I had mastered the art of cycling and was enjoying my bike, was doing well at school, had joined the "Cubs", and even got to go potato picking and earn a few pounds during the year. My leg and foot were stronger, but I still had to wear boots from the Crippled Aid Society that were designed to keep my foot straight, my Ma had tried ordering special boots from Bairds in Princess Street, but the cost was way beyond what we could afford at that time. My football skills never really matched my enthusiasm for the game but that didn't matter, "I was able to kick a ball" and I tried! How I tried. Doctor Low who by now was my teacher at the school felt I was ready to play for the Canaries (the school team) but Ma still said no.

As it happened that year our school class was scheduled to attend a camp called Broomlee near West Linton (20 miles from Edinburgh) for two weeks during the spring holiday arranged by our teacher Doctor Low and he had suggested to my Ma that I should be allowed to play in an exhibition game against the local school there. Ma agreed but only on condition that I play as goalie. I couldn't convince Ma that I wasn't a goalie, but she stuck to her decision, goalie or don't play.

I played goalie and we were completely outclassed and got beat 12-0, but I loved just being involved. You can imagine my surprise at the small ceremony after the game that Doctor Low paid me the most wonderful compliment when he said that had it not been for me the score would have been much worse, of course I gobbled all this up at the time. Ma and Dad put it all in perspective when I got home when they commented on what a nice man Doctor Low was and a very compassionate individual, he must be to have made me feel good about letting in 12 goals. Oh well I guess we live and learn about life.

One other pleasant memory I have of Broomlee Camp was when the teachers (who know everything that is going on) had become aware that my pals in class and I had developed a funny routine (we thought anyway) about a group called the Scots Brigade. Every night after lights out we would all get out of bed and march up and down the dormitory with sticks, broom handles, or pieces of wood representing "rifles" singing songs and generally acting daft. The duty teacher caught us one night but instead of giving us what for she said, "If you lot are willing to do this on the stage for the going away party, they always have on the last day of camp I won't report you" we accepted the challenge and fine-tuned our little skit and wouldn't you know it, we were a big hit. From then on till we finished Primary School our wee group was known as "the Scots Brigade".

Between potato picking, Broomlee Camp and getting a bike from Uncle John and playing cowboys and Indians in Princes St Gardens with my improving mobility I thought I had died and gone to heaven. The bike had broadened my horizons and I could cycle most places I wanted to go to with the constant caution from Ma "you be careful now". School work was going well and my left leg-ting stronger due to the cycling so of course I had to keep Ma in constant turmoil, "I want to play for the school team", "I want to get a milk or paper delivery job", "I want to cycle out to Uncle Johns near Stenhouse", poor Ma she would say "talk to your Dad". Dad was very supportive of my adventurous nature but of course he hadn't had to deal with all my early problems, but he had sensed that I was a "doer not a dreamer" even at this early age.

BALKYMOR 6

I was about to enter the last year of Primary School and I desperately wanted to play for the school team that year, so Ma had agreed to let the Doctors make that decision when I went for my annual checkup. We took the bus up to Fairmile head and then walked along to the Princess Margaret Rose Hospital, I was full of optimism but poor Ma, she had her own thoughts on the matter. Both Doctors, Professor Stirling and Doctor Aird seemed to be pleased with the progress I had made but the bad news at that time was I would need one more operation called a Triple Fusion if I wanted the foot to be as functional as was possible under the circumstances. Ma said she would have to discuss it with Dad and would let them know as soon as possible, "but can I play football for the school team in the meantime" I asked and to my delight the Doctors said, "If you can get on the school team son you go right ahead, you will only strengthen the leg". Both Ma and Dad agreed we should go ahead with the last operation but disagreed on letting me play for the School team. Betty reminded me on more than one occasion of what Ma had been through with me all these early years, but Dad and I prevailed, if Doctor Low said I was good enough for the team I could play in my last year at Castlehill School. Little did I know that my Ma and Doctor Low had conspired for me to be a goalie.

When I challenged Ma about it, later she apologized but said she wouldn't be able to live with herself if I got hurt while waiting for the final operation. It was to be some time later before I had the operation.

1950 Turned out to be a memorable year for one reason or another, I think I fell in love with my cousin Ann (Uncle John Currie's daughter), she was in my class and had the most beautiful red hair. Dad said not to worry about it as it was just a passing fancy, how could he have known? Both Grannies went to heaven that year so I was told but I couldn't really understand why everybody was crying if that was so, but I missed them almost immediately and soon it sunk in they were really gone forever, death is so final I found out. Some good news that year was to find out that we might get a new house in Broomhouse (near Sighthill) in the near future.

In the meantime, even although I'm not quite 12 years old, I'm out looking for a wee job because I have already decided that I'm going to buy myself a new racing bike with "the money I earn". I got wind of a bakery shop up in Morningside that needed someone to deliver rolls at 6am each morning including Sundays, Ma said "You need your head examined but go see if you can get the job". I did and I was off to the races so to speak, I hadn't realized what getting up "every morning" had meant but I soon found out, very tiring to say the least.

My schoolwork didn't suffer but between playing for the school, cycling, going to the cubs, delivering rolls, going for messages for Ma to the store (St Cuthberts) and Davy the butchers life was becoming very busy and a bit complicated.

Both Ma and Dad had this habit of sending me for 5 Woodbine cigarettes at different times to the paper shop on the Lawnmarket with specific instructions not to tell the other one, it was one of life's mysteries to me at the time, but I did as I was told as I thought this must be part of being married? During this period of my life, I was having weird dreams and not all of them were to do with girls who I had begun to notice and think about more than I should have. Somebody described this feeling as having raging hormones whatever that meant. However, I do remember waking up the odd morning with a damp stain on my pyjamas and a "nice feeling". The weird dreams that were recurring had more to do with being trapped in situations that I had no control over and left me in despair when I woke up. The dream I still have to this day is having been selected to play for Scotland in an International football match and not being able to find my football boots while the rest of the team were on the field, pipe band playing, crowds roaring and the referee set to start the match and I'm crying as I try to get through a swamp with no boots on and sinking slowly. Never did make the pitch but the dream still occurs, oh well! Betty claims I used to sleepwalk a lot too and was often found standing at the room window fast asleep, she also claims that our parents locked the windows at night, "just in case".

Although I had become a "sixer" at the Cubs and really enjoyed my time there I had decided that I would soon join the Boys Brigade and not the "Scouts" which would be the normal progression. I had heard that the Boys Brigade had a football team, and the Scouts didn't, easy decision for me and also had heard that Captain Madden was a great leader in the Tollbooth St Johns "BB's". The only rule they had was you had to attend the BB Sunday school to play the following Saturday game, this seemed ok to me.

At the end of the school year in June 1950 I was quite embarrassed to find out I was Castlehill "School Dux" and would receive the grand sum of three pounds and a special book for my efforts. My cousin Ann was third but apparently her parents were disappointed because they felt she had worked much harder than I had, personally I agreed but Dad said it was just sour grapes and for the first time I can remember, my Dad and his brother John had a disagreement. It didn't last long and had little effect on Ann or myself. Ma was as proud as could be and both her, Dad, Doctor Low and the Headmaster had decided I should go to a High Education Secondary School (Boroughmuir or James Gillespie's, the "posh schools) in order to realize what they said was "my potential".

Without having given the issue much thought I had expected to go with my pals to either Darroch or James Clarks where Betty had gone and couldn't believe what all the fuss was about. As I look back now, although I have had a very rewarding life, I often wonder what my life might have been like if Dad had insisted on the High Education School. However, I was allowed to go rather reluctantly by all involved to James Clark Secondary school.

My wee brother Alan was at a great age for annoying and having fun with, we played a lot in the lobby of the house and developed a great relationship while he was growing up, but our time together was also impacted by me going to Secondary School. Betty and I had to walk a considerable distance both morning and night and occasionally at lunch time if it happened Ma didn't have our lunch-time "piece ready", school dinners were out of the question for us.

Because of my scholastic record at Castlehill Primary School expectations were very high for this to continue at James Clarks Secondary school and for some reason it did, such wasn't the case with my "football career?". Mr. Moise was the metalwork teacher and also the coach for the first-year football team called the "B" eleven; he had heard I played in goal for my Primary School Team and also the Boys Brigade team. His assumption was I must be ok, and he asked me to come to the team practice after school, I sensed he was less than impressed but since nobody else wanted to play in net and Ma still insisted, I couldn't play out I was delighted when the team went up on the notice board on the Friday morning for games the following day at Meggetland.

The selection system used for second and third-year boys was very simple, second year was the "A" eleven and third year was the "First Team", that became my first major goal in life. I was surprised to find out I was in a Technical Course, which included subjects like woodwork, technical drawing and of course Mr. Moise's metalwork class and they were all interesting subjects, but I still seemed to prefer regular subjects like Math, English, history and geography.

We had lots of fun that first year at Secondary School and some embarrassing moments too, one boy in our metalwork class was teaching some of us how to masturbate behind a work bench when Mr. Moise caught him, he was ranting and raving about all of us going blind if we did this terrible thing and sent the boy to the headmaster. Needless to say, the boy got what for from the headmaster but later in the playground he assured us with a mischievous grin that we "wouldn't go blind".

Betty and our friends used to play on the Castle Esplanade at nights and on weekends, this became significant late in the 1940s when the Edinburgh Military Tattoo was born and became world famous in the years that followed. Because of Betty's "connections" with the soldiers we were fortunate enough to see all of the early productions of the Tattoo including the first few with Pompey "The Famous Drum Horse", what a magnificent proud animal it was. We were also lucky enough to be given passes to visit the temporary stables which were located at King Stables Road where the Mounted Military Band were stationed and where the horses were groomed. Ma wasn't too excited about Betty's interaction with the soldiers, but we all benefitted from it.

BALKYMOR 7

Shortly before my 12th birthday we received the most exciting news from the local council office, our family name was at the top of the list for relocating from the "Auld Toon" to a brand-new housing development on the west side of Edinburgh called Broomhouse and we were to select which house we wanted in a block of four in a street called Broomhouse Court. Ma was beside herself and couldn't wait to tell Dad who by now was working with the Gas Board in a good steady job. We had a nice tea that night when Dad got in from work and we discussed the implications of such a major change in our lives when and if we did decide to move. Not a hard decision we thought, jump on the bus and go look see. The decision on the choice of house was easy, Dad said the bottom right would be just perfect, garden in the front, garden in the back, 3 bedrooms, kitchen, living room, bathroom, and 2 fireplaces, we thought we had died and gone to heaven. With the decision made we jumped on the bus on our way back to the "Lawnie". Then came the doubts? What about school? What about our pals? It's a long way to travel to Dad's work, where is the shopping For Ma? We don't know anybody there! do we really want to leave the "Lawnie", panic stations setting in for all of us!! The next few days were just a blur as we tried to come to grips with the decision, but Ma and Dad felt this was to be a new beginning and just too good a chance to miss and we could work out all the issues given some time and patience. Broomhouse, here we come! And wouldn't you know it we received the keys for our new house on November 12/1950 my 12th birthday, now we had to plan "the flitting".

It hadn't really sunk in yet, we were really leaving the Historic part of the city for a new housing estate, sort of, out in the "boonies" and who knows what kind of neighbours we might have but we were all excited as Ma and Dad went about planning the move and us kids tried to get on with school and come to grips with the prospect of transferring to new schools, Alan would be going to Stenhouse Primary and Betty and I would be going to Carrickvale Secondary School, both schools within reasonable walking distance from our beautiful "new house". All of this going on and I was still waiting on word for what hopefully would be my last operation to rearrange the bones in my left foot and then we expected I could then look forward to what the Doctors described as a fairly normal and active life. They did say, however, there was a chance that the stronger right leg might pay the price in later years, how prophetic that turned out to be. I must confess though I was really looking ahead to the day when I could "play out" on the school team, now going to be at Carrickvale where I had heard 2 outstanding soccer players at the school were being scouted by the Pro's, Davie Mackay and Alan Finlay. Both would in fact go on to play for the "Heart of Midlothian" or to be more precise rivals of my "Hibs". Everything went as scheduled with the flitting, an old truck my uncles had borrowed was loaded with all our meagre belongings and off it went down Johnstone Terrace and heading to Broomhouse, Ma had insisted that she would take us "bairns" on the bus "just in case!" There was an accident, and we would meet Dad and the Uncles at Broomhouse.

Ma was obviously upset at leaving the Lawnie and all her friends and neighbors but as it happened, they were all now anxiously waiting on word on new houses too and would soon be flitting, the choice was like a raffle it seems, depending on your luck it could be Pilton, Craigmillar Broomhouse or any other council development.

The other concern bothering Ma was we didn't have much furniture and the "new house would look empty". If there was something to worry about it seems Ma would find it much to Dad's despair at times. Anyhow we arrived safe and sound at Carricknowe #1 bus stop and walked up to Broomhouse Court where all the men were unloading the truck, after about an hour my Uncle Wullie said they needed a wee break and off they went to "The Silver Wing" for a pint with strict orders to come back soon and to bring fish and chips for tea. They all came back feeling no pain and of course "nae" fish and chips.

Ma gave them all what for and walked up to the chip shop for our supper herself and "you lot make bloody sure this truck is unloaded when I get back" and of course it was, Dad and my uncles had the fish and chips Ma had bought and it happened they had got a "carry oot" which included several cans and bottles of beer. So started our new life in Broomhouse! Not much furniture, Dad under the weather and, in a wee bit of bother for the moment, but we had a "new house" and a new life to look forward to.

We settled in quickly and Dad got started on "his" garden, he seemed so pleased to have a wee bit of land to work on, Ma sorted out her bits and pieces of furniture and started a list of things to get when we had some extra money. Betty and I had transferred to Carrickvale and Alan was settling in ok at Stenhouse and some other families were starting to arrive in Broomhouse Court as the houses were being completed. We all seemed to miss our Lawnie friends at first, but they would often jump on the bus and come visit us and we would all play on the housing site and have lots of fun in the half-finished houses.

It wasn't very long before more families were arriving and although the occupied houses were a bit scattered around the "Court" we started to make contact with our new neighbors and soon to be new pals. One of the first families to arrive was the Taits who had picked a house around the corner from us and an upstairs which surprised us a wee bit at the time. Alastair Tait the second son in the family was to become my best pal for years to come and we hit it off right away. Shortly after the Taits came the Browns and the Watsons who had picked a house across the road from us and then a family called the "Roseberry's" who had picked the house directly above us. Seemed a nice family and had 4 kids under 5 which proved to be a disaster for us as the floors had no deafening installed and the children running up and down the lobby upstairs became a major problem. Alastair, whose dad had been sick with the chives when they arrived explained to me when I was telling him about the awful noise from upstairs in our house that it was this very reason they had been advised to pick an upstairs house. Our decision for downstairs house played a huge part in our family's future as it turned out and within the next year, our dream had become a bit of a nightmare especially for my poor Ma.

Dad was working extra hours as often as he could with the Gas Board to get more money for things that Ma had on her list, plus he was trying to grow vegetables in the back garden and get grass to grow in the front garden(small about 10 x 20ft) with a small walkway between but he tried to get me to Easter Road to see the Hibee's as often as he could. Just loved getting on the bus to go to the Tron on match day, the excitement was almost unbearable for me. The Special buses would just fill up and off they would go in an endless string to the match, at Easter Road Dad would pick a pub, have his nip and pint and get me my packet of Smiths chips and a drink while I waited outside the pub for him. We tried to get to the match about 15 minutes before kickoff and after lifting me over the turnstile we found our favorite spot behind the south net on the west side so we could watch Gordon Smith the right winger displays his many talents for the Hibs. It was just “MAGIC”.

Although we had moved to Broomhouse I continued to go to the BB’s at Tollbooth St John’s Church up at the “Lawnie”, this meant at least 2 trips a week on the #1 bus from Carricknowe to Johnstone Terrace. I was still enjoying the BB’s but more importantly by going to the Sunday School I was also able to play for the BB’s on Saturday afternoons and although it was a very modest league I was “not” telling Ma that I was playing “out”, she would have given me what for. So here I was playing in goal for the Carrickvale “B” team on Saturday mornings and playing out at right back for the BB’s in the afternoon, I just loved being involved in “fitbae”. One of the earliest achievements was the BB team reached the Final of what they called the League Cup and although we got beat 3-1 we did get a wee medal that was presented by a famous “Hearts” player by the name of Wullie Bauld. My secret thought was I wished that it had been Laurie Reilly the Hibs centre forward at the time, oh well such is life. Captain Madden our BB Leader was so proud of our team. Betty was enjoying her life out at Broomhouse but still spent a lot of time with her friends up at the Lawnie but unfortunately was always in trouble with Ma and Dad for coming home late and having to walk down a very dark Broomhouse Crescent. Dad had warned her over and over again to be home by 11pm at the latest as Ma had to go up and wait at the bus stop, some nights it would be midnight when she got home, and Dad would rant and rave before “retiring” to the bedroom where he and Ma would continue discussing the matter. About this time Betty told me she had started smoking, “if its ok for Ma and Dad it should be ok for me" she said to me, I never did try smoking, who knows why?

Betty, Alan and I played a lot at the farm just up the road from us where eventually a new school was to be built, we had lots of fun there and also round the corner where there was a row of shops that included a "paper" shop and this is where we bought sweeties, ice cream and of course picked up the "Edinburgh Evening News" at night for Ma and Dad. The row of shops had what we called a wee dyke immediately behind it and we often played there at night, and it became a favorite meeting place for all our friends in the future. Across the road on Broomhouse Crescent there were larger houses designed for families who needed 5 bedrooms and soon we began to get to know some of the boys and girls who had moved there.

I met a chap by the name of Norman Mackay in my class at Carrickvale School and it turned out he lived round the corner from us on the Crescent and he seemed a bit aloof but friendly enough, anyway through him I got to know his brothers, Alistair and Tom. Alistair became a close friend of ours, so our small group was expanding and at future parties Alistair we found out was a piper and very good at it. Our little colony of friends now includes Alastair Tait, John Brown, Alex Watson, Alex Lawson and now Alistair Mackay. For some reason I had evolved to being some kind of spokesman for the group, quite often as we sat at the dyke near the shops, we would ask each other "what do you want to do?" Nobody ever seemed to have an answer, but I always seemed to have a thought and offered it and lo and behold the response always seemed to be "let's do it". Informal leadership I guess even at this early age.

So here I was with a whole bunch of new friends, still friendly with the guys from the Lawnie and playing football for 2 teams and living in a new house and my "gammy" leg was getting stronger by the day, does life get any better than this I wondered? Then we got the news! it was time for the "Triple Fusion", the last operation on my left foot, I cried a lot but as always Ma was there for me providing all the love and support a child could ask for, "it will make your foot straighter, and you will be more like all the other laddies" she said. As expected, the operation at the Princess Margaret Rose Hospital by Professor Stirling was a success and he predicted after physiotherapy I would be as "normal" as any other boy although the left leg would always be thinner, and my left foot would be a bit smaller than the right foot. One decision that had to be made was whether to remove my second smallest toe as it was sitting up a bit between the small toe and the third toe and could be a nuisance in the future. Ma and Professor Stirling decided to leave it alone and I am glad they did, although over the years it has been caught and bashed more than any of my other toes.

My memories of the few weeks at the P.M.R. Hospital were all good although the friends I made, Ian Aitken, Tony Tortallani, Squirrel Brownlee and I were always in trouble with the nurses and Sister Douglas (The "Black Douglas"). She didn't like it when we all locked ourselves in the bathroom and wouldn't let her in because we were naked and didn't want her to see us that way, boy did we get a row. I was pleasantly surprised that we had schooling while in the hospital as I was still getting good marks and actually enjoyed "learning". I was 13 years old now, but I still cried my heart out unashamedly when Ma and Dad (but especially Ma) left me after visiting the hospital at the weekends, what a great relationship I had with my Ma and no doubt she spoiled me rotten by some definition.

Soon I was home with the family, on crutches, fairly mobile but with limited activities and able to get to school under my own steam. Ma was busy again making sure I was doing my exercises as described by the Doctors and I was working hard to manage without the crutches as soon as possible. During this period, we were meeting more and more people and although I wasn't mobile, I began organizing all kinds of games for the kids in the street, so between that and getting to watch the black and white Television at John Brown's house the time went by quickly. TV was fairly new and his house was the only one that had one, we watched all kinds of stuff but what I enjoyed the most was the Wimbledon Tennis.

With more and more people arriving in Broomhouse as houses were being completed it was only natural that we were getting to know more and more people, Johnny Craig had moved into the Grove and a girl by the name of Pat Poole was becoming quite friendly on our walks to school. The Lawson Family had moved into Broomhouse Road and Alex and his brother Jimmy had become involved with our little colony of friends Dad was really working hard at making our little garden look good, he had managed to "acquire" some bricks for garden edging and some nice link chain with posts for a fence around the front garden and I was encouraged to be a helper. It looked nice when completed and around the back of the house the vegetables were starting to grow nicely, much to my Ma's surprise. Unfortunately, as all these good things were happening Ma was having serious problems with her nerves due to the continuous racket from the 4 kids upstairs, it was driving her daft (literally). Dad had tried in vain to talk to the Roseberry's and even offered to buy rugs for the lobby's where the noise came from, not accepted. We tried to get the Council to deal with the problem, but they seemed to think we were a bit unreasonable which Dad reacted to rather badly and became unpopular with the council and now it seemed "we" were the problem. It really was a shame as we loved the house and the neighborhood at that time and all the concerns, we had had about moving were all gone. Ma had taken to banging on the ceiling of our house with a broom handle at nights as the noise went on and on to all hours and that of course affected her relationship with Mrs. Roseberry, soon Dad would have to decide whether we could continue like this or put in for a transfer to another council house for the sake of Ma's health, what a dilemma.

It was about this time I had noticed that a group of cyclists often would cycle past the Court on their way to a house on Broomhouse Crescent just up the road from the row of shops, the house was noticeable by a bird bath in the front yard. All the bikes were racing models, and this got me to thinking about finding a wee job again once I had recovered from the operation, now I couldn't wait to get the cast off and get back to football and cycling as soon as humanly possible.

As my future was starting to look promising unfortunately my dear Ma was really struggling, and Dad continued to be on demand by the Gas Board on 24 hours' notice which on one hand was great financially but only compounded my Ma's deteriorating health. Doctor Bignold told Dad that Ma was heading for a nervous breakdown and we should seriously consider looking for an "Exchange" to another house. We were all devastated by this possibility, but Dad has to be complimented on his decision to do what was best for Ma in spite of all our naive and selfish protests about how this would change our lives again.

The fact that we had a three-bedroom ground floor front entrance house with a front and back garden made it appealing to lots of folks in other Council houses but unfortunately, we weren't interested in moving to another new estate so that limited our choices. The Council finally told us we better move soon so we settled for a two-bedroom flat on the top floor of a fairly new 12 in the block building on Stevenson Drive opposite Saughton Park, Dad explained the word "compromise" to us when we claimed it wasn't fair to give up our house for a tenement. The move proved to be successful for many reasons in the years to come.

Our move to 61 Stevenson Drive went quite smoothly and our small amount of furniture seemed more suited for the older 2-bedroom house. The biggest impact was on Betty who really needed a room to herself but had to sleep in the living room in a fold down settee, needless to say there were some battle royals as we tried to adjust to this arrangement. Alan and I slept in the back bedroom where the north wind blew through the window and wall to maintain a frigid atmosphere. Ma and Dad had the front bedroom, smaller room but a nice view of the park and the Pentland Hills away in the distance. The real irony of all of this was when we found out the Roseberry's had left the upstairs house at Broomhouse Court and emigrated to Australia. To say my dad was "upset" would be a major understatement when he heard about it, maybe just as well they had moved to another country. Once Dad had "cooled" off a bit all he could say was "why didn't they tell us?".

The move had little impact on our school arrangements, in fact we had a shorter walk now from Stevenson Drive. Having the park across the road from us was also a blessing in disguise as I continued with my rehab from the operation and once the cast was off, I made great progress with short walks and cycling around the neighborhood. Contact with my newfound friends at Broomhouse was maintained at school and cycling up to see them. School work was going great, and I had been selected to be a prefect in "Bonaly House", apparently school marks, sports and being involved in organizing activities had not gone unnoticed at Carrickvale Secondary School, amazing I thought rewarded for doing things that I really enjoy.

Before I knew it, I was kicking a ball again and although I had a strange gait to my run was able to move around fairly well but still in my mind, with very limited skills but huge desire to "do well". So before too much longer I was playing football again for the

2nd school team at Meggetland every Saturday morning (in goals Boo-Hoo) and the BB's down at Warriston Park in the afternoon (at right back Yippee) without my parents' permission, they would have only worried I thought. With all this football and cycling my leg was getting stronger by the day and now it was time to find a job to save money for a new racing bike like the guys who cycled by us at Broomhouse had. Mum was agreeable and said if I could find a job before or after school, I could keep whatever I earned as long as I "saved" a quarter of the wages and put it in what she called a piggy bank. This simple piece of philosophy along with the advice she gave me away back then about not spending more than you earn has had a major impact on my life and has proved its value at least to me over the years. Turns out I was a good saver anyways and after I got a job up at Corstorphine delivering papers I was literally away to the races. Things were going so well at this time I decided to have a go at cricket and actually made the 6th Eleven, quite chuffed I was bragging too Dad about my achievement when he asked, "how many Elevens are there?" I replied with a huge smile "six Dad", he gave me a huge hug and to my dying day I will never forget his few words, "you are ok son".

My schoolwork was progressing very well and I was now getting quite good at subjects like woodwork and technical drawing, in fact I had made a neat looking coffee table for Ma and a small stool that was actually a "bank" and Ma suggested I use that for saving my bike money so every weekend I would religiously put whatever I could save in the "bank" that now sat on the bedroom mantlepiece. Unfortunately, my Ma and Betty were often a wee bit short and would borrow a few shillings to get them by till pay day, this became a weekly habit and I soon had to develop an understanding of "bookkeeping" as there were always different opinions on who had borrowed what. Dad was quite helpful with the discrepancies and insisted that if "you want to borrow off the laddie, make sure you pay him back or try to manage without borrowing". Dad was always able to give Ma her housekeeping money but seemed to keep enough to have his pint, go to the football and have a wee bet on the horses. I am not sure how they managed their money but there were long discussions on where the money should go! I think these discussions lead to Ma going back to work as a cleaning lady (Charwoman) and this seemed to give her a bit more independence, she got a job at Patrick Thompsons working with Uncle Alex Fell's wife Martha and they became even closer friends. They used to tell people that they would pick up all the cigarette ends (butts) in the ash trays on the job and take them home and roll homemade cigarettes, claimed it saved them a fortune on "fag" money. Dad thought this was a great idea and soon he was making homemade cigarettes too. Anything to make "ends" meet so to speak.

Ma's health had improved dramatically with the move to Stevenson Drive and she was getting to know some of the neighbours really well and had become quite friendly with the lady next door, a Mrs. Roy, and this helped her to settle in quickly. Dad was quite pleased she had got a job and had gone back to work too as this eased the money problems a wee bit. The only problem was a really early start at 4:30am which meant Ma had to leave the house to catch the 4am bus into the Bridges and got home about 8:30am usually to find Dad was off to work, Alan and I were leaving for school and Betty was still asleep in the "living" room much to my Ma's dismay. Most mornings were a battlefield for Ma and Betty and after Betty left Ma would sit down exhausted with her cup of tea. This situation continued on for years even after Betty had gone to work for a living, Alan and I always tried to make sure we were out the door shortly after Ma came home. Alan had made friends with some of the kids at school and around the neighborhood but we continued to have some fun together at times too although I was now getting "too big" to play with my wee brother or so I was told by my friends. About this time, we really started to notice the great music that was on the wireless and "fancy" haircuts were the order of the day. I asked Ma and Dad if I could go up to Grove Street where there was a well-known Barbers shop called Phil's, he had already became well known for the "Flat" top and I wanted to try it. Talking about cool I thought it was great, but all my friends laughed at me since it was quite different than the side score, I had had most of my life, didn't bother me a bit. Can you believe that years later we found out the great Scottish actor Sean Connory actually lived on this same street (Grove Street) and he also used Phil's barber shop. This fact was a great source of pleasure in years to come for us as he was to become Sir Sean Connory, the chap who used to deliver milk on Grove Street. My brother Alan liked my "Flat" top and decided one day when he got a bit older, he would go to Phil's barber shop.

With about one more year left to go to Carrickvale Secondary School and my sister Betty now working at Grant's Furniture Office at the west end, girls were becoming less of a nuisance to us guys now and we began to notice how all the wee lassies were starting to develop a bit and actually quite pleasing to the eye. Some of these suddenly noticeable wee lassies had in fact been all around us at different times as we played up at Broomhouse near the shops and over at the farm and other places. Up till now we had just been pests and annoyed the girls as they played on the estate but now, we wanted to talk and interact with them and we got to know some of them over time, the McFarlane's, Lawrence's, Kirwan's Ann Fraser and a girl by the name of Pat Poole who I seemed to get on quite well with. My pals all had their own choices of who they "fancied" at the time, but it was all boyhood fantasies, I guess.

Although my Ma and Dad were both busy with their own lives, we always had lots of time for chats at meal times (mostly what we called tea time) which is actually supper or dinner time in other cultures and they just seemed to sense where we 3 kids were at as we were growing up and I was surprised one day when Dad for once wanted to talk to me about something other than sports. It wasn't about the "birds and the bees" as such it sounded more like a warning not to get any girls in trouble? Wasn't sure what he meant at the time. Apparently, he had found out I was becoming quite friendly with the Pat Poole girl from up at Broomhouse (sister Betty me thinks). Anyway, no need to worry I was a "good wee boy" wasn't I? My Ma continued to give me more attention than I deserved or now needed, we had developed such a great relationship and communicated very well and of course since I enjoyed talking to her there were no secrets and I told her everything I did. Unfortunately, this caused a problem for Betty and Alan as they got older as Ma expected the same from them and they weren't as free with their thoughts as I had inadvertently been over the years. Ma had overlooked the fact that her children were all quite different and possibly I had had more attention than my brother and sister due to my circumstances. Ma would probably argue that it wasn't the case, but I certainly took up a lot of her time and energy in my early years.

1953 came along very quickly and I had no idea what I was going to do when I left school, hadn't really given it much thought but Dad had said all along that the very least I should consider was to be a tradesman, my teachers and Headmaster strongly recommended I go on to fulfill the potential they thought I had (academically). We didn't give much thought to that option for a variety of reasons and personally I felt it was time to go to work and start to earn a living. As I grew older, I never regretted this decision but eventually realized that one of the greatest achievements one can have in their life is a formal education, no one can ever take that away and the doors of opportunity are much greater to you. After I graduated with the Scottish Leaving Certificate, I started job hunting, basically knocking on doors at all the shops and asking if they needed a laddie to help, no science to the job search it seemed, whoever needed help might determine your future occupation unless you became selective in the search. Some significant events occurred during 1953 that will be with me for the rest of my life, the Coronation of Queen Elizabeth 2nd, Edmund Hillary and Sherpa Tensing became the first humans to climb Mount Everest and then Sir Stanley Mathews finally won an English Cup winners medal with the Blackpool Football Club.

My search for a job was rewarded by being hired as a warehouse boy in a company called Simplex Electrical Supply on Frederick Street in down town Edinburgh, they seemed to be impressed by my school record and suggested that maybe once I got to know all the bits and pieces in the electrical trade that I would have a chance to get an apprentice job in the trade once I became 16 years old (the official start age). Needless to say Ma and Dad were absolutely delighted. The job went well, and I was anxious "to please", the fact that I rode my old bike into work was a bonus as I didn't have to pay bus fares and also helped me get some exercise. It wasn't too long before I had become familiar with most of the stock items in the warehouse and the tradesmen got to know me and it seems they were fairly happy with my ability to prepare their orders quickly and efficiently. Some of the contractors asked if I might be interested in working for them but I felt I owed it to Simplex to work a bit longer for them. To bring me back to earth I had discovered I had trouble with some of the cable colours but I kept that to myself and I also had a bad experience while experimenting with an electrical heater that had a small bar wound with an open cable, I had stuck a screwdriver in the heater and held the screwdriver against what they called the element (the small bar)and the protective grill, how was I to know it would go to "ground" and destroy both the heater and the screwdriver? Life's embarrassing moments I guess, natural curiosity the warehouse man had said but you are bloody lucky you didn't get electrocuted. Seems the wooden handle did not conduct electricity, boy was I learning all about "this electric stuff", great lesson in life for me Dad said. In spite of several learning experiences, it seems that a couple of contractors were willing to give me an opportunity to become an apprentice, so I finally accepted the offer from a chap who worked for himself called Angus Innes and his shop was up at Newington just past the Meadows. So, I started my apprenticeship before my 16th birthday with great trepidation (still concerned about the colour problem). I am sure had I mentioned it I would not have got the job, oh well!

The job went quite well at first, but I quickly realized that Angus was a grumpy unhappy man and no matter what I did or how hard I tried he always seemed to "moan" about everything. Most of the jobs were small jobs for older people and it seemed money was always an issue, we went to one job where a nice old lady had lost her electric supply and this had never happened before she said, anyway after some preliminary research Angus discovered that there was no money in the meter, he put a shilling in and of course the lights came on, surprise. As we drove away, he muttered to himself "what a stupid auld bugger, how can I charge anything for that". An hour of his time, my time and transport costs, no wonder he was mad. We also worked a lot on small appliances but not much profit in that either, he claimed. Why is he in this business? I thought.

Another incident was in Rosslyn in a pensioner's house and I was to tell him when I heard the noise of a plumb bob against the inside of the wall (he was up in the attic), I was scared shitless and couldn't detect the noise so I just said ok, well there was hell to pay when he came down and knocked a hole in the wall and never did find the plumb bob, Jim's fault of course.

While I had been working at Simplex on Frederick Street, I had found out about this really neat bicycle shop at the foot of Frederick Street down near Stockbridge which was run by a nice man by the name of Jimmy Gilchrist, with all the cycling my friends and I were now doing we were always having to repair or replace parts and he became very helpful in providing spare parts and keeping the costs down. I had mentioned to him that I was saving up for a new bike and he sensed I had more than a passing interest in cycling and told me he was a member of the "Dunedin Cycling Club" and was I interested? Jimmy was instrumental in my friends and I getting involved with the Dunedin Cycling Club and also in advising several of us on what to look for in a new bike, especially if you want to tour or even get into racing, little did we know how important all this would turn out to be. Pretty soon we had started to go away for weekends on the bikes and decided to join the Youth Hostels which provide overnight accommodation at a very reasonable price, we were now seriously considering joining the "Dunedin". These weekends were life savers for me as Angus Innes was becoming a major nightmare to work with and Dad suspected I was very unhappy and couldn't sleep at nights.

So here I was, no football since leaving school and the BB's, working as an apprentice, probably having to go to night school 3 nights a week for Math, Practical and Theory, getting into cycling big time and more than a passing fancy for Pat Poole who I had had a few dates with, some of my friends were now talking about going to the "Palais de Dance" to learn how to dance and meet the "talent", does life get any busier than this?

My Dad encouraged me to start looking for another job as soon as possible and although I felt some loyalty to Angus Innes for hiring me out of The Simplex Electrical Supply outfit, I knew a change was necessary for me to get back to enjoying life again. There was an Electrical Engineering Company on George IV Bridge just round the corner from where we used to live on the Lawnmarket so I decide to try there and as luck would have it they were in fact looking for a "Showroom Boy" to help with cleaning the shop and help with small appliance repairs with a view to starting an official 5 year Electrical apprenticeship which in those days meant you had to start by your 16th birthday. My school record came in handy, and I was offered the job much to my Ma and Dad's delight. Angus Innes as expected was not a very happy camper since he was losing cheap help but strangely enough and to his credit, he told me this would be a much better opportunity for me and wished me all the best in the future. So, the job switch took place and I cycled from Stevenson Drive every morning to the showroom on George IV Bridge (about a half hour ride) in rain, hail sleet or snow saving the cost of the Bus fares and getting fitter at the same time.

My first day on the job I met a Tradesman by the name of Bill Pearson who was responsible for my training and development, this seemed to be a match made in heaven as we connected immediately. He guided me through the early days of setting up a routine for the daily vacuuming of the showroom, making the coffee and looking after the needs of the office staff (mostly ladies it seemed). I tried so hard to please (be good and do good philosophy) since I was really enjoying my new job and they all seemed to appreciate the effort.

Soon Bill was getting me involved in the small Appliance repairs in the workshop under the showroom and he told me that if I was serious about the "Electrical Trade" I should soon be looking at going to Bellevue Technical School on Broughton Street in the near future as my apprenticeship would start officially on my birthday in November 1954 and finish in November 1959 if I worked really hard. I would also be required to take a 4-year course to get the City and Guilds Certificate at night school taking 3 subjects on separate nights, Mathematics, Electrical Practical and Theory, if I thought I had been busy before I had a challenge coming up. Bill had got me started on small jobs in the showroom but as always my sense of adventure often got in the way and I got a few "shocks" along the way, one of them from the top of a stepladder that could have been serious but we all got a wee laugh out of how stupid could Jim be touching live wires that were 240 volts, how was I to know I should have shut the switch of first, lesson learned and not forgotten.

Life seemed really busy, but I was quite happy, and content now and apparently was often seen whistling and singing on my bike as I traveled to and from work at George 1V Bridge. It was about this time of my life that in spite of having a reasonably happy home and family environment I started having thoughts of a "better" life in another country such as Australia, Denmark or Canada. Australia at that time seemed to be beckoning as I had a wee notion to be a Sheep Farmer but really didn't know why. All I could think of was that the merchant ship Dad had been assigned to had been dry docked in New Zealand for repairs during the war and several of the Royal Artillery gunners on board had been sent to a sheep farm for some R and R.

The "better" life I refer to was based on my perception of my Ma and Dad's hard work and struggles to make ends meet over the years, even with both of them out working, at the end of a given week there was "nothing extra" and little hope of them having additional cash to put aside for the future. We always had food on the table and clothes on our backs, but once the Council rent was paid and Ma bought the groceries there wasn't much left for cigarettes, a nip and a pint, the odd Football match or a bet on the horses, but as I recall these items were a low priority, at least they were for Ma, this caused a wee bit of conflict on the odd occasion as you might imagine. Somehow, we always managed a few days away for a holiday each year, but Dad was never far from a Pub.

On the social front my friends and I had decided that if we were ever going to go to the dancing at places like the Palais de Dance or the Cavendish or the Assembly Rooms we would need to learn how to dance, my sister Betty provided us with the answer, go to the Edina School of Ballroom Dancing up at Surgeons Hall for basic steps. Well, that went over like a lead balloon with my pal's "do you think we are all a bunch of wee lassies?" Anyway, we eventually did go to the Edina a few times and really enjoyed it as there were some very good-looking young lassies learning to dance too. We graduated after 3 sessions and moved on to the Central School of Ballroom Dancing at South Bridge and then The Afton Club down St Mary's St and now we were getting closer and closer to actually going to the "Palais de Dance" and meeting all the talent that we kept hearing about.

Cycling was also becoming a major hobby for my friends and I and we were actually starting to have weekends out of town at various Youth Hostel locations within about a 30-mile radius from Edinburgh, we had in fact joined the Scottish Youth Hostel Association and they provided a bed and kitchen facility for the princely sum of two and sixpence for an overnight stay. We had also started making serious enquiries about the "Dunedin" Cycling Club with a view to getting involved in longer distance cycling trips and who knows maybe Bike Racing?

BALKYMOR 8

Monday nights at the Palais de Dance at Fountain Bridge with the Jeff Rowena Quartet on one side of the Stage Roundabout and on the other side was the famous Basil Kirchin Band, we had all this to look forward to when we could get up the courage to go. One Saturday night after a few pints at the Wheatsheaf Inn we were enjoying Fish and Chips on the way home when Johnny Craig said to Alistair Tait, Alex Lawson and myself, right "let's do it" so after much humming and hawing we agreed that on the very next Monday we would "bite the bullet" and go see what all the fuss was about at the dancing. Alex informed us that his older brother Jimmy had shared some great stories with him and that there was "lots of talent" available.

It wasn't the next Monday or even the next two after that as one thing after another kept getting in the way of our proposed foray into the Palais de Dance world, however eventually we did manage to get there but we didn't have the courage to venture on the dance floor for fear of rejection from the many lassies who were there. We spent the next 3 Mondays hanging over the balcony looking forlornly at the dance floor where everyone seemed to be having a good time, but we just couldn't find the courage to take the plunge. It was about the fifth week when we decided it "was time". We hadn't really realized how difficult this process would be, where do you start? We were all rejected several times before we realized, the girls actually had a choice too, they could accept a dance or say no. We had not figured on this, how could they refuse "us", another lesson in life it would be. We had spent some time at learning how to dance but now we had to learn how to seek out and ask a girl who you felt might just want to dance with shy newcomers and eventually we made it on to the dance floor and the lessons certainly helped out as we actually could lead the girls and stay in step to the surprise of some of them.

We had some great laughs in the early days going home from the dancing late at night, sharing our moments and comparing notes on the "talent" with nary a thought to what the girls might have said about us.

Work at James Scotts was going well and I was developing a great relationship with Bill Pearson in the Appliance Repair Shop and in fact he was coaching and counselling me toward an Electrical Engineering apprenticeship starting in November 1954 and arranged for me to enroll at Bellevue Technical School for the 4 year City and Guilds course requiring 3 nights a week at night school, subjects would include Mathematics, Electrical Theory and Practical work, I was excited not realizing what a commitment this was. Bill had a longtime girlfriend named Helen and they lived in a flat on Broughton Street, just round the corner from the night school, so I spent a lot of time with him during the day and with them on the 3 nights after I started the classes.

I really enjoyed this period of my life as I was cycling from Broomhouse Court into George 1V Bridge in the town for work and then on to night school some evenings. My left leg and foot seemed to be improving daily and the limp I had for most of my life was less noticeable now and my inner thoughts and love of football was very strong but how does one fit all this "stuff" into their life. Ma and Dad were very encouraging in all my endeavours and true to their word let me keep all the bus fare money I received in my pay plus I didn't have to pay dig money at this time, but they did insist I save 25% of my take home pay and agreed I could someday consider buying a "racing" bike since I had so much interest in cycling. I think now when I look back, they were still a bit nervous about my "fitbae" notions. Dad would have loved to have a solid soccer player and secretly was delighted in my interest in the game BUT! Maybe cycling would cause less stress for dear auld Ma. Brother Alan was growing up like a weed at this time and had a good group of friends from around the Balgreen, Stevenson Drive area but they seemed more interested in things other than football. Alan really enjoyed music and the Cadets and Dad was ok with that but Alan and I for different reasons over the years always felt Dad didn't get the "Football Player" he so badly desired.

My friends and I were really getting into the swing of things at the dancing now and actually even starting to ask some of the girl's "home" afterwards with thoughts of a date in the future and all this was going quite well with no serious relationships developing we thought. I had got to know a girl from Lochend. Her name was Irene Mack (one of the few girls who didn't say NO to a dance request), and we got to dancing quite a bit together on Monday nights. On one occasion after a few dances, I asked if I could take her home, not thinking of where she lived. Well wouldn't you know it? She said okay and then I found out she lived at Lochend which is on the other side of Edinburgh. I was so embarrassed at the time, but she said "why just not walk me to the bus stop" so I did. She promised to save me a few dances the following Monday and so began my first sort of relationship that I shared with my big sister Betty and wee brother Alan, I was quite chuffed at all of this and could not wait to share these moments with my Ma. In the meantime, Johnny Craig and Alistair had met girls at different times and started dating fairly frequently so we had some good chats when we got together which seemed to be less and less these days, but we had great plans for joining the Dunedin Cycling Club and not only going hosteling on weekends but try to get into road racing or time trials on the bikes. Unfortunately, we weren't yet in a position to buy the type of bike we might need so were just getting by with the clunkers we had at the moment. We had been given some advice by the cyclists who went by at Broomhouse Crescent about the Dunedin and also mentioned when we were ready there was a chap who ran a Bicycle Shop at Stockbridge who could help us get started looking for better bikes, the Jimmy Gilchrist I had met some time ago who had suggested a 26 inch Rosendale bike frame for me when I had the money and he proved to be a great resource for both the building of our bikes and the Dunedin Cycling Club.

Irene Mack and I had started going steady and often went to the pictures when time would allow, she also got to know Helen and Bill Pearson quite well as occasionally she would meet me after night school, and we would visit their small flat just down the road from Bellevue Technical School. We met once or twice a week, went dancing on a Monday and enjoyed long walks near her house at Lochend. My schedule was becoming more and more demanding as my friends and I had really got serious about our cycling and had evolved to going away almost every weekend Youth Hostelling mostly down in what is called "The Borders" plus I was still trying to get involved with any football team that would give me a chance and we had approached the Dunedin Cycling Club to get information about what was required to join the Club and start racing.

Irene and I sort of went steady and my Dad had said what a nice lassie she was but that I was too busy and eventually she would get fed up and move on, "never I replied" but as always Dad got it right and we parted several months later, I was devastated, it got worse as she said she had started going out with Helen Pearson's brother.

Bill and Helen had married during this time, and I had been asked to be the Best Man at the Wedding which I accepted, and it turns out that was where Irene and the brother had meet, they have been happily married ever since.

My friends who still lived at Broomhouse had got to know the local lassies quite well and it turned out some of them had friends in the Dunedin Cycling Club. We had become members by then and combined hosteling with developing an interest in racing with the other members and it turns out Allan McFarlane and his sister Betty the ones who lived in Broomhouse Crescent that had advised us of the Dunedin Cycling were also very active in cycling and this began a very close connection to the "McFarlane" Family.

The next few years just flew by, my sister Betty and her friends spent a lot of time at the Cavendish Ballroom, Alan had developed an interest in musical instruments including the trumpet and the Cello, he actually played in a concert in the Usher Hall at one time. Ma and Dad were getting along reasonably well during this period. I had actually got an invitation to play for Longstone United, a Secondary Juvenile Team who was having a hard time fielding a team each week, we didn't have a lot of success, but I was delighted to be playing at right back. We were also taking part in the 10-mile Time Trials at the Mayberry Inn every Wednesday, and I was having some really good times e.g., 24 minutes and 26 seconds which seemed to impress members of the Dunedin Club at the time. I must admit I was delighted with the 26-inch Rosendale bike that Jimmy Gilchrist had ordered and assembled for me at a cost of approx. 50 British pounds (parents couldn't believe this!).

Work was really going well, Bill Pearson had arranged for me to spend 2 years in the "office" training to become an Electrical estimator, he thought I had potential it seems.

New Year 1956 or as we called it Hogmany was to become a very important occasion in my life although I didn't realize it at the time. The McFarlane family and the Frasers had arranged a party at the Lawrence house and to this day I am not sure how we ended up there but Johnny Craig had a crush on Aileen McFarlane's pal Margaret Kirwan (a wee bit snobby), Alex Lawson had a crush on Ann Lawrence, Alastair Tait had been going steady with Margaret Gillespie for a while and we "all" had an eye on the Lawrence sisters (Ann and Betty) as they had really "good figures" and of course I am still on the rebound from a major rejection from Irene Mack.

We all had the most fantastic night, and I had several dances with Doreen McFarlane and really enjoyed her company, the music was mixed, and we had slow dances and faster ones, but the slow ones were "really good".

Doreen was an attractive young woman, quietly fragile and an innocence about her that was noticeable who had developed a tidy little figure after being one of the scrawny wee lassies who used to hang around the shops in the earlier years at Broomhouse. She wore a fascinating perfume at the party that night called "American Cream" that seemed to haunt me for days afterwards. I thought we got on quite well and enjoyed dancing together but as I recall there was no immediate "fireworks" for either of us.

Before the night was over and we had all kissed and cuddled at midnight, some dates had been set and Doreen and I were to meet with some of the other couples for a night at the Astoria picture house in Corstorphine at some future date. Was never sure how Doreen ever agreed to this, but I was really glad it happened.

Back at work after the New Year things were progressing well in my apprenticeship and before I was to be assigned as a Trainee Estimator, I had been working regularly with one Tom McCabe (Electrician) on some new Esso Petrol Stations all over Midlothian, Broxburn and Dalkeith. During this time, I continued to visit Bill and Helen Pearson at a wee flat on Primrose Terrace and then one on Gorgie Road as they seemed to move house frequently.

All the cycling to jobs plus weekends away at Hostels allowed me to become very fit and we were now involved with the Dunedin Cycling Club and attempting time trials of 10,25,50 and 100 miles. This allowed us to enter times for the Dunedin Junior Championship, I actually managed to achieve the "Runner Up" medal in 1958 would you believe with an average speed of 22.78 mph much to my surprise.

Touring was a major part of our lives at this time (the guys). All over Scotland, many parts of England including "YORK" (where Doreen and I would go for our honeymoon in 1959), North Wales including Collwyn Bay, Prestatyn and Lhandudno via the Mersey Tunnel from Liverpool. Johnny Craig and I also had a 2-week tour of Ireland arriving in Larne from Stranraer on the ferry, our tour included overnights at Belfast, County Armagh, Dublin, Waterford, Cork, Galway Bay to name a few.

As you can imagine as I was slowly getting more and more involved with Doreen, It seemed there wasn't enough hours or days in the week and it became very difficult to attend night school 3 nights a week striving for City and Guilds Certification, a very busy job at James Scotts, playing football for Longstone United, Youth Hostelling on weekends and some bike races plus beginning to realize that I had found a "Wee Gem" in Doreen.

Unfortunately, I did make some horrible decisions during this period, who knows why? I was very thankful that "we" survived because when I look back, I was a real "jerk". Can you imagine being out with your pals and bumping into your girlfriend at a bus stop where she was waiting to go to see a picture at the Astoria on her own and I went with my pals. "How could I do that?" This I regretted and have felt guilty ever since. Among the other embarrassing decisions, I made along the way was to be late for a reception being held in the Silver Wing at Sighthill in 1958, Doreen's brother Allan and his new bride Marg were on holiday from Samia in Canada. Not only was I late (out drinking with pals) but even after I arrived there, I didn't make contact with Doreen right away, still can't explain what happened but "I was cast as a villain" by Family and friends with no excuses. God bless Doreen what a really nice forgiving person she was, gave me the last dance and allowed me to take her home in spite of some serious attention from Bob Johnson who was a good friend of the family.

Doreen and I were developing a terrific relationship as we grew to know and understand each other, we loved each other's company and our time together which on reflection seemed to annoy some of the other sisters who may have resented what we had, late night kissing at the back door, cuddling, holding hands and oh yes missing the last bus home quite often.

Our love flourished, we were quite naïve but really enjoying our time together it was like "taking soup with a fork" couldn't get enough of each other it seemed, going to movies, dancing, long walks holding hands it was just "magic" We also had a deep respect for each other and as it turned out we both had the same philosophy about sex before marriage hmmm! although I must admit for me it was a challenge not to get "involved" during the latter stages before getting even considering getting married. My apprenticeship was moving along as I tried to pick up all the tricks of what seemed to be a demanding trade. For some reason I had been having thoughts of looking for a better way of life than what Scotland seemed to offer ordinary people. My parents had both worked most of their married life and provided for our family "but" here they were still living in a council house that was quite nice but barely making ends meet even with all the overtime that Dad worked at the Scottish Gas Board.

There has to be something out there that rewards hard working, taxpaying, community minded people was my thinking at the time. Loved Scotland but between the weather and lack of opportunities I thought, I started researching what might be out there as Doreen and I were moving closer and closer to getting "engaged". Australia, Denmark and Canada (Doreen it happens had relatives in Canada already) were options to consider when and if the time came. Sensitive issue as we both had really close families, what would they think? not really sure what Doreen would think either.

Doreen's older sister Betty and her boyfriend Alex Low both members if the Dunedin Cycling Club and I got to know each other quite well since we were racing and touring together. They were seriously dating at the same time as we were but didn't spend as much time at the "backdoor" of the McFarlane house as Doreen and I did so we always seemed to be in trouble, "what are you two doing out there" was often the cry, mostly good natured from Mrs. Mac and "some" of the sisters. Anyhow both couples were heading to marriage somewhere down the road. Betty being the oldest would be expected to get married first and started making plans in1958.

March 1959 and I was in the last year of my apprenticeship and earning reasonable wages, Doreen had moved from Fishy Thompsons shop in Corstorphine to a good paying job in Kinleith Paper Mill where her dad worked as a millwright Foreman. Time to get "engaged" methinks! So, in my infinite wisdom I go buy an engagement ring that I could afford Hm? One night after a date we are heading home to Doreen's house up at Blinkbonny where one has to cross a wee bridge that goes over the Water of Leith, and I went down on one knee and proposed as I so loved this girl. WOW she accepted thank goodness now we were a "couple" could not stop thinking about the physical side of our relationship now but thought "hold on" we are only engaged.

Both families were happy and excited for us but my dad reminded me that whatever we do make sure I finish my apprenticeship (made sense) before even considering emigrating and consider seriously where you might want to go and the effect it might have on Doreen, "not a problem" I thought. Betty and Alex were engaged by now but hadn't given much thought to a wedding date as yet. My apprenticeship would be complete in November this year 1959 so in my mind I am thinking that would be a good time to get married so discussed this with Doreen who reminded me that Betty would probably want to get married first, being the older sister. This could be difficult for the McFarlane family having z weddings in the same year. We discussed the option of me heading for Canada late November "maybe" and then Doreen joining me and getting married there, not a good option. Plans were then developed for Betty and Alex to be married earlier in the year and use for the November date, huge burden on Mr. McFarlane but he said he could manage it.

In the midst of all this Doreen's younger sister Margaret had been diagnosed with Hodgkin's Lymphoma a type of Cancer for which no cure had been found at this time, but research was on going and there was optimism that a cure would be found over time, but this issue was having a huge effect on Doreen's Mum and the Family.

Doreen and I had decided on a November 1959 Wedding to coincide with me completing my 5 year apprenticeship (I had fortunately been deferred from military service by learning a trade, probably would have been exempt anyway due to club foot) and we wanted to be married before heading to Canada hopefully in the spring of 1960. Betty wasn't too happy because it seems they had planned to be married in 1960 with Jeannette coming home from Canada to be her best maid we found out; it seems the elder sister should be married first and we had created a wee problem rather innocently by making plans for "our" wedding in Nov 1959. Doreen was then to be Betty's Best Maid in Jeanette's absence because she was the next in line as the oldest Twin even although she was to be married 3 months later.

Meanwhile I am happy as Larry with my busy life cycling, football, night school, and dates with Doreen and "socializing" in general, seemed like "good times" to me. Doreen was working very hard to maintain her virginity and finally making really good wages at Kinleith Paper Mill where her Dad had become the Plant Manager, quite an achievement from Millwright Foreman. Doreen was still not sure about the thought of immigrating to Canada even although she had a brother and sister there and leaving behind her Family and sick sister Margaret.

It appeared to me that since the McFarlane Family now had 2 weddings to plan in 1959 maybe I could get things started for "our" wedding, planner and organizer that I thought I was. Major BOO BOO #1, I had gone ahead and booked the Silver Wing at Sighthill Road for our Wedding reception, arranged buses for transport to and from Currie Kirk and was looking into booking a band or some type of music when Mrs. Mac got wind of my endeavors!' I was told in no uncertain terms that this was none of my business (the groom) and all the plans would be made by the bride's family. WOW. Talked this over with Dad and he said that although my intentions were good Mrs. Mac was "absolutely right".

Betty and Alex had a lovely wedding on Aug 29/59 at his Church down in Leith area with a reception held at the Milton House Hotel near Portobello. Good time was had by all with many memorable moments. Helen Manson who was a friend and neighbor to the McFarlane family had an American soldier boyfriend who was stationed at Kirknewton at the time were both at the wedding, his name was Cliff Doylan. After the reception he had offered Doreen and I a ride up to Blinkbonny where the celebration was to continue, my Ma and Dad would get a ride from Jessie and George Lee. Our car made a pit stop at the Railway Inn at Juniper Green where we decided to have a drink. A good Scottish custom is to buy a round of drinks so I decided to get the drinks since we wouldn't be there long as we had to get back to Blinky, imagine my surprise when Cliff said "well I think I will have a triple brandy", I was stunned but got him his drink. Yanks I thought to myself, money to burn it seems.

Our Wedding would be at Currie Kirk near Juniper Green, reception would be at Crawford Rooms near Stockbridge and Water of Leith, my parents offered to share some of the expenses with Mr. Mac possibly the Bar bill, but this was declined. At the reception many of the Currie friends and relatives weren't aware that the Bar was "free" and had found a Pub just up the road while filling in time before the meal. We had to send someone up to get them. They were a wee bit under the weather by then but delighted to hear about the free booze.

The reception went very well but Doreen and I had to leave early, which turned out to be a big mistake, I had arranged our train to York for 7:30 at the Waverley Station, how daft was that? Seems we missed a really great party. The train ride was very long and boring and here we were heading for our "honeymoon" but didn't get there till about 7 am as we stopped at every Station on the way down from Edinburgh, on reflection we should have arranged a room for the night in Auld Reekie.

We managed to get a taxi to our hotel "The Spotted Cow" which was just outside the walls of old York not far from the Cathedral, the name should have been a clue to what to expect! York is a beautiful City in England that I had visited in my earlier cycling adventures. The hotel was closed and in darkness, the taxi driver said, "are you sure this is your hotel?" and had a peculiar look in his eyes.

We had banged and banged on the door getting more and more frustrated at the situation when eventually the landlord came to the entrance door "what are you doing here" he said banging on my door at this time of night, when I told him who we were he said you weren't supposed to arrive till tomorrow morning, what a great way to start our first night of marriage me thinks.

We finally got booked in and made our way up to what only can be described as a "modest" on the second floor we were both a bit tired and totally not in a romantic mood. We had what could only be described as an "awkward" first night, neither one of us knew what to do, (no experience) and eventually fell asleep exhausted only to wake up very early in the morning both slightly embarrassed about our first night and listening to cattle/sheep noises coming from outside the window. Yes, you guessed it "The Spotted Cow" was in the middle of a huge marketplace. But wait it gets worse and worse, after we had showered and dressed careful not to look at each other in underwear we headed down the stairs for breakfast, I think every farmer in York was sitting there looking at us with a smile "this would be the Honeymoon Couple" from Scotland. We were both totally embarrassed again as they probably all had an idea about what we were trying to do last night.

Turned out to be a very long week in York as we were both quite uncomfortable as we wandered around York Cathedral and all the other history in the City wondering "what happened" to us after such a wonderful, affectionate and terrific courtship? Is this really what being married is all about, not a good start by any definition.

We arrived back home after our "honeymoon" both pretending we have had a nice time and shared some of our memories with friends and family, but the truth of the matter was a nightmare experience for both of us as we discussed it sometime later. What happened? No experience! There could be an argument here for pre-marital sex but really how were we to know.

The plan to immigrate to Canada in April 1960 was even more sensitive than ever due to the awkward relationship after the honeymoon and of course Doreen's younger sister Margaret's situation was deteriorating. We moved into a small apartment on Primrose Terrace that had belonged to Bill and Helen Pearson, and we were both working hard to save the fares for the trip as we did not want to go on "assisted package" to Canada. Doreen contacted her brother in Sarnia Canada for the sponsorship letter required to get us into Canada.

We were slowly recovering our innocent love for each other over time but then I was sent to Jedburgh to work on a farm by James Scott's my employer, it was a good job for me now that I was a journeyman "but" I said look I have just got married and can't really be gone from Monday to Friday every week, I was told basically sorry but you have to go. So, we gave up the Primrose Terrace apartment, Doreen moved back home to Blinkbonny and continued working and earning good wages at her Dad's paper mill at Kinleith while I worked in Jedburgh.

By now Doreen and I had figured out the sex thing and were recovering our strong feelings for each other again. So, every Friday I would get the bus home from Jedburgh about a 1-hour drive, and we would go to the pictures and have a drink and something to eat afterwards. I was always kind of anxious to get to bed and have sex (been away for 5 days) but once again I hadn't consulted Doreen who had also been working all week, living at her Mum and Dad's all week (very emotional status) PLUS people can hear us in the bedroom. This marriage thing was a bit of a challenge it seems.

Although I had a club foot and would not likely to be conscripted into the Forces for 2 years it was still a bit of a concern for me and also my Ma, Conscription was scheduled to finish at the end of December 1959 and my apprenticeship finished in November 1959 as I would then be a Certified Electrical Engineer, wonder what would happen?

The next few months went by rather quickly as we continued to work during the week and enjoy our weekends together and started planning for our big adventure to Canada, Doreen with some trepidation it must be said. We had heard from her brother Allan with some useful advice to follow including bring lots of money and try to make sure that Doreen was not pregnant? as we would not be covered by the Ontario Health system for at least a year after arrival. We had been saving hard but mostly to pay our airfare to London Ontario (about 60 British Pounds each) and have some extra cash for living expenses for a few weeks at Allan and his wife Marg's house in Sarnia. We did go to the City Chambers in Edinburgh to talk to the Canadian Emigration Officer looking for any help he could give us regarding our move to his country. We were absolutely astounded when he asked where we were heading for and when we said Sarnia Ontario he had "no idea" where that was, oh no! where are we heading for.

April 26, 1960, came around in a hurry lots of excitement and emotions at the McFarlane and Currie households, especially the 2 Mums, Betty McFarlane had gone through this 2 times before, but it was new to my Ma and of course Doreen's Mum was dealing with Margaret who was very sick and Doreen was struggling with leaving home at this time. Doreen's Dad had helped us with the planning and built a small wooden crate for some of our personal stuff that would be shipped ahead of us.

There is absolutely no way we could have possibly been prepared for the "big day", we all gathered at the Waverley Station in Edinburgh, friends, families, neighbors and work mates the emotions were brutal as we patiently waited for the Train coming from Newcastle that was to whisk us away to Prestwick Airport on our way to a new life. During the emotional turmoil someone heard an announcement on the PA system "train from Newcastle has been delayed and would not arrive for several hours" what now? we had to be at Prestwick Airport to catch the Flight to Canada. After some tense discussions Terry Shanks and Walter Fraser two very good friends of the McFarlane's offered to drive us (more emotions) so off we went but as we waved cheerio to all and sundry with lots of tears, we couldn't help but wonder when will we ever see them all again.

The 2-hour drive to Prestwick Airport was uneventful, fairly quiet except for a few sniffles and some idle chatter, Terry and Walter made sure we were checked in for our flight and settled in the waiting area at the airport before heading back to Edinburgh, they wouldn't take any money for the petrol, said with a smile we might need it in Canada. Once we were on the plane, we were told the flight could take approximately 13 hours to reach our destination. The plane was not exactly state of the art it seems, (turbo-jet). We went through all kinds of emotions and even I who had wanted to do this had a wee cry thinking "what have we done"? leaving behind a beautiful country, good friends and great families. Doreen had a few sick moments on the way and had to use the brown bags on the plane that were provided for this purpose "but "what we didn't know until sometime later was that she was pregnant "oh no".

Landed in Montreal to refuel and then headed for Toronto Airport and then hopefully on to London Ontario but unfortunately had some engine trouble and had to go back to Montreal where we had to wait until the plane was fixed and ready to go again.

We had been scheduled to land in Toronto Airport for about 11 hours where we had hoped to spend some time with my old pal Johnny Craig who was now working and living here in Toronto but because of all the delays along the way we only had 30 minutes to say hello and cheerio, he had been waiting almost 10 hrs. to see us poor bugger. Off we went again on our way and as we approached London Airport it seemed very small and the trees looked very dry and there didn't seem to be much habitation or houses in the area, hmm, what next? After we got off the plane, we were surprised to find nobody waiting for us at the arrival's terminal, anyway we waited and waited but after a couple of hours and still nobody to meet us we decided to call Sarnia. Both Allan (Doreen s brother) and Jeanette (Doreen's elder sister) were surprised to hear we were in London Ontario they thought we were in London England. Apparently, they had got the dates all wrong but would send a car down to get us and it would take at least an hour or more.

So, we had a cup of tea and waited for them. Two and a half hours later Allan arrived with Norm Fairbairn (Jeanette's husband) they had had car troubles on the way from Sarnia but at last they were here, and we loaded the car before heading down the Highway to Sarnia. What an adventure, things can only get better if our life in Canada is to be a success.

BALKYMOR 9

CANADA, 1960-1983

We arrived back in Sarnia (the Chemical Valley) several hours after landing in London Ontario. Allan's wife Marg, who was pregnant with Cathie at the time, their son Steven, Jeanette and her 3 kids Douglas, Tania and Colin were all anxiously waiting at the Fairbairn house on Brock Street for our arrival. Lots of excitement as you could imagine as we all sat around and chatted about our trip and catching up on family news, having a few drinks and some nice food the ladies had prepared. Doreen and I were both exhausted and needed a shower before we started unpacking so off, we went to Allan and Marg's house on Parsons Street where they showed us to the bedroom, we would be using till we managed to find a place of our own somewhere down the road.

The following morning, we were up early suffering a wee bit jet lag and had a coffee with some toast as we tried to come to grips with the events of the last few days, bit much to take in. We were surprised to find Allan still at home that morning as we knew he worked at Polymer as a Lab Technician, what we didn't know was he had been on strike for 3 months and hadn't wanted to tell us. So here we were living at Doreen's brother's house, he is on strike has a wife a bairn and another on the way and no income to speak of and now he has Doreen and I living with them, hmm interesting developments it would seem.

Doreen appeared very confused and unhappy the first few days, away from her home in Scotland and family, not feeling well in the morning? spent a lot of quiet time in our room reading. I had some very embarrassing moments in Marg's kitchen spilling milk, dropping eggs out the fridge and other clumsy actions, felt really uncomfortable for a while. Allan took me down to the Unemployment Office to register where I managed to pick up a wee job "sod busting", I was willing to take anything just to get started and earn a few dollars. Ed Sullivan had a contract to lay grass at some of the new houses in the area. All he needed was cheap labor, but I took it anyway for $1 an hour and work as many hours as you were able to but no overtime rate! First week I worked 80 hours and almost died, it was heavy work, and I wasn't used to that, but I hung in there. Got my first paycheck at the end of the week and scurried down to the CIBC Bank at Northgate to open an account and get some cash. "Sorry sir" Ed Sullivan doesn't have enough money in his account to cover this "what" you have to be kidding? The Cheque bounced but Ed said there would be some money in the bank the following week and could I just be patient and work the next week. The girl in the Bank was very kind, took Allan's phone # and said as soon as Mr. Sullivan makes a deposit, she would phone me immediately and if I went straight over to the bank, she would make sure I got paid and I did, what a nice young woman.

Allan and I seemed to get on well right from the get-go, Norm gave me the impression that he was a different cut of cloth, but we still got on quite well. They both told me that there was plenty of work in Sarnia for Electricians and I should start looking as soon as possible as "sod busting" wasn't a promising career. Meanwhile Doreen and Marg were doing ok but Marg was awaiting the birth of the second child and Doreen was struggling with life in general, a new home, a new country, a new husband and missing her Family in Scotland.

One night after my work we had supper (dinner in Scotland) and Allan, and I had had a few beers after playing with a football out on the street much to the amusement of several neighbors when we had a wee chat on how things were going generally. He asked me if I remembered the advice, he had given us before emigrating and I said yes so, he then asked, "how much money did you actually bring with you"? I told him $90, now keep in mind he had been on strike for 3 months and hadn't made any mortgage payments, I thought he was going to faint, although that $go seemed a lot to us it was not a lot by Canadian standards. Then he asked about Doreen who had been sick most mornings and I said I think she might be pregnant wow another bad reaction, after a few more beers and a couple of shots of whisk he told me of the predicament they were in financially due to the strike at Polymer. Ever the optimist I said, "we can work our way through this". I realized that I needed a better paying job sooner than later so as not be a burden to Allan and Marg.

Went back to the employment office and asked a guy by the name of Jack Easedale about a job in the electrical trade, he said he would do what he could for me. He then asked if I had ever played football (soccer) in Scotland and when I told him I had played for Longstone United Secondary Juvenile team Edinburgh Amateur league he seemed impressed and told me to get Allan to take me to Norm Perry Park when I had time as Sarnia had a local soccer club that may be looking for some players (not sure that I was good enough) but no harm going some Tuesday or Thursday and kicking the ball around. He said he had helped lots of the lads on the team find good work.

Doreen had to find a doctor so we went to see a Dr. Gladdy, who had an office near Northgate and made an appointment, he confirmed that in fact Doreen was pregnant and also confirmed what Allan had told us, we wouldn't have OHIP coverage until 1 year in Canada, this could be a problem financially it seems. Nice man that he was he said not to worry about finances at this time as we had enough to worry about trying to settle in Sarnia. Got an interview for a job with Delta Electrical Services, a guy by the name of Terry Jongsma said he would hire me at $1.10 hr. but would have to learn armature winding as they had no electrical contract work at the moment, so I took the job working 40 hours week and settled in quickly to this new aspect of the electrical trade.

We now had to think about getting a place to rent since we couldn't stay on forever at Allan and Marg's house, Norm and Jeanette rented a big house on Brock Street that had a wee apartment attached (converted garage) that might soon be available, that was encouraging news. Allan and I had given some thought to going to Norm Perry to check out the soccer team but there was just too much going on it seemed at the time. Got a phone call from Jack Easdale asking how things were going and he said that Dow Chemical might be hiring early in 1961 and if I was interested, he would keep me in mind but suggested I try to go the soccer practices as they would get the priority.

Although neither Allan nor I had actually played a game for the Sarnia Soccer Club during that summer of 1960 we got to know some of the players by going to practices on Tuesdays and Thursdays. Tom Finlayson who had emigrated to Canada in 1929, Syd Harris and George Edwards were the 3 older men who ran the team all from the UK, but Tom was the only Scotsman, Doreen and

I developed a very close relationship over the years with Tom and his wife Morag.

The small garage apartment attached to Norm and Jeanette's at 254 South Brock Street was to become available to us after about 3 months living with Allan and Marg, the rent was to be $50 month, so we agreed to take it, especially with Doreen's sister living next door. The timing was good as Doreen, and I felt it was time to move on as our relationship with Allan and Marg was becoming a wee bit strained. We had been getting to know the neighbors at Parsons Street, socializing, playing soccer, headers keepy uppy, and throwing a baseball on the street and would miss them.

A wee place of our own "WOW", we moved a few weeks later with minimal furniture to start with "bare bones" actually, not much space to fill but we needed basic stuff. Managed to pick up some stuff at Hudson's Bay Dept store, Bed, Dresser, Kitchen table and 2 chairs and other odds and ends to get started. Jeannette and Marg had given us some extra kitchen pots pans, knives and forks etc.

Doreen was due with our first baby in late December 1960 and Dr. Gladdy had somehow arranged that the Hospital Bill would be taken care of even although we really didn't qualify for OHIP? Work was going well for me, but salary was poor at Delta Electric, and I had actually been doing Electrical contract work for them and not armature winding as Terry had originally said I would be doing but that didn't matter as I was working and doing okay financially, we thought. Jack Easdale at the Employment Office was keeping an eye on any opportunities at Dow Chemical for me since I had committed to playing for the local Soccer Team in 1961, really wasn't that good but what the heck football/soccer in Canada was a growing sport.

We got settled in the apartment having a busy time sorting out the apartment and Doreen although pregnant was feeling a bit better about life in Canada but still struggling with all the changes in her young life.

Around this time a guy by the name of Dave Butt who turned out to be the Electrical Union Business Agent had got wind that I was working non-union and wanted to have a chat with me, could we meet soon. He had discovered that I was a fully Qualified Electrician from Scotland and wondered why I hadn't gone to Union Hall looking for work instead of working for Delta Electrical at such a low salary $1.10/hr when I could be earning $3.25/hr working for the Union. No answer really other than I took the first job I could get, "right" he said after checking my credentials, you start work next Monday at get this Dow Chemical of all places "but" as an Electrician on a new Unit they were building. Told him I had to talk to Terry Jongsma at Delta and give him 2 weeks' notice, don't do that he said go in and hand in your notice asap. I couldn't do that but did give Terry 2 weeks' notice, Dave thought I was nuts, Terry was angry but did agree it was a great opportunity for me and wished me all the best.

Meanwhile back in Scotland Doreen's young sister was struggling with Hodgkin's Lymphoma and this had a huge impact on Doreen who was dealing with our first pregnancy and all the other issues related to the culture shock of emigrating.

After moving into 254 South Brock Street Doreen and I would often take a walk in the evening since we didn't have a car and I couldn't drive anyway and one night we walked past a building on our street that looked like a big barn, and we heard lots of noise coming from within. We paid $1 each to go in and see what the noise was all about. This was our introduction to Ice Hockey Canada's National Sport it seems.

About 300 people were shouting and cheering for a Team called The Sarnia Legionnaires playing in what was called Junior "B" hockey, little did we know that a young guy by the name of Phil Esposito (who eventually would become a superstar with the Boston Bruins in the NHL) was playing on what was called the "Sault Line". Dick Lakowitch and Jimmy Sanko were the other members of this prolific scoring line, they were from a place called Sault Saint Marie somewhere up north. Doreen was so excited? ho hum, little did we know then what an important part of our lives this sport would play in our future.

I had been working on the Construction job at Dow Chemical for about 3 months and Norm suggested it was about time I learned to drive, he took me out a few times and taught me the basics of driving in a very large car called an Oldsmobile, allowed me to drive around the block a couple of times and said "ok Jim your reading for driving test" my reaction was "are you kidding me?" He wasn't I took the test and much to my surprise passed the test with a few nervous moments. Now I have the license but no car but at least I could drive when given the opportunity.

In Nov 1960 I had decided that in spite of the higher wages in the construction trade I had been told that there wasn't a lot of work in winter months due to inclement weather, the option of working full time in Dow Chemical as a Trainee Process Operator might be a better choice for me. Besides I was concerned about being a color-blind electrician even though I had been doing very well on the construction job, had actually become a Foreman mainly because I could read electrical drawings and it turns out for some reason that not a lot of the Local Electricians could. Anyway, I contacted Jack Easedale at the Employment office, and he arranged an interview for me at Dow.

Went to the Administration Office on South Vidal Street and was interviewed by a guy named Jack Hornblower he asked about my education, and I proudly replied "graduated with Scottish

Secondary Leaving Certificate" also served 5-year Electrical Apprenticeship with 4 years at Bellevue Technical Night School during the 5 years learning the Trade. "What age did you graduate from school he asked?" "I left school when I was 15 years old, that is fairly normal in Scotland unless you are going on to University or College" was my reply. The Interview was suspended, seems I didn't qualify for employment as I needed to have a minimum Canadian Grade 12 education level (normally 18 years old to graduate) I was devastated. When I relayed what had happened to Allan McFarlane he said, "don't worry about it, go back in a couple of weeks, apply again and tell them you do have Grade 12 "equivalent". I anxiously waited for 2 long weeks, arranged another Interview and told them I had Grade 12 equivalent and to my surprise was told to get a medical and if it was ok you have a job. They did express some concern that I might jump ship in the spring when the construction picked up again, but I managed to convince them I was more interested in learning Process work and working year-round with some benefits even at a lower hourly rate.

All the guys at the Soccer Club were happy for me and Doreen but couldn't fully understand why I would take a job in the "Plants" instead of staying with the Electricians Union, who knows? It was a gut-wrenching decision, but I was more interested in a steady job for the future, with a good salary and benefits too. With a pregnant Wife and a Family to look after it just seemed the right thing to do at the time. Doreen got a part time job at the Dominion Store near Northgate about now Xmas 1960 was a major disaster for us, Doreen was ready to have our first baby late December we thought, but all we could think of was "what" we were missing in Scotland, Family, Friends, Xmas, lots of Parties the New Year Celebrations (Hogmanay) and all the good times that we had left behind to come to Canada. We went to bed very early, cuddling together for comfort, wanting all this to "go away" shed quite a few tears about what we were missing Traditions, "not a good time of our young lives".

Jeff our first son was due on Dec 27/60 but didn't arrive until Jan 3/61 at St Joseph's Hospital after a long and energy draining birth for Doreen, she had looked beautiful all during her pregnancy and I loved her to death and even more when Jeff arrived safe and sound with all his bits and pieces intact (no club feet, my big concern). I was in and out of the hospital as time permitted between work, going for a beer and table tennis matches as I was playing for the Sarnia Soccer Table Tennis team this first winter. Phil Turner, Don Bell, Bobby Copeland, and Arthur Walker were the other team members. In retrospect I had my priorities all wrong and really should have spent more time at the hospital with Doreen and the baby.1961 promised to be a great year by my definition after the miserable Xmas season, we have just had a new baby son, new job at Dow Chemical, our own apartment, involved with the Sarnia Soccer Club and maybe buy a wee car. Doreen probably had her own thoughts about our future, 1960 had been challenging for her to say the least even with some of her family close by.

We were delighted to get our baby home after a few days in hospital and felt like we were a "wee family" now, Doreen did take some time to recover from her ordeal, but she had a glow about her that suggested she was happy to be a Mum. Things went reasonably well for a few months with Doreen's cousin George Lee, his wife Jessie and their 3 kids scheduled to arrive in Sarnia from Scotland in the early spring but on April 10/61 we got news that Doreen's young sister Margaret had passed away at age 16 in Edinburgh, we were all devastated with the news. The rest of that summer was a bit depressing as you can imagine but we decided to proceed with our plans to spend Doreen's 21st Birthday with twin sister Aileen, new boyfriend Ron Phillips and both our Families at the Maybury Inn near Corstorphine while on our first vacation back in Edinburgh since immigrating to Canada. We had a really good time at the Birthday party, had some nice visits with family and friends during the vacation but thoughts were still with sister Margaret, Doreen's Mum and Dad were really struggling with the loss of such a young daughter. With bitter/ sweet memories and heavy hearts we headed back to Canada.

I had got used to walking to work at Dow getting the odd ride from a workmate and on occasion would take the bus which wasn't on a regular schedule at that time. The weather in the winters could be brutally cold especially late in the evenings on my way home and I actually suffered frost bite on my right ear one night, should have worn a hat, I guess. We were settling in well at Brock Street and began thinking about getting a "car" something we only dreamed about back home in Scotland but seemed a necessity here in Canada. Phil Turner had a very good friend called Eric Widdowson who worked for Bay View Chrysler Dodge at this time, and he said he would try and find me an older cheaper car to start with and he did, 1956 Pontiac for $300. I kicked the tires, didn't know what I should be looking for.

We decided to buy it and after signing the papers I asked if he could drive me home as I hadn't driven much up till then. Eric drove me home to Brock Street and now we had a car that would sit in the driveway for a while. Although I did have a valid driver's license, I didn't have the courage to drive the car on the road at first but spent a lot of hours meantime going up and down the driveway trying to become familiar with the car.

My job at Dow seemed very mundane at first, I was assigned to the "Track Dept" in a large Warehouse working for a Charlie Borthwick (the foreman), was shown how to safely and carefully fill drums with a variety of chemicals put the cap on and move it off the scale's "wow", getting paid for this, money for old rope it seemed. The days and afternoon shifts were very long and boring, but more was to come, soon I was shown how to load a Tank Truck then a Railway Tank car and then all sorts of other wee jobs related to transporting all sorts of chemicals. Felt very comfortable with this and Charlie soon was asking me "keep an eye on things" while he disappeared to do other stuff? Job seemed to be going smoothly so far.

Meanwhile Doreen and Jeanette were getting along very well for the most part and rebuilding a nice sister relationship, they spent a lot of time in each other's apartments looking after the kids and doing domestic stuff and shopping. We were really glad to have Norm next door one afternoon when I was at work, Doreen discovered a rat in the toilet bowl she slammed the lid and went running next door screaming and yelling. Norm who did a lot of hunting was quite calm and went through to our apartment armed with a hockey stick while Jeanette tried to console Doreen, seems he closed the toilet door, opened the toilet lid and beat the rat to death. Not being very brave I was kind of glad I wasn't there, but it caused us to think about how long we wanted to stay in Brock Street.

Some strange actions during my time working on the Track took place but I was advised to "just do the job" and don't ask too many questions, drop the level in this tank from 6ft to zft, open the suction and discharge valves and start the pump and stay here until the level drops, 3 hours later it was at zft. Was curious where the "stuff" was going, don't you worry about that I was told. Drain lead to the St Clair River but I had to do what I was told, strange conflict of interest I thought, my integrity told me this isn't right but "Environmental Issues" were not a priority back then it seemed.

Outside of work life was going well, Doreen and I were trying 10 pin bowling with Norm and Jeanette with his Catalytic Construction friends, it was fun getting out, but bowling didn't do it for me, as a sport but we played for the whole season anyway. During the summer I had signed and played for the Sarnia Soccer Club, they had a good team but always seemed to be short of players, so we went pub crawling looking for players most Fridays and found a player or two. The players we did have who were dedicated to training and playing included, Charlie McCracken, Phil Turner, Ray Thompson, Roger Letham and a German chap Johhny Eischolz. We picked up a really good player when Doreen's cousin George Lee and his family arrived late in the season, he had played Junior level in Scotland and had a trial for Aberdeen in the Scottish First Division. Doreen was enjoying having Jeff and we later found out she was pregnant again and we were both happy about that.

Lots of soccer in 1962, playing for Sarnia and London & District All Stars travelling to places like Chicago, Hamilton and Windsor for exhibition games as soccer seemed to be growing in Canada and the USA. This activity was taking up a lot of time much to the dismay of our wives who didn't mind us playing but not too excited about the boozing and late nights afterwards which obviously caused some conflict.

On April 27, 1962, our second son Mike was born, 2 boys where I chuffed or what!!! These were busy times with Doreen having 2 young kids and trying to keep the apartment reasonably clean, my work/soccer etc, trying to get to the beach for picnics and family breakfasts as often as possible now that we were now using "the car". On top of this we were trying to raise funds for the Soccer Team, and I got deeply involved with arranging Dances and 50/50 draws with Phil Turner who had become a good friend and his wife Peggy who had 2 young kids also and got on well with Doreen. We were beginning to feel the apartment on Brock Street was too small for our growing family and started looking for a larger flat.

In August 1962 we had found a nice 2-bedroom basement apartment and made the move to 1100 Lakeshore Road after negotiating with a really nice Dutch couple Mr. and Mrs. Vandenheuvel who gave us a break on the monthly rent as they had themselves emigrated to Canada understood the challenges we faced and seemed to take a liking to us. They had a nice back garden with lots of flowers and vegetables plus an old wooden rowboat sitting to the side that provided hours and hours of fun for Jeff and Mike in later months. Next door there was a nice Canadian family the "Frasers" who we would get to know really well, and our kids played together a lot in both yards, they had a little girl who had been born with Down's Syndrome, but our boys seemed oblivious to this, and they played happily with "Cathy", who was their friend.

Somehow or other our new apartment with a rear entrance from the back garden became the "social" place for work mates and the guys on the soccer team, we had many wonderful occasions and evenings, and I am sure the Dutch couple wondered what they had let themselves in for. Doreen for the most part was quite supportive of all these activities and was a gracious hostess but as I look back what with New Years parties, Dow guys dropping in after working 4-12 shift and the soccer guys coming back after dances, games and practice in retrospect it must have been a lot to deal with, what was I thinking? There was one incident one night after 4-12 shift, we had gone for a drink on the way home and I invited the Dow guys back to the flat and one of the guys was a bit forward with Doreen, so she slapped him and that put an end to that night, the guy apologized later but things were a bit awkward after that.

Doreen and I would try and get out for a date at the odd time with one of the Fraser boys babysitting, Jeff and Mike, we also still managed to get out bowling with Norm, Jeanette, Allan and Marg once a week, quite a busy life at the time. Things had been going so well we invited my Ma and Dad to come visit us in Sarnia in 1963, Dad proud old bugger took the position he would only come when he could afford to pay "his own way Doreen's Mum, Norms Mum Mary, his sister Moira and a friend of Jessie Lee had also planned a trip to come to Canada that year. Dolly, Betty, Mary and some of the others although coming and going on different dates all seemed to enjoy our lifestyle here in Canada. We had trips to the beach, breakfast in the park, house parties and even a trip to Niagara Falls that everyone enjoyed. We went over to Buffalo in USA one night while visiting Niagara to try and see Nat King Cole concert, got lost on the freeways and never did see the show, ended up in a grungy wee Pub before heading back to Hotel in Niagara. One wee incident my Ma will never forget at 1100 Lakeshore was the day she was in the toilet and screamed for me to help her, she had been to the toilet and flushed as one would "but" the toilet bowl over flowed much to her embarrassment, don't think she ever got over that, couldn't convince her it wasn't her fault but we did have some fun about it later after she calmed down ha ha. When my Ma shared her many holiday experiences with my dad after arriving home, he said he regretted his decision not to come "but" he would come next time "even if he couldn't pay his own way" such is life.

We had a nice trip to Detroit in 1963 while Mrs. Mac and my Mum were here visiting, they couldn't get over the height of the sky-scrapers and how busy downtown was but somehow, we managed to get to the Detroit Zoo and really enjoyed the experience. We had a nice picnic lunch, and both the Mums shared a wheelchair as they got tired as the day progressed, had a really good time but tiring. We really missed them when they headed home to Scotland several days later.

Our life was becoming very busy as we settled in here in Sarnia just seemed like a bit of a blur at times, managed to write an airmail letter to Ma and Dad once a week to keep them informed on how things were going. Sarnia Soccer Club was doing well, George Lee and I had become the best of friends as we both played on the soccer and table tennis teams. Jessie and Doreen seemed to go get on well, so we did a lot of social activities together with other team members. Lots of parties, bus trips to some of our games and Dances to raise funds for the team that we all enjoyed. Occasionally we would head out to Brights Grove area on Sundays and have picnics, at first it was Wildwood beach and then later we would go to Brigden Sideroad beach as it was a bit quieter for our young kids, good times!!! I was now the Team Captain and getting involved probably more than I should have but got on great with the committee and as they were getting a bit old for all the duties require to run a team, I guess I was "willing" to get involved. Oh, by the way Doreen was handling z kids now and very busy at home and by hook or by crook we were pregnant again hmmm.

Sometime in the late summer I managed to get a week off my work at Dow with short notice, we borrowed a tent, packed some stuff, exchanged some Canadian dollars for USA dollars (got $1.10c not bad, eh?) and headed for Kentucky USA. We had never camped before, with a borrowed tent, and in the rain we arrived at Colonel Carter State Park 7 hours later. After spending hours trying to put the tent up, not fun I must add we had a terrible night with not much to eat, Doreen pregnant and not very well, the boys a wee bit grumpy we decided the next morning "to hell" with camping, packed the bags, headed for Sandusky Ohio, got a nice Motel and had a great time at Cedar Point and Sandusky beach for the rest of the week.

1965 turned out to be quite an eventful year, Jeanette who hadn't been too well and Doreen were both pregnant, on March 31st Elaine was born, about 3 weeks late "we did get our girl" but it was a difficult time for Doreen, now we have 3 kids. Jeanette had a seizure during her pregnancy at just over 7 months in March and was taken to London Victoria Hospital where she was diagnosed with a brain tumor and almost died, her baby Jan was taken during the pregnancy on April 3rd barely 5lbs, but Jeanette survived and was sent home after about 5 or 6 weeks still having seizures.

Around this time Aileen and Ron, now married, had arrived in Sarnia and stayed with us until Doreen went into the hospital to have our baby girl just before they moved to Allan and Marg's house on Parsons Street. The arrival of Aileen and Ron would at some stage in the future have a significantly negative impact on our social lives here in Sarnia even though we did have some great times together. Aileen, being the stronger willed twin (squeaky wheel) made things happen while Doreen was the gentler twin who quietly went about her business and in my opinion was more thoughtful and considerate of others. Norm later asked Aileen if she could move into the Fairbairn house on Nelson St and help him take care of his family since Jeanette had been sent home from hospital and was still quite sick and that Doreen would probably have her hands full with a new baby and 3 kids to look after, seems also that Jeanette had a limited life expectancy and would be in and out of hospital as her health deteriorated.

Mr. McFarlane visited our Families during the summer of 1965, he was on a quest to trace some of his Family members who had settled in Hamilton Ontario many years ago, had some minor success but think he was a little disappointed with the results. Ron and Aileen had now gone off to Petawawa where Ron had found some work on the DEW Line, and we felt at that time Norm expected that Doreen should have done more for her sick sister even though she had her hands full with her own family. Doreen felt her efforts may not have been fully appreciated but always gave 100% of what she could under very difficult circumstances.

Doreen was beginning to struggle big time with everything that was going on at this time, doing her best for the Fairbairn's, trying to cope with our 3 kids and all that was going on at the time. I thought I was doing what I could but again my priorities seemed to be in the wrong place, soccer, table tennis and getting involved with the SMAA trying to develop kids' soccer, not enough support for my wife and kids when she needed it? seems to me now that even working at Dow Chemical then was for me just a "hobby" that provided us with a good income.

The rest of that year we were in the survival mode and Xmas and New Year seemed to come and go very quickly but Doreen and I tried to get out on a "date" once in a while, I always liked our anniversary night out at the "Golden Hind" restaurant at Northgate, food was good and reasonably priced but by the time we paid babysitters and had a couple of drinks it started to add up but it was our once a year (at that time) night out.

Doreen had encouraged us to consider buying a wee house soon since the Lakeshore apartment was getting to be too small for our growing Family.

In the spring of 1966, we seriously began looking for a house, discussed what we thought we might want and how much we could really afford and tried to estimate what the expenses might be and then contacted a real estate agent. He showed us a few houses based on what we had decided and wanted, e.g., a brick house, one floor, 3 bedrooms, nice bathroom, basement, and possibly a garage up in the North End of Sarnia. "Well," he said how much money do you actually have? We replied rather proudly enough for a $900 down payment and we would consider something called a 25-year mortgage. He gently told us we were looking in the wrong place and took us to some smaller storey and a half frame house around town and we landed at 794 Pineview Ave just off Rosedale Ave (houses that were built many years ago after the war it turns out) but in our price range. Lovely small 3-bedroom house, large basement with a beautiful yard and some really nice shade trees that was owned by a nice older Dutch couple who wanted to sell and instantly seemed to take a liking to us. Unfortunately, they died sometime later in a car crash and their son had to hold the second Mortgage for us.

We had wanted better but this we thought we could afford so Doreen said let's go for it and after much discussion and the old couple giving us a break on the down payment, we agreed to make an offer. The house was priced at $10,700 and we could only get 75% of that as a first mortgage which left us unable to come up with all of the 20% down payment which we didn't have so the nice old couple said they would carry a small second mortgage so we made a deal, exciting but very scary "we owned a house" something we had only dreamed about in Scotland. The house was going to need a lot of work and lots of painting (house was all in dark colors) but we were ok with that. By the way "owning" the house wasn't quite right as it really belonged to the mortgage company till, we paid them all the money back over umpteen years! We were able to get a mortgage with Canadian Trust over a 17-year period @ 7% whatever that meant. Think the biggest shock Doreen and I got was when we received a statement after living one year in the house, the status of the mortgage! we had paid approx. $100 a month for over 12 months and all that came of what they called the principle was $19 "what a shock?", the rest of the money went to Interest on the mortgage, I cried for the second time in a year, such is the life of naïve land owners. However, kudos once again to Doreen as this turned out to be probably one of the best decisions we have ever made in our lives. We now had a "HOME".

We should have been over the moon after buying our first house but so many changes in Doreen's young life over the last few years was taking a toll on her emotionally, physically and mentally it seemed a breakdown was imminent according to Dr. Gladdy. Getting married leaving her home and her Family in Scotland, settling in a new country, sickness in her family,3 kids in 5 years, early marriage issues, buying and trying to settle in a new house while spending a lot of time on her own as I was enjoying life in Canada with lots of activities at work and play were all contributing factors to a major meltdown. Dr. Gladdy insisted on hospital for Doreen as she was on the brink of a nervous breakdown, so life suddenly became quite complicated as we all tried to cope. Doctor advised me it was about time that I gave serious consideration to our Family affairs and spending more time looking after Doreen and the kids as my wife needed more support from me at "home".

Everybody we knew gave us a helping hand in one way or another during this time, my activities were severely adjusted to meet commitments with work and looking after the kids. On one occasion I was asked to look after Aileen and Ron's family as they had planned a trip to Niagara Falls, I looked after the 5 kids for a couple of days and somehow managed ok. Doreen's Mum visited that summer around May and June, but Doreen can't remember much of that trip as she was in the hospital and had EST (electric shock therapy) losing a bit of short-term memory during the visit. We were allowed to pick up Doreen from the hospital for the McPhee Family wedding at that time provided she was returned to the Ward by 8pm. Jessie Lee had been quite unhappy and having difficulty adjusting to her life in Canada and seemed to be a bit cool toward Doreen for some time toward the end of her stay, she seemed desperate to go back to Scotland even although by now George had finally found steady good paying work at Polysar. She went home for a holiday in July with her kids and decided not to return, George reluctantly would join her later that year and stay with us in the meantime to earn some extra cash. Doreen really missed her and her Family when they left, seems she had not really settled to life in Canada and of course George was involved in even more activities than I was including the Pipe Band, Lodge, Golf and "never home" so I was going to lose a very good friend soon it seemed.

George and I were an integral part of the Sarnia Table Tennis team, we were also part of the very successful Sarnia Soccer club for several years in the early 1960's which still included some very good players including Mike Devenny, Charlie McCracken, Walter Di Odorico, Roger Letham and Phil Turner. Our Team won several League Championships, Ruppe Cup, play offs and the Cosmos Cup in the London and District Soccer League. The Scottish players on this Sarnia Team also were fortunate enough to win the International Cup in 1964 which was played at the end of each season. George certainly was going to be a huge loss for me.

Later that summer we had a soccer game down in Stratford against "Fischer Bearings", I had worked the night shift on Friday evening at Dow Chemical where I was now working as a Process Operator in the Ethylene Unit, didn't get much sleep in the morning before heading for Stratford around noon with 5 players including George in my car (an old Ford Meteor). Won the game and went to a local Pub where we met a former professional soccer player called Sammy Cox who was wearing his Glasgow Rangers sports coat with the "badge" on the left breast, he had played against us in the afternoon. We had a great old time, had a blether and more than a few beers but we had to leave around 5:30pm as I was scheduled to go back in on nightshift that night. Rather stupidly I took the driver s seat and off we went but soon I realized I was too "tired" to drive to Samia so George said I will drive, the other 3 in the car were either sleeping or pretending to. We were rounding a bend near St Mary's when we side swiped a car coming towards us and ended up in a ditch, fortunately no one was seriously hurt, 2 cars came from Sarnia to pick us up after the cops finished investigating and I never did make it to work but my reliable old Ford was wrecked. The payout on an old car was next to nothing so now besides having a new house, very little furniture, living from pay cheque to pay cheque we had "no car" George was in no position to help so we just got by as well as we could. George stayed with us and worked till early December and then headed back to Scotland to be with his Family and start all over again in Edinburgh.

In the meantime, Doreen and Sister Jeanette were still very sick, but her older kids all dug in and helped at home while Norm was working, probably they should have had home help and a nurse in the house.

Doreen's recovery was slow and steady after her EST Treatment which at that time seemed fairly aggressive stuff but with some "adjustments" in our lifestyle and trying to do as Dr. Glady had suggested plus occasional visits to a psychiatrist, she seemed to be making progress and Jeff, Mike and Elaine were quite well behaved and helpful during her recovery stage. As she got stronger, she joined a "Recovery" group that really proved to be very helpful over the coming years.

To expedite Doreen's recovery, it was suggested she might want to consider a part time job to get her out and about, so she pursued part time employment and secured a wee job at Zellers and later at a Fabric Sewing store for several years and this definitely proved to be instrumental in restoring her self-esteem and confidence. The salary wasn't great but allowed her to spend more "freely" on personal stuff and extra household needs as I was a bit of a tight wade and still hadn't recovered from the shock of how much money we paid monthly for interest and how little against the principle on the house mortgage, didn't sleep well for several months, oh well, I had a decent job at Dow Chemical. Jeff was now getting involved in ice hockey this winter as well as having played SMAA soccer in the summer and doing quite well at both, Mike would follow soon when he was old enough. The house league games were played at the old Children's Arena on Christina Street and it was obvious that Jeff had a bit of talent right from the start. We were soon approached by Wayne Cousins who was the coach of a "Travel" team and wanted Jeff to try out for his team, this was the beginning of a long and rewarding hockey experience for Jeff, we were proud and happy. Expenses were a bit of a challenge on Travel teams but somehow, we managed. Jeff apparently was a bit embarrassed about some of the less expensive equipment we were able to buy in particular he tells the story about walking into the dressing room with his "kit bag" when all the other players had lovely looked proper Hockey Bags, however it didn't seem to affect his developing hockey skills. That winter went by quickly with Doreen continuing to improve then we heard that my brother Alan and his wife Helen were emigrating to Canada and arrived in London, Ontario in the spring of 1967 with their son Scott who was 10 months old. They stayed with us at 794 Pineview Ave until Alan found work and sometime later, they found a wee place of their own. He seemed interested in getting involved with our soccer team and came to a few practices and enjoyed it. By now I was kind of the player coach, manager by default. We had combined with a young team called the Collegians coached by Roy Powell and were now sponsored by the German Canadian Club, so Sarnia Soccer Club disappeared and the German Canadian Soccer Team with some experienced and youthful players went on to be quite a powerhouse for several years in the London and District First Division Soccer League. Helmet Herter and Helmet Gross provided the financial support we needed to run the club and were deeply involved in Club business. Brian Harris and I looked after running the Team and Administrative issues. This was a great arrangement both socially and sports wise, we had dances, 50/50 draws and lots of fund-raising activities "but" not too many German soccer players which eventually became a problem, in the meantime we had enough players to have an "A" and a "B" team which brother Alan got involved in and from all accounts really enjoyed the camaraderie, Pete Shaw was the successful coach of the "B" Team.

1967 was the Centennial year for Canada and every house in Sarnia was given a "Tree" cutting to celebrate the occasion, we planted our cutting in the front yard right in the middle of the lawn, we were quite chuffed and would watch carefully over the years as it grew. The other main significant event for me was I was named Most Valuable Player by the L&D Soccer League for this year and was fortunate enough to be also selected for the All-Star Team and played games in Hamilton, London and Chicago against some very good teams. Work at Dow Chemical was rewarding, I enjoyed doing my job and had progressed from filling Tank trucks and Railway cars on a 2-shift system (days and afternoons) to becoming a Process Operator in the Ethylene Unit, unfortunately this meant 3 x shifts. (24 x 7 continuous process work) but it did have a better salary plus a shift allowance. The good part of the 3 shifts work was being able to take Doreen and the growing Family to the park on certain shifts, also to the beaches in Sarnia and grocery shopping during relatively quiet times. Social life was still fairly good, and we were settling in very nicely at 794 Pineview. Both the boys were playing SMAA Soccer and Mike would soon be getting into ice hockey and Lainie was just a happy wee baby with not a care in the world, so life seemed to be good at the moment.

The time was flying by so quickly now with fairly normal activities and before we knew it my dad was talking about making his first trip some time in 1969 and we suggested we could help out with his "expenses' so to speak and he was ok with that this time. The World Cup of Soccer (Football) was scheduled to take place in Mexico in 1970 and some of the German Canadian Soccer Team were making plans to go "so" Jim came up with a plan to start saving some $$ every month and then feeling a wee bit guilty suggested to Doreen that she might want to go to Scotland with our 3 Bairns for a vacation since I was hoping to go to the World Cup with the guys, what a great deal I thought ho hum Doreen accepted a bit reluctantly anticipating what a challenge it might be with 3 kids on a long flight, no problem says I lots of help when you get to Edinburgh hmm.

The trip to Scotland for Doreen was scheduled in the spring of 1969 around the time when Neil Armstrong did the Moon Walk which we all watched in amazement on the TV, great stuff. Doreen s trip home was another story as it turned out, where to start? Well Jim broke his left ankle playing football and decided that Mexico just wasn't going to happen for him, driving was possible but not comfortable, but we had to get the family down to catch the London Celtic Bus in London, the bus left for Toronto, and I headed back to Sarnia with very mixed emotions so much for my wonderful plan, no Mexico and Doreen off to Scotland. Doreen called me later in the day that the 3 kids had slept all the way to Toronto, this was the good news, the bad news was that the flight had been delayed and they were staying in a hotel overnight. She tried hard to keep the kids happy but since they had slept all the way to Toronto, they had no plans to go to bed early. Those passengers who had no kids went for a meal/drink but she had decided to have room service with the voucher the Airline provided because of the delay, guess it was a long night trying to keep the kids happy.

The flight the following day was 13 hours on a Turbo-Jet and something of a nightmare as you can imagine with 3 kids under 8 years old, she eventually arrived in Prestwick Airport tired and in tears where her Dad picked her up in his old Bentley Car and drove her home to Blinkbonny, really don't know how she survived, another good idea gone wrong but she did make the most of her visit to Auld Reekie.

When Doreen came back from her visit home to Scotland where she had been kept busy running between both sets of Grandparents and visiting relatives in Edinburgh and Bo'ness, she went right back to work fulltime at Woolco. She was determined to contribute to all our living expenses and buy what she called "extras" for our modestly furnished home, and I loved her for that along with all her other domestic chores and responsibilities. The money certainly came in handy when later that year my employer Dow Chemical refused to meet the Chemical Union Local 975 demands for increased salaries and some improvement in benefits, personally I was one of only 3 employees who voted against strike action, 907 voted for it? During the strike which lasted 3 months I also refused to picket but I did find a job with Ed Heath Paint Co painting Storage Tanks on Plank Road which now belong to Enbridge Pipelines and was reasonably well paid but I had to contribute 10% of my salary to the Union Strike Fund. I had no problem with that as I had followed my personal integrity/principles and gladly paid up. Also managed to secure a job with Rocco D, Andrea (President of the Labor Union) working as a laborer on the St Clair River shore protection job due to my current connections with the Dante Club and the Senior Men's soccer team who had now moved from their sponsorship with the German Canadian Club to the Italians. Tommy Ogle from Newcastle by way of Hamilton was instrumental in bringing about this change and he turned out to be a terrific coach, but I was still looking after Managing and Training the local Team, another nice English chap who came to Sarnia with Tom Ogle by the name of Alan Williams looked after the Clubs finances. Doreen had always been great about helping out with washing and ironing the strips for the Team, the 3 older guys (Tom, Syd and George) had basically "retired" from looking after the old Sarnia Soccer Club, but they were still great supporters of our Team.

By now Jeff was playing AAA all-star hockey and doing very well playing with Dino Ciccarelli who went on and scored over 600 goals in the NHL, Pat Crombeen, Billy Aberhart among others who went on to careers in Junior "A" and Junior "B" leagues, Mike was also doing well but somewhat restricted by breathing problems and Asthma, played District Hockey and scored some interesting goals for his teams along the way. Mike didn't seem overly interested in playing on the All-Star Hockey or All-Star Soccer Teams with his older brother that I was coaching at the time as he seemed more interested in tinkering with motor bikes and lawnmower engines. Obviously, our Family spent a lot of time at hockey rinks and soccer fields during the early years and Elaine was now starting to show some interest in figure skating. It happened that our neighbor on 794 Pineview Ave had a daughter who was involved in the Point Edward Figure Skating Club so guess what? Elaine started skating lessons. She took part in a couple of Shows for the club but did not pursue the very rigorous challenges of this particular sport, we weren't too disappointed as it was really expensive.

I had ordered a Middle East Newsletter around this time, having become a Chief Operator in the Ethylene Plant in Dow I was interested in opportunities overseas much to Doreen's dismay (bit of a gypsy in me I guess). Ron who was working at Catalytic by now had read about some opportunities in the magazine and since he wasn't that happy in his job at the time while living in a modest rented house in Grove Street decided to write after some jobs in the Middle East. Before we knew it, he had a response and Occidental out of Bakersfield California offered him a job in Libya. Before we knew it Ron, Aileen and the Family were off to Libya via Scotland.

The strike at Dow Chemical had by now been resolved, not to everyone's satisfaction I might add, but back to work we went, the Plant that had been run by Management and Dow people from out of town was in immaculate condition and being run very efficiently and safely "much" to the surprise of the Union personnel who had predicted "they didn't know what they were doing". Was really very impressive because not only did they know what they were doing but the place was spotless, and all the machinery was running at optimum rates. I was really impressed but had rd to keep my thoughts to myself since I wasn't a believer in needing a **3''** Party to obtain a decent wage but obviously in the minority. Three months lost wages and small adjustments to the contract didn't make sense to me at the time.

With all the kids' activities and family stuff going on Doreen working plus a fairly busy social life Doreen seemed to be in a "good Place" but she describes her 30th Birthday as the worst ever for her, a bit overwhelmed she described it at the time, only old people are 30 years old!!! Meanwhile Aileen and her kids had joined Ron who was now working in Libya, this turned out to be a bad experience and she went back to Scotland to live after 3 months. Living conditions were poor in Tripoli and the kids were being subjected to harassment by the locals who didn't take too kindly to people from other cultures and religious beliefs living in their communities.

Time was slipping quickly by now here in Canada and we had more visitors from Scotland in 1971, Jeanette was poorly, and her parents visited from Scotland staying at the Nelson Street house where Norm and Jeanette were now living. Norm and his older kids were doing the best they could under the circumstances with lots of help from friends and relatives but eventually after many epilepsy seizures compounded by a brain tumor Doreen lost her sister on Oct 4th, 1971.

1972,73,74 seemed like a bit of a blur as we managed through life's many challenges with our 3 kids heading to school when each one became 5 years old, Rosedale Public was the school our kids had to go to as we were right on a boundary as it happened, too bad really as this meant they had to cross a busy intersection at Indian Road, this turned out to be not an issue. Our kids were heavily involved in Travel soccer/ice hockey at a high level/figure skating and all sorts of other activities during this time which kept us extremely busy, still not clear how we managed to afford all the travelling etc. but somehow, we managed. Ron and Aileen had a visit to Canada during 1972 and Ron who was and is a bit of an entrepreneur asked me about some houses being built in Assiniboine Park near Maxwell, I couldn't really help him other than to say he could buy one for a $zoo deposit which he promptly did and a few years later he wished he had bought more than one because he made a handsome profit on the one he had bought, renovated, rented while overseas and sold for twice the money he had bought it for. Sometimes I wish I could have been that adventurous, but I have to "sleep at night", very cautious person that I am.

It was around this same time that I realized that although I had a good job at Dow Chemical and in fact had become a "Chief Operator" at a very young age simply because some of my fellow workers had settled into their Operating positions in the Ethylene Unit and decided they did not want the heavy responsibility that went with being in the Chief Operator position, not sure why I felt so comfortable about moving up to that position but can only conclude that I was ok being a leader if you will. So, the question was why was I becoming bored in this demanding job, "is this all there is to life?" Really not sure what the answer was but I started looking at overseas opportunities, am I nuts or what?

After Ron and Aileen s vacation when they bought the Assiniboine house they went back to Scotland and made a decision to emigrate back to Canada in 1974, bought an expensive lot in the exclusive Lakeshore Road and started building a new house. They rented quite a few different houses in Sarnia during this process.

1975 proved to be a critical point in our lives my active days playing and managing in the London and District soccer league were coming to an end, table tennis days were over, Coaching soccer for the SMAA had become a chore, the job at Dow wasn't very satisfying anymore. Coincidentally Doreen's life had improved dramatically, she had started jogging, played table tennis, enjoyed lunches and played Bridge with a host of friends and was really enjoying watching our young family develop their natural skills and doing well at school.

At Dow Chemical my boss "Unit Manager" Peter Fink informed me that a World Scale Ethylene Plant was being Proposed and Designed to be built here in Sarnia, might I be interested? "Certainly, was my response" I thought why not, turns out that Dow had a 25% share in the proposed multi-million-dollar Ethylene Plant to be known as SOAP (Sarnia Olefins Aromatic Project) to be built near Corunna and the small Ethylene Unit we currently operated in Dow was to be closed down. The really neat part of the communication info that caught my attention was it would be non-union, and they would use a new method called Participative and Results Oriented Management. Needless to say, I was "hooked", on the downside I would have to give up over 15 years seniority at Dow Chemical and cash in my pension "if" I made the move to this grass roots organization, salary and benefits were very, very attractive. Promotion was a real possibility in this People Oriented Philosophy set up. Huge decision to consider, what effect if any would this have on our Family? Prospects of promotion to even a Process Foreman at Dow Chemical appeared to be very limited so, why not?

Needless to say, Doreen and I had many long discussions about the pros and cons of such a move, what are we giving up and what is to be gained? I was very excited about this opportunity and Doreen could sense I probably needed a change so eventually "I think" we agreed to pursue this, Job. My Boss was delighted and put my name forward for a Shift Supervisors position in the new Company which had already changed its name to Petrosar (Petrochemicals Sarnia) and had started recruiting. As it happened I was the second Supervisor hired after an interesting interview at the RBC building on Christina Street 3 different people conducted the interview and I was delighted they agreed to hire me as soon as I could be released by Dow, I was asked several times during the Interviews why are you willing to take this position as it seems they felt I should have gone after a job at the next level? My response was I was very happy to be hired as a supervisor and if that worked out well, we would see what the future had to offer, I signed the offer that day and Doreen and I celebrated the occasion that night and told Jeff, Mike and Elaine about our good fortune. Giving up 5weeks vacation with Dow was not pleasant but I felt the overall benefit package from Petrosar would more than compensated for this.

Since my interview process had gone so well, Cliff Crossland one of the 3 Process Engineers who had interviewed me and later kind of adopted me as his personal Project was happy to take me to the Plant construction site and introduce me to some of the others who had been hired "early" and arranged for me to work out of a

Construction Trailer starting on Feb 25th, 1976. During this transition period I was fascinated by a wee bit of philosophy that I had come across over the years that seemed to fit this particular occasion. A guy by the name of Patanjali (Einstein in the world of Buddha and author of Yoga Sutras) from the 3rd Century BC had written these words about being inspired.

"When you are INSPIRED by some great purpose, some extraordinary Project, all your thoughts break their bonds, your mind transcends its limitations, your consciousness expands in every direction, and you find yourself in a new great and wonderful world. Dormant forces, faculties and talents become alive, and you consider yourself to be a greater person by far than you ever dreamed yourself to be". This is what Petrosar did for me, there was a reference in this gentleman's writings that talked about Life Balance or the 3 circles of life e.g., Family-WorkSelf, none of these should dominate the other, this was to be a great challenge for me during my years at Petrosar 1976 to 1983. Work would take over my life during this period. I was very well rewarded within the organization, but it eventually took a toll that was recognized by Doreen, my family and my Dear old Ma among others.

Doreen and I were trying to make the adjustments required from such a significant event in our lives, the kids were all doing well in sports and school, interaction with Doreen's Canada family continued with picnics in Canatara Park and events like breakfast in the park and annual trips to Rock Glen in April to roll the Easter eggs, build a fire to roast marshmallows, and hike down to the river, life seemed to be good during this period. We got word that Moira (Doreen's youngest sister) and her new husband Bryan would be immigrating to Canada in August 1976, so we were all looking forward to that. Moira and Bryan would stay with us for a while and then move over to the Phillips house till they found a place of their own. Bryan was able to find work as a plate welder upon arrival to get him started in Sarnia. About this time Allan McFarlane became quite sick unfortunately and was diagnosed with Cancer in the bowel around Xmas time and the prognosis was not good, another unexpected devastating blow to this family. Meanwhile in Scotland Doreen's Mum was also sick and passed away September 1st/1977 Doreen and Aileen went to Scotland for the Funeral and with Ron in Libya that left me to manage the Phillips kids and our kids as well as I could, difficult times for all Families. Allan eventually passed away shortly after his Mum. What a cruel world it seemed at this time, how this McFarlane family have suffered over the years, but they seem to be resilient all things considered.

My career at Petrosar was developing into something "special" during the construction phase, an English chap by the name of Tom Hughes (hired as an Assistant Dept Head, ADH) had enlisted me to become what he called the Punch Out Co-Ordinator which included setting up Teams using drawings and Piping & Instrument Diagrams (P&IDS) to check all the construction going on within the site, it was right up my street and Tom had what he called a Commissioning Procedure Plan for all the "Systems" under construction and he said you can handle this, worked out well had great teams, I loved the work and interaction between all the trades personnel and Operations staff. As each system was punched out and commissioned, we moved to the next system over the next few months, Tom knew what needed to be done and made it all happen and carried me on his coat tails to a successful Start-up of the Ethylene (Olefins) Unit in 1977.

Prior to the Plant Start Up all the Supervisors were provided with Interview Training and Partner Plant Training. The Interview Training prepared us for trips to places like Montreal, and out west to Calgary, Edmonton, Banff Springs and Lake Louise where we conducted as many as so Interviews with some success. We were looking for Process Operators who had a minimum of 10 years' experience in the Ethylene Manufacturing Process. The Partner Plant Training was to be conducted In Taft New Orleans and several groups/teams would be sent down there with all expenses paid to see how a Single Train Operating Plant functioned. My group was the first group to go and included 10 Shift Supervisors and 2 Administration workers. We spent some time in the Taft Plant but more time in New Orleans downtown and Fat City, the hub of great entertainment. Reconciling expenses for the trip would later become a challenge even although Petrosar was very generous, but somehow, we sorted that out. Tom Hughes and I conducted many of the interviews out of town and continued to develop a great relationship as we recruited a number of well-qualified experienced Process Operators who were willing to relocate to Sarnia.

Doreen's Mum and Dad had come to Canada for a wee holiday during this busy time for me and I don't think Betty was too impressed at how much time I spent at work and other activities with Doreen having to manage all the domestic chores and arrange all the kid's sports, it was an awkward time for all of us.

Tom was eventually rewarded with the Department Head (DH) of the Olefins Unit job for all his hard work and I was rewarded with the Hot Side Shift Supervisors job, plum job on days and another increase in salary. George Milne was named the Cold Side Shift Supervisor at the same time. Tom, George and I continued to work well together with the On-Shift Supervisors and their Teams over the next months after the start up then during the Run and Maintain Phase and we all became very good friends at work and socially. Somehow or other George and I were later considered the Commissioning and Start up Project Co-Ordinator's working closely with the Process Engineers assigned to the six Operating Areas.

During this period when I was consumed by this wonderful Project, I had become involved in, Jeff was playing some high-level hockey and in fact went west to Kamloops to a very important AAA Midget Hockey tournament on a team coached by former Junior B Star Fred Pageau. The team had done well and actually had advanced to the Final, but Jeff had an unfortunate accident while skiing and broke his leg up on a mountain the day before the final, naturally he was devastated, they had a hard time getting him off the mountain and getting him home to Sarnia, this incident took a lot out of Jeff and he really never totally recovered and his promising hockey career was to suffer a bit.

Elaine by now had been involved for several years in the Point Edward Figure Skating Club and was doing very well in other sports, Kim Johnson our neighbors daughter was a good skater and had been teaching Elaine all about the sport and in fact Elaine was in a few Xmas Skating shows over this period, we were quite proud of her but somewhere along the way she seemed to lose her enthusiasm and interest and moved on to other sports, e.g. cross country running and soccer. Mike meanwhile had shown a keen interest in "machines, lawnmowers" engines and motor bikes. Mike was born with asthma which had impacted his involvement in ice hockey and soccer, too bad really because he was a very good athlete.

Mike had a go at dirt bike racing/riding along the way but in his very first race up at a place called Varga near Goderich he fell off his bike at the first hazard and damaged his shoulder which put a damper on his brief racing career, he was very unhappy on the way home after the "race" Doreen and I made a decision that year that instead of buying a big new fancy home as my salary had continually improved annually, we would build an 8ft x 12ft extension to our modest "home" at 794 Pineview and hired building contractor Fred Van Reenan to do the work, he had some really good ideas that suited our budget and soon we had a beautiful new dining room with a big bay window, a display cabinet and upgraded kitchen area for our growing family. We also decided to upgrade the forced gas furnace and put new shingles on the roof, guess what? This work cost more than the original price of the house when we bought it, but we were happy with the end result as my job at Petrosar seemed secure and we were doing very well with the generous annual increases.

Early 1977 Doreen's brother Allan had become really sick, Moira's first child Claire was born in January that year so Doreen's Mum decided she would come back to Canada around June to spend some time with her dying son and when she left to go home, she had said to us "I could be gone before Allan", little did we know that on Sept 1st that year she would pass, another tragedy. Doreen and Aileen went home for the Funeral, Ron who was home on leave from Libya at the time decided he would go to Scotland and join them for the funeral so Elaine, Karen P and I were left to look after all the "bairns".

The timing could not have been worse for me as I was up to my eyeballs at Petrosar with Start Up/Commissioning procedures at work, the kids were all involved in one thing or another and needed to be shuttled around here and there however we managed thanks mainly to Elaine and KP. Shortly after Doreen and Aileen returned home Allan McFarlane was moved home from St Joseph's Hospital to Parsons Street where he died on Oct 1st and the grieving Mr. McFarlane had to make every effort to be here in Canada for his son's funeral shortly after losing his wife whose predication had come true, she had died before her son. There were some thoughts that maybe Mum "Betty" had died of a broken heart, she had so many tragedies to deal with in her life.

Somehow or other life does go on, "the circle of life" moves ahead and the remaining McFarlane family members in spite of all life had thrown at them, the surviving siblings and their partners were to go on and make a good life for themselves. Doreen and I were no exception as the kids were all doing very well, Doreen was "blooming" and my job at Petrosar was rewarding but demanding all my interest and energy. Little did I know that I was being consumed by my work but emerging as some kind of leader or "workhorse" and unfortunately it seems losing sight of the "life balance" and neglecting my Family and Self.

February 1978, we decided I needed a vacation and arranged to go to the Nassau/Bahamas for a week of R&R, talked to the kids and agreed we could trust Jeff and Mike to manage the house while away and Elaine could stay with Aunt Marg. It took me 4 days according to Doreen to unwind in this beautiful island resort and return to "normal", the rest of the week we really enjoyed. lots of time on the beach, lovely meals/ drinks, a visit to the old town and Paradise Island Casino. Soon we were on our way home and arrived to 2 very quiet and subdued boys. Elaine was delighted to have us home.

794 Pineview Ave it turned out had been the "party place" for some of the Northern High School party crowd while we were away, the impact on some neighbors and our house and basement "Bar" was significant. Needless to say, we were very disappointed with the boys, Jeff took most of the blame/responsibility at the time, but we found out some time later that he had accepted the blame as the older brother but had tried to prevent some of the activities. As parents it was a significant learning experience. We also arrived home to find one of our wonderful back yard willow trees had been blown over in a storm while we were away, yes, a memorable trip.

Later this year on Nov 12th we celebrated my 40th Birthday party in the basement "Bar" at 794 with all our closest Family, Friends and work mates, it was a great party, and a good time was had by all, we made some tapes of the singers during the evening sing along. One of our closest friends at the time had prepared a "Roast of Jim" but somehow or other she wasn't quite up to it, having too good a time and didn't feel well.

1979 came storming in as the Commissioning of this World Scale C2H4 Plant was executed in an efficient professional manner over several months and we settled into what is called "Run and Maintain" with an eye to optimizing all areas of operations, it was challenging but a fantastic experience as we responded to all the upsets, the experienced Operators we had hired had "seen it all before". Promotions after Start Up came fast and furious with personnel changes responding to people moving on and other situations developing in the organization, I was moved to Day Supervisor in Olefins almost immediately but within 3 weeks I was asked to become Plant Shift Superintendent that lasted one month then a move to Utilities Dept as the Department Head (DH). Starting to feel this is too much too soon but was told by Management not to worry about it? Three months later after a stressful but successful time in Utilities I was appointed to Olefins Hot Side DH and my good friend George Milne was appointed Olefins Cold Side DH, maybe this had been the plan all along, but I was delighted to be back working with George and Ray Arseneault who now held the position of Process Manager. In retrospect both George and I were feeling the strain of the workload but doing the best we could, lots of long chats in the evenings at the local pub "Ups and Downs" which wasn't well received by our wives.

The impact on our families was beginning to show success, if you call it that was having an effect on our personalities and we were losing touch with our families and home life, is this the price you pay? for being willing horses? It was about this time I came across a magazine called "The Middle East Newsletter" and my interest in overseas work surfaced again (am I nuts or what). Anyway, in my inimitable fashion I contacted a company in the Newsletter called Aramco (Arabian American Co) who had several major Petrochemical projects in Saudi Arabia. Had an all-expenses paid trip to Detroit, good interview, nice meal later and the promise of a response within 48 hours as they seemed to be impressed with my resume and participation in the Petrosar Ethylene Project in Sarnia. Anyhow wouldn't you know it I did get offered a job "but" about this time Iran and Iraq decided to go to war, so I gracefully declined this opportunity. My brother-in-law Ron Phillips had sent away to another address in the Newsletter to Occidental Co in Bakersfield California and ended up getting offered a job in Libya as an Instrument Technician and started work within 6 weeks of applying.

Petrosar was churning out Ethylene (C2H4) in 1980 as per design along with other by-products to Shareholders satisfaction, the challenges memorable trip.

Later this year on Nov 12th we celebrated my 40th Birthday party in the basement "Bar" at 794 with all our closest Family, Friends and work mates, it was a great party, and a good time was had by all, we made some tapes of the singers during the evening sing along. One of our closest friends at the time had prepared a "Roast of Jim" but somehow or other she wasn't quite up to it, having too good a time and didn't feel well.

1979 came storming in as the Commissioning of this World Scale C2H4 Plant was executed in an efficient professional manner over several months and we settled into what is called "Run and Maintain" with an eye to optimizing all areas of operations, it was challenging but a fantastic experience as we responded to all the upsets, the experienced Operators we had hired had "seen it all before". Promotions after Start Up came fast and furious with personnel changes responding to people moving on and other situations developing in the organization, I was moved to Day Supervisor in Olefins almost immediately but within 3 weeks I was asked to become Plant Shift Superintendent that lasted one month then a move to Utilities Dept as the Department Head (DH). Starting to feel this is too much too soon but was told by Management not to worry about it? Three months later after a stressful but successful time in Utilities I was appointed to Olefins Hot Side DH and my good friend George Milne was appointed Olefins Cold Side DH, maybe this had been the plan all along, but I was delighted to be back working with George and Ray Arseneault who now held the position of Process Manager. In retrospect both George and I were feeling the strain of the workload but doing the best we could, lots of long chats in the evenings at the local pub "Ups and Downs" which wasn't well received by our wives.

The impact on our families was beginning to show success, if you call it that was having an effect on our personalities and we were losing touch with our families and home life, is this the price you pay? for being willing horses? It was about this time I came across a magazine called "The Middle East Newsletter" and my interest in overseas work surfaced again (am I nuts or what). Anyway, in my inimitable fashion I contacted a company in the Newsletter called Aramco (Arabian American Co) who had several major Petrochemical projects in Saudi Arabia. Had an all-expenses paid trip to Detroit, good interview, nice meal later and the promise of a response within 48 hours as they seemed to be impressed with my resume and participation in the Petrosar Ethylene Project in Sarnia. Anyhow wouldn't you know it I did get offered a job "but" about this time Iran and Iraq decided to go to war, so I gracefully declined this opportunity. My brother-in-law Ron Phillips had sent away to another address in the Newsletter to Occidental Co in Bakersfield California and ended up getting offered a job in Libya as an Instrument Technician and started work within 6 weeks of applying.

Petrosar was churning out Ethylene (C2H4) in 1980 as per design along with other by-products to Shareholders satisfaction, the challenges were many, but the employees always seemed equal to the task. However, lots of hard work and long work hours plus The Participative Management style were having a decidedly negative effect on all of us. Department and Core Teams were meeting daily, and manpower was being reduced to try and improve efficiency and be more cost effective, my workload was being increased almost weekly looking after Operations/Administration/Maintenance Coordination/ and Training. Guess I thought I was up to it and continued to give my best, but I was paying the price mentally and physically, the "willing horse" was slowly collapsing at the knees.

Doreen's Dad had a 70th Birthday approaching in May of this year Doreen, and I planned a trip to Scotland the 3 kids were boarded out with Aunt's in Samia, the boys attended a soccer camp and Elaine was busy with her figure skating. Turned out to be a really nice visit and we did all the usual stuff in Edinburgh plus we rented a car and took Ma and Dad for a trip up to a lovely wee town called Crieff where Donald was working at the time with a stop at Gleneagles Hotel for afternoon Tea, we had hoped to have it in the Main Hotel but Ma decided it was too posh for her when the door-man with his top hat and fancy gear asked her to "please step out the car Ma, m". Quote "I am not gone in there". We ended up in the Golf Course Clubhouse for tea and sandwiches which according to Ma "we could have bought a house for") Oh well such is life. On the way to Crieff Doreen loves to tell the story about me trying to organize the sheep so that I could get a nice picture of the scenery near the Devil's elbow "but" the sheep wouldn't cooperate, so Jim got mad, damn sheep don't listen I thought. We walked up a famous trail called the Knock to the waterfalls just past another big hotel called the Hydro where we got a spectacular view looking south of the Ochill Hills and surrounding area.

After visiting Donald and Jennifer's rented house in Crieff we enjoyed a Fish and Chips lunch at a nice restaurant on the main street we headed northwest to the Isle of Skye, crossed the new Prince Charles Bridge that had recently been built and enjoyed a grand night in one of the local Pubs listening to old Scottish music and having a few drinks before heading to a B&B for the night.

That little trip plus celebrating Mr. Macs 70th Birthday was memorable but as usual the time goes in too quickly and soon, we were on our way back to Sarnia. Later this same year we had a nice 4-day trip to Las Vegas with Dick and Audrey Fletcher, originally several couples at a drunken New Year's party had thought we should all go to Las Vegas together and have a ball. We organized the trip but almost everybody dropped out eventually after sobering up, so it was just two couples who went. We had a fantastic time and caught several great shows including Wayne Newton, Siegfried and Roy and the Pointer Sisters. Dick and Audrey enjoy playing the machines and had some success but me thinks Las Vegas won, we headed home relaxed and having enjoyed our time together.

The two breaks from work were wonderful and Doreen and I both felt the benefit of no stress from work but unfortunately the workload did not go away and before long it was more of the same and soon our lives were being challenged again. What did we have to look forward to in the next few years, can we see this through, great job, great salary but the economics of The Petrochemical Business had changed dramatically, Crude Oil feedstock prices going through the roof, Ethylene prices dropping like a stone and Petrosar debts were climbing, gloomy outlook for this progressive grassroots company.

In the spring of 1981 in spite of what was happening at my work Doreen and I decided that we were going to go back to Florida for another trip, we invited my Ma and Dad to come to Canada and bring my sisters daughter Fiona with them and since Doreen's Dad was going to be here in Samia anyways for Kathy McFarlane s wedding we would take all of them to Florida with us, Jeff and Mike would stay home and were ok with that. Mr. McF walked Kathy down the aisle, and we all had a great time at the wedding. We did have a wee problem with Fiona getting paperwork for her going into USA, this was resolved with a quick trip to the Canadian Embassy/Toronpassport office. So off we went, flying to Orlando from Toronto with a large, air-conditioned Station Wagon waiting for us at the Airport. We had rented a nice Villa in Port Charlotte on the Gulf of Mexico side of Florida from a friend of Eric Ritchie. We drove about an hour and a half, and we were all stunned on arrival by this beautiful Villa where we were going to stay "but" once again Ma was "very uncomfortable" with the "posh" surroundings, Dad was fine he found a box of whisky under the kitchen sink, place was really upper crust to say the least. We stayed 2 days in this wonderful home but realized Ma was not enjoying the discomfort of being in this upscale elitist environment. Doreen and I decided to drive up to Clearwater Beach which was more down to earth and Family Oriented and found a Motel right on the beach at a place called Indian Rocks. We moved the next day with some happy and some not so happy to the Motel on the beach. Dad said, "but what about all that whisky under the sink?"

We had a wonderful time at Indian Rocks, found lots of nice attractions in the area, breakfast places on the beach, and of course a few nice Pubs where Dad settled in and soon forgot about "the box of whisky". Had some really nice day trips and a boat ride, spent a lot of time on the beaches, one in particular was memorable at

Boca Grande peninsula, hot, beautiful and golden sand. Was great to see the two old Grand Dads cavorting in shorts and cowboy hats, my dad even jumped into the deep end of the pool at the motel, so what? You say? "He can't swim" silly auld bugger said Granma.

Back in Edinburgh Betty Low's husband Alex had been very sick for several months and was dealing with cancer in one of his main organs. His health was deteriorating fast so when we got back to Sarnia from Florida, we had to arrange an earlier than planned return trip for Mr. McF. Unfortunately, Alex passed away early in June before Doreen's Dad made it home to Edinburgh.

Doreen now had to deal with another loss in her family circle just at a time in her life she had evolved to being in a reasonably "happy place", although I was very busy at work and soccer, she had got a couple of wee jobs that provided her with some extra cash to do things she wanted to do around the house, our kids had done or were doing well at school, sports, part time jobs etc. and she was into exercising and running almost daily. Jeff had developed into an excellent ice hockey player and had played for Mooretown Flags Junior C and then Sarnia Legionnaires Junior B. Mike who had been troubled with asthma played in some senior leagues as he struggled with breathing limitations in those years but still loved "motor bikes". Elaine had participated in several Point Edward Figure Skating Shows by now and had done very well but eventually moved on and excelled in cross country running, soccer and many other athletic endeavors.

Work for me continued to be a bit of an anomaly, exciting, challenging, a position I could only have dreamed about, but very exhausting and seemingly endless demands and it was taking a toll.

Doreen s sister Phyllis who seemed to have had an exciting young life and worked in London with a decent job had met a nice German chap called Gerhard Christ on a bus tour while in Canada planned to be married in April 1982. The wedding and reception in Edinburgh apparently went very well on April 21 but the Family was shocked the following morning, April 22 when poor Mr. McF was found dead in his room at the age of 72, he had seemed well and really enjoyed the wedding reception but no one had expected this, another tragic event. Poor Phyllis and Gerhard, what a difficult week they had.

We struggled through the coming months, but it was apparent that I was "losing it", ill tempered, angry, reactionary with Doreen and out of touch with the kids and had lost what had always seemed to be a good sense of humor, Doreen my Ma and several work associates asked the question "where has Jim Currie gone". The summer months were miserable for everyone at 794 as I struggled for survival both at work and home, Doreen suggested I take time off work and go home to Scotland on my own to sort things out in my head as our lives seemed to be crumbling. Difficult decision but finally I agreed to go "home alone" and spend time with Ma and Dad and try to get things in perspective again and booked a flight flying from Sarnia to Toronto and on to Edinburgh on Sunday Oct 24th.

GOING HOME OCTOBER 1982 (SCOTLAND CHAPTER)

On Sunday Oct 24th as the plane took off from Sarnia heading for Toronto then on to Edinburgh, I was more confused than ever, the purpose of the trip was clear in my mind but I was leaving two people behind who I love very much (it reminded me of the day that Doreen and I had emigrated to Canada). Something seems to drive me to a "goal" that isn't yet clear in my life, the results to date seem to suggest success (depending on how you measure it). Why then am I not experiencing inner satisfaction? Sitting in Toronto Airport my ever-active mind has taken care of the mundane details like duty free, books and other stuff. I called Doreen since I felt both her and Elaine probably were worried about me and my frame of mind. How can anyone "not be happy" with great people around me in Canada and Ma and Dad in Scotland? Really must strive to look for the best in people and be positive try to deal with problems as opportunities "to help" others.

Sitting in the plane I am watching "auld folk" struggling with wheelchairs, coats, bags, duty free and gifts, all looking very worried "what in heaven's name am I worried about". Another thought! In life you should always be going somewhere, maybe you never reach it you just change where it is you are trying to get to. So far 5 older couples have had words and fallen out, wonder why we do that to each other surely this should be the time to understand and help each other. Maybe that's just life "but?"

Monday Oct 25th. Great flight Boeing 727, had a drink up in the bar and the service was fantastic, had little or no sleep as a nice old lady from Lancashire with a cousin in Sarnia wanted to talk, talk, talk. Arrived at Glasgow Airport at 6:45am was out of the Airport in 15 minutes and arrived in Auld Reekie at 8:45am much to Ma and Dads surprise. As the day wore on, I became very tired but patient with my parents, they were excited like you wouldn't believe but I had to have a wee sleep for an hour.

When I woke up, we took a drive in the car I had hired up to the Pentland Hills and Hill End Skiing area, stopped at the Phillips but nobody was home. Drove around Blinkbonny, Currie Kirk, Dolphin Gardens and stopped for a drink at the Riccarton Arms. It is now 9:30pm and I have had 1hours sleep in the last 40 hours and "listened" a lot but trying to understand want to talk but don't listen. Fiona, my niece from Redcar understands them a lot better I found out later.

Tuesday Oct 26th, Weight is 205lbs, had a great sleep for about 10 hours, went jogging in Saughton Park, picked up some rolls and morning paper, feeling much better. Repaired some lights in the house then took a drive to George Street, on to Meadowbank, Kings Park and then a visit to Joe and Kate Spowart (Kate was in hospital) but we met son John at the house. We drove back up to Blinky and decided I love that area, visited the Kirk again, High Ponds, Marchbanks, Kestrel and then had a Pub Lunch at the Riccarton Arms. When we got home about 9pm I had to be careful not to "SCREAM" Ma and Dad keep talking over each other, the radio and the TV very frustrating in my fragile state. Unable to relax, too much attention and really haven't had a chance to read and just chill out. Ma won't listen and doesn't hear much, Dad is a perpetual talker and they both want to reminisce not surprising I guess but I sense shades of hostility but they have their own ways it seems.

Unemployment is rampant 17-18% in Scotland, 21% in Ireland, lots of violence on the TV and vandalism all over the place,

Broomhouse (council housing) is a disaster area, would you believe iron bars on the living room windows. Try to relax Jim, I remind myself, but I can't, the world seems to be in a mess, some areas less of a mess than others.

Wed 27th Oct (203lbs). Had a great sleep, listened to Ma and Dad complain and grouch about everything it seems. I had a jog in the park and feeling quite good, just remembered 2 jokes from Joe Spowart, 1st joke 2 guys at the bar the chap that is unemployed says I will buy the beer you can't afford it you are working, 2nd joke, I remember the days when the first kids up in the morning got the best choice of clothes, Joe just loved telling jokes.

Ma Dad and I left for a drive at 8:30am headed over the Forth road Bridge to the Fife area up through Dunfermline/Gleneagles (coffee 50p each)/Comrie/Crieff and on to Lochearnhead where we had a Pub Lunch. Headed up the Pass of Killicrankie to Killin/west to Balquidder (where we had had a couple of memorable vacations when younger)/Callander/ Stirling/ and stopped in Linlithgow to visit my cousin Moira and her husband John for a couple of hours had a few drinks and laughs before heading home to Edinburgh. It's now 11:30pm, Ma and Dad refuse to go to bed, too excited about our day out.

We are trying to arrange a birthday party for Dad on November 4th but Moira and John "not sure", Liz and Sandy will need a babysitter, still not sure of Auntie Jean yet but feel certain that Doreen's sister Betty will be there. Ma and Dad doing lots of "complaining" about why they can't just come and stop "complaining", careful Jim??? Losing it. Ma says "nobody ever visits us, why do we always have to go to them, nobody ever left us anything???, the council don't care about us, Moira and John come sometimes etc etc etc" is this normal for elderly people?

Thursday Nov 28th, have to have the rented car back by 8am, got back home by 8:30am for more listening and patience for 3 hours. Fortunately, I had a good sleep and time is slipping by. Dad seems to know everything about everything, and Ma continues to interrupt him calling him a blethering bugger. We went shopping at Fine Fair Grocery Store Dad complaining about prices, bus fares, and the unemployment situation. Had a pint at the Clock Inn with Ma and Dad and left them for a long walk into town along Princes St up the Bridges to the High St and on to the Lawnmarket. Ma had a nice dinner ready when I got home unfortunately Dad was a bit under the influence by now and looking for arguments. I have come to the conclusion that Scottish people generally speaking really "enjoy moaning" but don't seem prepared to do anything to improve things so that they can continue moaning.

Unable to read or listen to the news as Ma and Dad continue to talk. Decided to call Liz about Nov 4th and they are ok to come to Dad's birthday" hang in there Jim". Met Mike McLenagan today and got the impression he would be glad to get together for a pint but didn't seem to want to put himself out, got the same feeling with John Roy yesterday.

Friday Oct 29th, up at 7:30am for 2 mile run and exercise, blether for 2 hours in the house, Ma and I then went for a wee walk, visited my Auntie Bella who lived up the road near Stenhouse Cross. Later in the day my sister Betty's daughter Fiona who had come up from Redcar to visit with me went downtown shopping. Dad and I went out for a drink that night to "Luckie's Bar", went from there to Rose St to catch some night life ended up at the Abbotsford Pub a bit pickled by 11pm, had a really good night together with my Dad. Needless to say, Ma who had stayed home with Fiona was not very happy when we came home "Happy".

Sat Oct 30th up at 8:00am jogging and exercising, Fiona is heading back to Redcar today, when Johhny Craig, one of my best pals dropped in to visit, he offered to drive us to the station. We had a pint at the Waverly Station (10:30 in the morning yugh). Took Ma and Dad for a pint at the Abbotsford Pub, haggis and turnip it was great. Unfortunately, Ma and Dad were damp and cold and headed home in the bus, so I went to see the Hibernian football game at Easter Road myself. The language and violence at the game was terrible, what a mob of animals they appeared to be. Was I really from the same culture and heritage or is it just changing times? Got home about 5:30 pm, had a beer and settled in for the night. "Saturday Night" is this for real.

It is now Sun 31st Oct, would you believe it's 9:45am and I just woke up, another great sleep. Ma has been in and out my room for 20 minutes now, getting me coffee, the morning paper, what clothes need washed? She is just loving having one of her sons home.

Really starting to miss Doreen now, what an important part of my life she is these days, I have had several dreams with the same theme, she has found someone else, I woke up sick to the stomach with the thought. Generally feeling a bit better about myself but inwardly still doubts about my self-esteem and still dealing with lost confidence. Time is slipping by quickly, really enjoying jogging and exercise the soft ground is kind to my knees and I feel in good shape. Johnny Craig came by the house at 12:30 to take Dad and I to Merchiston Hearts Supporters Club, after a few drinks he took us to his house at Carricknowe where we met his wife Margo and their kids. Tea and scones were great but then Johhny opened a bottle of 14-year-old Scotch Whisky, Dad loved it, me not so much, not a whisky fan. Phoned Doreen later and that made my day, really felt excited talking to her but it's difficult to express in words. We agreed that we miss each other badly and that was no surprise. When we got home, we found that Auntie Jean and Uncle Davie were visiting, they both looked really well and obviously glad to see me. I had called Connie McKean earlier today and she said that her Mum Betty would be home late Monday. Had a nice quiet night at home watching TV and listening to Dad explain every show we watched (the anger and frustration that has been in my stomach slowly disappearing though as I adjust to making allowances for their habits). Ma is dead on her feet but won't go to bed so I decided at 11pm I would knowing that then they would too.

Mon Nov 1st, up at 8:00am jog in the park starting to enjoy the slower pace living but Ma and Dad are trying so hard to please me it's almost unbearable, so I have to watch what I am saying and doing. We left the house about 10:00am heading to Leith to do some shopping before visiting Mrs. Low at 11:30. Effie, her daughter dropped in to visit and we left around 1:00. Took Ma and Dad to "The Persevere" Pub for lunch, the waitress knew Betty and Alex Low who were regular clients on Fridays.

Put Ma and Dad on a bus after lunch then I went for a long walk from Easter Road up to, Leith Street, the Bridges, High Street, Lawnmarket down the Mound to Princes Street, I was really needing some quiet time and then walked home to Stevenson Drive, a really good walk.

I am finding as I settle in that Ma has really changed and is quite a difficult person to be around, continually correcting and contradicting Dad, issuing orders and forever planning our time and including herself in almost everything. We have just spent an hour trying to watch and listen to a Barry Manilow TV Special and Ma and Dad had 4 different arguments, occasionally they seem to have no respect for each other nowadays, maybe they are ok on their own. Called Betty Low at 7pm and she was home from Germany but very tired, she mentioned that the Ron Phillips parents had been trying to find our address to visit.

Philosophical thought "life is a constant obstacle course" and one must wend their way through it with consideration to others, people and themselves, I am reminded of Doreen's sister Betty who once said years ago "you can't please everyone but if you can please yourself, you are half way there" (Jim was starting to become very frustrated again, try to remember why you are here). PATIENCE, UNDERSTANDING, KINDNESS. It is now 11.30pm and I just had to go to bed as Ma and Dad were sleeping on their feet but wouldn't give in. I was looking at them both very closely tonight as they watched the TV, two old lonely people who have brief snatches of happiness once in a while, they have their own ways but appear to be "just putting in time". It is a wee bit sad they don't have many friends but then they don't want to it seems, soon they won't be able to get out and about, what then? They only live for the brief moments when their kids and Grandkids are able to visit them, we have all flown the nest with their blessing but what a price to them. Granma Low says she is a very lucky old woman and now I really know why, Betty and her kids visit several times a week, Effie (Alex's sister) and her kids visit on different days (very significant).

Tuesday Nov 2/82, up early again really sleeping well and getting a good rest, after jogging in the park Ma and I took the bus to Betty's and arrived at 10:30am, had tea and biscuits, nice visit. Had a good blether with Betty and she is doing away ok and seems to be getting back into the mainstream again after losing husband Alex to cancer. She mentioned Phyllis is quite heavy at the moment and sounds a bit out of sorts with all the changes in her life, married, living in Germany and having a baby, she is loving having the baby but spends all her time looking after her Sara Jane much to husband Gerhard's dismay. Later that day after leaving Betty's we stopped at my Uncle John Burns house at 63 Stenhouse Ave on our way home, he is still going strong at 82 years old, nice old gentleman former Pipe Major in Royal Scots Pipe Band.

More evidence of the level of vandalism and hooliganism in Edinburgh, Betty Low's neighbors had a break in last week, this makes the fourth in the last 3 months. The newspapers are full of more unemployment and government misspending and there doesn't seem to be any incentive for people to find work, a married man with two children earns more being out of work than working.

ICI in Tweedside is paying thousands of workers 141 British pounds a week rather than make them redundant because of job security agreements made when times were better.

The men clock in at "work" and watch TV or play cards till it is time to go home. An article in the Daily Express said it all "To Work or Not to Work?", Unemployment and Social Security are over taking wages. A married man with 2 children needs to earn more than 132 British pounds a week working to be better off. The Institute of Economic Affairs says that Government should curb benefits and cut taxes to get people back to work. Present social policies have had perverse economic effects by destroying incentives to work. A clear result is to encourage, extend and prolong dependence on social benefits which are themselves an increasing cause of higher taxation. Living standards from work should always be higher than living standards from "idleness" and this would preserve work incentive.

Would you believe that on Wed Nov 3rd I slept from 8:45pm last night to 11:30am this morning. My weight is still hanging around 14st 9lbs (205 lbs.) but it is becoming more and more difficult to control my eating habits here, Ma and Dad don't eat a lot but they seem to eat often.

I went jogging as usual in the morning and enjoyed some exercise and freedom to run but my knees are still acting up a bit. Later Dad and I went for a walk to Corstorphine via Carricknowe, I showed him Fishy Thompsons where Doreen used to work (can't seem to get her out of my mind, must be missing her I guess.). Played snooker for a couple of hours with Dad, he really enjoyed that, "signs of an ill spent youth" I joked with him, had a bowl of soup and a roll at the Oak Inn before he took a bus home, and I walked home via Glasgow Road and Balgreen. Picked up a few odds and ends for Dad's upcoming birthday party e.g., Playboy magazine, cigars, Teachers Highland Cream Whisky, a few cans of Tennants Lager and a Birthday Cake with a wee golfer on it saying Happy Birthday.

As I continued walking home, I reflected on my perception of Edinburgh (Auld Reekie), a beautiful city with a depressing atmosphere created mostly by the damp windy cold weather, the inhabitants, and a society that seems to encourage idleness and mostly negative attitudes. If you can look beyond that though there must be some really good people who make an effort to provide a satisfactory life for themselves. My parents seem to have chosen not to change and stay current with the times, I must discuss this with Doreen when I go home as I sense I am also like that, and I don't want to stifle Doreen and her potential to change and develop with the changing times in an ever-evolving society. I will have to be more receptive to new ideas and our ever changing Social and Domestic scene. I am also finding out it is more rewarding letting people "do their own thing" and not interfering or providing advice "unless" you are asked.

I am thinking of going to see the Elton John Concert on Friday night and Ma and Dad are trying not to control "but".

Tomorrow we have Dad's Birthday, Friday is the only day you can see the Phillips, sister Betty is coming up on Friday, need to visit Betty Low's on Sunday, we want to take you to Portobello, Tues "free" day, Hearts v Rangers game at Tynecastle on Wed and on

Thursday "we" are not sharing you with anyone, we are going out to lunch "other than that you can do what you want".

NOW TRY TO REMEMEMBER THE PURPOSE OF YOUR TRIP JIM AND DON'T FORGET THEY ARE GETTING OLD AND TO THEM YOU ARE VERY SPECIAL.

Thurs Nov 4th, jogging in the morning and then Ma, Dad and I went shopping at the Finefair Store in Dalry Road and then on to the Clock Inn for a pint, a blether and back home so Dad could get a wee sleep in the afternoon (resting up for his 70th birthday party). Called Alan in Canada and Ma and Dad had a wee greet and we went over to "Luckies" for a late afternoon pint before the Party. The Party went well, and everyone showed up and seemed to have a good time, Betty Low, Johnny Craig, Auntie Jean and Uncle Davie, Moira and John Roy, Liz and Sandy Masterton. In spite of the great time, we had all dad talked about the next morning was "can you believe Jean and Davie taking their bottle of whisky home with them last night" they probably thought because we had lots of drinks on hand it wasn't really needed. "Oh well" such is life.

Woke up on Friday Nov 5th around 9am, feeling good, jog in the park, exercise and home for a roll and cup of coffee, Dad on the other hand wasn't feeling so good and just "had" to go for a drink (he has got the taste for it now and starting to become a bit obnoxious), Ma gets a bit concerned when he reaches this point, happens a lot she claims. Had a pint at the Haymarket Bar and then walked to the Playhouse to pick up tickets for the Elton John Concert and walked home. Betty Low went with me to see the show and it was fabulous, really enjoyed her company and she obviously had to "talk" about losing her husband Alex and I listened, she really is missing him but trying to adjust. I got home to 61 Stevenson by about 11.30pm, had a blether with Ma, Dad was sleeping by then and then off to "beddy byes" (where is Doreen?).

Sat Nov 6th, Its Sat night and we have had a very enjoyable day, no jogging in the morning as my knees were sore, Ma and I went in to Gorgie Road for groceries and then Dad and I went into Waverly Station to pick up sister Betty and her kids. We bumped into cousin Alex Fell on Princes Street and went for a pint, had a good blether and a "few" more pints before meeting Betty off the train from Newcastle. Went for a coffee and had a good laugh while reminiscing about the "auld" days. Had a good day With Betty, Anita and Paul, Dad took Paul to play snooker up at Corstorphine while Ma, Betty, Anita and I went for a walk in the Rose Gardens at Saughton Park. Late in the day I dropped Betty and Family off at the station as Dad had been dipping into the Scotch, didn't want to go with us and Ma won't leave him in the house alone!!! Had a good "greet" when Betty and Family were boarding the train, Anita and Paul were quiet but very respectful of our emotions. Went for a walk along Rose Street and visited a couple of Pubs (discos), the music was great, got a bus about 8 pm and was home by 9pm to watch Scotsport on TV.

Sun Nov 7th, up at 8am, jog in the park, picked up Sunday Post and morning rolls. Dad really has the shakes today, the worst I have seen him in years. Ma claimed he had drunk a whole bottle of whisky yesterday in the house and probably had a few more drinks at Saturday game, she is mad at him as he isn't able to go to Betty Low's, she is worried about him so I suggested he go back to bed and rest (seems he thinks I am his passport to extra drinking, loves my company). Ma and I went off to Betty's still mad at him, she claims that nobody will ever understand what she has gone through over the years due to "booze" but is quick to add that he has been really good these past 10 years except when they are on vacation or when we visit him, just doesn't know when to stop and then he is over the top. We did have a nice visit with Betty Low and her Family, she is a fantastic hostess, soup and rolls then a smorgasboard lunch and wine from Fellbach that Phyllis and Gerhard had sent home from Germany with her.

We also met Connie s boyfriend Colin, Liz's boyfriend Paul, Alan's girlfriend Susan, Granny Low, the Phillips, Donald, Jennifer and their kids plus Doug Strang and his daughter dropped in to visit. It was a full house as you can imagine and a bit overwhelming for Ma who was having a hard time explaining why "Geordie" wasn't with her. Tried some of Alan's homemade beer and then Harry Phillips offered us a ride home as they were going past our house, both he and Betty also offered the use of their cars the rest of my time in Edinburgh but I declined, these people sure make one feel special. The parcels and gifts for home are starting to pileup.

Mon Nov 8th, up at 8am, 14st 8lbs 204lbs doing ok, jog in the parkand then into town for 10am, meeting Ma and Dad at the Victoria and Albert on Frederick Street for lunch at 1pm after we have done our shopping separately. We had a nice lunch and headed home about 2:30pm. Visited Mrs. Craig and had some of her famous gingerbread with her son Robert then headed home, she is a great lady. Ma and Dad wanted to talk about their upcoming 50th Anniversary and also to check out some Insurance Policies they have had for years. They have 15 separate policies between them that cost 15 British pounds a month total value of all the policies was about 1700 pounds, suggested they cash them in, but they felt they would rather keep them. George and Jessie Lee dropped in for a visit later after our chat and stayed for about 3 hours we had a good blether and George gave me a 12-year-old bottle of whisky "Grants Royal" to take back to Canada with me much to my Dad's dismay.

On Tues Nov 9th, Ma and Dad are showing some improvement in total outlook in life, at the moment they seem to be more relaxed and getting on a wee bit better with each other and certainly both the better for all the activity. Slept till gam from 11,30 last night and feeling champion, we jumped on a bus to Cramond and had a walk around, walked along the River Almond to the falls and then another 40 minutes' walk to the Ferry Road and Cramond Brig Inn for lunch. Called Betty Low and she joined us for a drink but didn't want lunch, she brought along some fish for their Tea and drove us home to Stevenson Drive about 3pm. Betty had brought along some Xmas cards and a cup and saucer for Doreen, God only knows how I am going to get all this stuff home to Canada. Having another night home and enjoying the chit chat and more relaxed atmosphere now plus I am trying to keep the eating and boozing down to a minimum. It's now midnight I am feeling great, a clear head, parents seem happy and off to bed, reading a great book but my thoughts are of Doreen and going back home to Sarnia. I am actually excited and looking forward to something. Feel I am ready to face the future with some optimism now and capable with any circumstance, it is OK.

Wed Nov 10th, woke up about 8am feeling good, haven't been up much during the night so I must be cozy. Went jogging and ran twice as far as usual and twice as many exercises. Ma and I went into Gorgie shopping as I had forgotten to get a gift for Paula no luck so decided to go into Princes Street and see what we could find. Did some shopping and had a half pint in the White Cockade with Ma and then home by 1 pm. We had a good laugh and blether as we tried to wrap the gifts. Ma decided I might need another bag for all the gifts going to Sarnia.

Had supper then Dad and I went to see the Hearts V Rangers game at Tynecastle, bumped into Harry Bunt (Doreen s Uncle) who lives at Balgreen and we then went to the Stratford Bar for a pint, game was good and a fair crowd. Had an unexpected visit from Jimmy Hogg later that day, unfortunately Auntie Bella had passed away at noon today, so Ma was very upset. After she regained her composure, she was glad that we had managed to visit her last Friday as she had not seen her in years. Funeral is expected to be on Saturday and Ma and Dad had a healthy discussion about what the funeral arrangements should be and fell out as they could not agree on what should happen, "oh well such is life".

Thurs Nov 11th, I woke up at 9am today to the sound of the postman with mail from Doreen and brother Alan, had a wee greet as I read Doreen's letter as it is obvious, she misses me as much as I miss her, what a lucky man I am. After my greeting I went for a jog in the park then I went round to Uncle John Burns with the news that Auntie Bella had passed away, we had a large Napoleon Brandy and chatted about years gone by. Ma, Dad and I then went to Finefair shopping, stopped in at Luckies Bar for my Birthday drink and some lunch, I had French onion flan? They had Hungarian goulash and of course a few "nips", Auntie Jean and Uncle Davie arrived a bit later joining us for a drink. We had a nice visit and chat about things and they decided they would try and visit Ma every other Tuesday in the future, some progress me thinks. Parents by now were half "chowed" and ready for a nap by 4.30pm and hoping that we would have no visitors as they wanted Jim all to themselves tonight.

I can't believe the excitement within myself in anticipation of going home to Doreen and the kids (especially Doreen) I know I will feel bad about leaving Ma and Dad again, but we have had a really good 3 weeks with each other and benefitted from it (Doreen should be a psychologist) and I am feeling much better all round now. At tea time we had a phone call from Jimmy Hogg regards funeral arrangements for the coming Saturday. Ma and Dad are showing signs of "end of vacation syndrome" what with Auntie Bella passing away and me heading home they are becoming a bit sentimental and emotional. Ma has enjoyed her day today and felt good about buying the lunch and drinks, but she is very tired and ready for bed. Betty Low arrived about 8pm for a few minutes with more gifts and cards for Canada.

Dad almost got me into an argument watching TV regards politics as he said "I KNOW THAT THEY ARE ALL WRONG" (the politicians"). I didn't respond much to his dismay, nice going Jim good control, I must be ready for home. Interesting trip and I feel the better for it, will have a clear mind when I get home and will consider all the options regarding our future.

When I returned from Scotland I felt I was in a better place, had spent some quality time albeit a wee bit challenging with my dear Ma and Dad and returned to the love of my life Doreen and my family with the future seemingly clearer in my mind, a change was going to be necessary for me to survive at the position I had evolved to at Petrosar. Basically, I felt there was no more I could give of myself to this Major Project that I had embraced. We had tried to save crumbling marriages at the Petrosar Plant by using an Industrial Psychologist named Anne Nolan on a 3-day seminar supported and budgeted for by management at the Chatham Wheels Inn with the Ethylene Dept Supervisors and their wives or partners (70% divorce rate, on Projects of this magnitude 25% seemed to be the normal and expected?). We had convinced our management to pre hire and staff for an upcoming Major Project called the H.F.O.U (heavy fuel oil upgrade), then it was cancelled after spending almost $50M Canadian dollars on Engineering, the future was now looking bleak as even the Government wouldn't bail Petrosar out of some of our current financial difficulties. The clincher for me and my future was when we (Petrosar) had to decide we would have to "let go" personnel when the HFOU Project was cancelled.

This decision was not going to be easy as we were a "non-union" organization and some of the original employees who had given up long term jobs on other sites to join us would possibly have to be released based on Performance Appraisals not Seniority. My immediate Manager had told me I "had" to be involved in the decision making of "who to let go", I said I just couldn't do this and the option I was given was if you can't we will have to move someone into your current position who will. All I could think of was the employees and their families who had given up careers to join us in the beginning could be compromised.

One of the many wonderful "tools" they provided for Management at Petrosar was a Decision Analysis/Potential Problem Analysis/Problem Analysis method called Kepnor Trego. When I returned from Scotland, I had decided that we would use this tool to make a Decision on what "we" should consider doing in the near future. Doreen and I went through this process and low and behold the simple answer was to apply for a different position (less demanding) at Petrosar or look for another job. I jumped all over this and my Middle East thoughts came to mind again, was it time? Keep in mind that Doreen had reached "a comfortable life" at this time in her life, so why would we move? I really wanted to go to Saudi Arabia, but once again "am I nuts or what?" The seed to move seemed to have been planted, but to where? Doreen was obviously frustrated as she really was in a good place in her life and to quote my dad "why in heavens name would you consider going to Saudi Arabia when your wife already gave up so much to come to Canada in the first place you owe your wife big time as it is". As it happened, she sacrificed a lot more over the coming years, with moves to Saudi Arabia, Australia, Korea, and Japan with her gypsy husband who was slowly "losing it".

Petrosar decided to go ahead with lay-offs in late 1982 but did offer most employees an exit package that was quite generous, obviously I did not agree with this approach as we were encouraging "excellent workers" to take the package and run, my integrity and principles were at risk and not to be compromised so I declined the Authoritarian Approach that had been used and decided "not" to take the exit package but would move on at the earliest opportunity. (a very expensive decision much to Doreen's dismay).

Our family was in a bit of a turmoil since I had decided a "change" was necessary for me to get some semblance of order back in my life but what effect was this going to have on Doreen, Jeff, Mike and Elaine. We spent several months round the kitchen table discussing pros and cons of several options, but I was determined that Saudi was our best option and the kids seemed ok with that and Doreen was prepared to support me whatever the decision was.

I continued to do my best as Production Superintendent in the Olefins Dept early in 1983 and although I was very proud of this position Doreen, and I recognized I was struggling to keep my head above water however the Plant was running well, and we were making maximum quality products. Our social lives were now being impacted along with our Family life with the demanding workload.

I decided then to respond to an opportunity identified in a Middle East Newsletter early spring of 1983. I received a phone call from an Ed Evola who was a Personnel Consultant in Houston Texas around about May 15/83 regarding a Petrochemical Chemical Co being formed in Al Jubail Saudi Arabia called SADAF (Arabic name for Shell). Al Jubail was a small fishing village on the Arabian Gulf side of Saudi Arabia "was I interested?"

The Project
Shell Oil/Saudi complex 509%/50%
Fluor Corporation building the Plant
Bechtel building the community
Plant Complex/Ethylene and four other Units

Generous Salary/Benefits/housing provided
High growth Area, lots of opportunities
30 days Annual Vacation/Fares paid to Sarnia or other
We will contact you within 4 weeks with an offer
Supervisory Position, promotions likely

After discussion with Doreen, I responded and said we were interested, was the "Saudi Adventure" about to become a reality, now I am excited and looking forward to the future again, Doreen still not sure about all this.

BALKYMOR 10

THE SAUDI ARABIA ADVENTURE, 1983-1988

We received correspondence from Ed Ebola within the 4 weeks with more information on the Project and Interview dates set for early July at the Inn on the Bridge (Port Huron). We were to be interviewed on July 6th by a Mr. Amin Al-Shubbar and other Engineers who had already been hired by SADAF. Doreen and I did another Kepnor Trego exercise and concluded this could be a great opportunity and decided to pursue it further. GOAL, Early retirement, be able to afford and enjoy our time together but also maintain our own interests at the current elevated standard of living. Basically "enjoy life" while we can "Now".

The interview went well, and I received an offer of Operations Supervisor in Saudi Petrochemicals Co and Engineering Organization (SADAF) on July 26/83.

Salary was very generous American $s and Car Allowance, good benefits, generous allowances for shipping/packing/storage and relocation allowances. Housing is provided and he confirmed the 30-day annual vacation with paid trips home, or destination of choice twice a year.

The offer was contingent on successful medical examinations including an Aids test, obtaining Visa's and Residency Permits for Saudi Arabia.

Somewhere around July 31/83 Doreen and I discussed the why? And why not? Still both a bit apprehensive but slowly reaching a position of accepting the fact a "change" might be necessary for both of us for different reasons. We also did a financial analysis and concluded it would be very beneficial to seriously consider this opportunity, but we were still not very clear on the longer-term implications.

The financial incentives were, higher income, no income tax if we declared non-residency for 2 years in Canada, USA dollars salary (+20% against Canadian dollar at the time), free housing, all utilities paid, car allowance, shipping and storage allowance, (very attractive).

Called Doris Shoemaker in Detroit 1-713-241-0450 August 9th gave her a verbal ok and to please send on more information and a contract. We arranged another family discussion this same day regards the house, car, Jeff's status, Mike's status, Elaine would stay at our home till Brock University, our future etc. and we reached the conclusion we should seriously consider going overseas. Round the kitchen table vote was 5-0 to go. Some of the kids' responses were, good challenge, an adventure, see the world, possibly retire early, go for it, concerns about Mum, will miss you, haven't a clue it is your decision.

On August the 12th we contacted an old friend, George Duthie who happened to be on vacation home here in Sarnia and had been working for Aramco in Dhahran near Al Jubail.

His comments were all very favorable about the living and working conditions in that area, benefits and compensation were excellent and both he and his wife were really enjoying the opportunity to travel and see the world. His parting comment to us based on their experience was that "after the culture shock you will love it", the heads up about the "culture shock" was quite profound as we would find out in the coming months.

By now I had received a letter from Ed Evola saying that I had a confirmed verbal offer of employment and wants to hear from us whether we will accept or not as soon as possible, "we" hadn't really decided just yet, but I think I had. We went to see a Chartered Accountant for advice on the house status, income taxes and non-residency issues. We filled in a form for non-residency that he would process, signed a letter of authorization for income tax purposes and he said we would need a copy of my 1982 Tax return plus a letter from Payroll at Petrosar for 1983 earnings and any interest earned with our bank accounts.

Things were starting to happen real fast now, and I actually received a call from a Nick Reeves in Detroit that Doreen and were set up for a 1week Orientation Session Oct 2nd-7th, at BCIU an Institute in Washington and then depart for Saudi on Oct 8th and I still hadn't seen or signed a contract yet.

Called Doris Shoemaker but she was on vacation till Aug 29th. Her office said not to worry a package with the contracts and info on transfer to Saudi would be included.

On August 24th we finally received a contract that have to be signed and returned with approval and all medical information, guess we were going but I was a bit nervous by now about the slow paperwork. Need to draft letter of resignation for Petrosar soon wow.

We received an information package from Sadaf on Aug 30t h with work permit/residency check lists, biographical forms, Visa applications, and brochures about life in AI Jubail.

On Aug 31st still not a "final" decision made by us but I called Doris Shoemaker and informed her that I had had a medical and Doreen was due for hers on Sept and. Also informed her that Oct and to Oct 7en at BCIU (Business Council for International Understanding) Institute in Washington would be very tight with all that still had to be done and requested that Oct 16d1 start date at BCIU be considered. I also requested that, if possible, Doreen and I would like a one-week stopover in Scotland to see family and friends after BCIU before continuing on to Dhahran, I could not see that arriving a week or two late would make much difference as the Plant was still under construction. She had to contact a Roger Sullivan (Plant Manager for Shell and Sadaf Project) for approval which she did, and we got the ok. Try to imagine the turmoil that Doreen was going through during this emotional Process, when I look back now, she should get a tole medal just for considering this move.

We were told by Sadaf that we would need 30 passport pictures (contacted Elliot Crocket) in Sarnia and arranged to get 3o photos taken), my Canadian Passport was currently being processed, Doreen had applied for and was patiently waiting for a British passport (finally received it Sep 28th) we would also have to contact Dixon Van Lines soon regards our shipping arrangements. We seemed to be being carried away like a leaf in the wind. STILL STRUGGLING WITH THE DECISION, we both have said yes but "GUT WRENCHING" nevertheless, haven't yet put pen to paper. Primary Concerns? Everything it seems.

Doreen was leaving a great life now in Canada, Jim giving up a position that he had only dreamed about. We started to scrutinize an information package that had arrived from Houston, and it looked "overwhelming" to say the least.

- Letter to BCIU Dates for Orientation and Wellington Hotel
- Transfer to Al Jubail information
- Yellow work permit/residency check list
- Foreign Employee Biographical Data
- Photograph address in Houston TX
- list of cars available in Al Jubail
- Personal Auto loan information
- Information regarding International Driving license
- Office shipments information
- Furniture that was available in provided housing
- Life in Al Jubail book.
- Letter with helpful advice

We still had a multitude of things to consider, not the least was to sign the "OFFER" soon and send Resignation letter to Petrosar.

By Sunday Sept 3/83 all the information was in our hands now but still having nightmares trying to come to grips with what is right? I really wanted to go, Doreen will support me, but I am scared for some reason. Why? nerves maybe. Anyway, we set out a tentative schedule of everything that "needed" to be done in the following week, we would sign and return the z contracts and all the necessary paperwork to Houston by Thursday Sept 7/83. Some minor issues however still had to be resolved.

We received a call from Doris Shoemaker on Sept 8th with our proposed travel dates and when we would be expected in Al Jubail (Nov 6. We were tentatively scheduled to leave Houston Texas on Thursday Oct loth for Washington to attend BCIU Institute

Orientation on Oct 23rd to Oct 28th staying at the Wellington Hotel then depart for Scotland Oct 29th till November 5th and then leave for Dhahran Airport in Saudi Arabia via Amsterdam where we would be met by some Sadaf personnel and escorted to the very posh Dhahran Hotel. Doris was also pursuing Elaine's status as an unmarried dependent for Medical and Dental coverage, apparently our Jeff and Mike were too old to get any benefits coverage by Sadaf (Saudi Petrochemicals as it would be known as now).

Started preparing a draft letter of resignation on Sept 14th, intend to give Petrosar one month's notice but still had no "contract" in my hands. The finished letter was delivered to my boss at the time Ray Arsenault several days later, it was no surprise for him as we had had many lengthy discussions about my future options both at Petrosar and other organizations. Dixon Van Lines finally contacted us with rough estimates for Air, Sea shipping and Storage costs, thank goodness these expenses were being covered by Sadaf, we had about Soo lbs. of "stuff" to ship. Received a couple of letters from friends who had already arrived in Al Juba", and they had some really interesting comments about the community, how they were feeling after arrival and what they were currently involved in on the construction site.

Meanwhile life goes on in Sarnia, be it somewhat chaotic, many of our friends still couldn't believe we were making this move. Peggy and Phil Tumer had arranged a potluck supper for our small golf group, mostly people from the old soccer group and associates not knowing it would be a few weeks before we left, we had a great night anyways, quite an emotional night I might add. Why would we leave was on all their lips.

Soon after this Doreen started preparing packages and boxes with itemized lists for Air and Sea freight, our decision was to send "valuable and need to have" stuff by air and everything else by sea. Lots of phone calls reshipping from Abdullah Al Anway (the clearing agent for Sadaf) and Abdul Karim Al-Derwesh (the purchasing agent for Sadaf). We should notify them when our "stuff" was on its way, can you believe this?

Several people expressed an interest in our relatively new K-Car that was state of the art at that time, small but efficient, we had it appraised, and we had 2 people who said they would like to buy it when we left Sarnia, Jessie and Alex Mackay two of our closest friends showed the most interest at the time.

On Wednesday Sept 21st we received a phone call from Mary Ann Rogers in Houston that they were working on finalizing arrangements and considering sending someone up from Houston on Oct 20th for us to "sign on. Their intention, she said, was to fly Doreen and I from Sarnia to Washington together if possible and be in Washington for Sat Oct 22nd for the BCIU Orientation session on Oct 23rd. Further to this a Mr. Nashwa? was trying to ensure our trip to Edinburgh / Prestwick after the orientation and then on to Saudi for Nov 6th was taken care off.

By now we were both basically basket cases but moving things along as well as we could and Doreen continued in her efficient way to pack and list items, needless to say our basement now looked like Paddy s Market with stuff everywhere. Hope we will be within our shipping allowance?

Lots of people who had heard of our proposed "adventure called and asked us if they could come over and talk to us about their interest in "going overseas to work", we had to tell them we were buried in paper-work and would get back to them sometime in the future but I kept a list and thought if we ever do get there I should contact them and share our experience that was currently bordering on a "nightmare".

Tuesday Sept 27/83, Dixon Van Lines sent a representative to our house at 794 Pineview, they were still trying to finalize the shipping arrangements for us. It looks like the costs will be higher than anticipated (surprise, surprise). We told them to proceed with the agreed upon arrangements as we were going regardless of the price and Sadaf said they would pick up any additional costs incurred.

Donna Barclay the Dept Associate (Secretary) at Olefins Dept, Petrosar invited Doreen and I over for dinner with some of our workmates on the 27th and the Ladies Bridge group took Doreen out to lunch the following day and gave her a beautiful Royal Doulton figurine as a going away gift.

- We had needed to sit down and prepare a schedule for social events as everyone it seems wanted to see us off in style.
- Sept 22 Moira and Brian dinner
- Sept 24 Golf and dinner
- Sept 27 Donna's dinner
- Oct 1 Ron and Aileen dinner Oct 4 Shift Leaders Party
- Oct 7 Marg's reception
- Oct 8 Alan and Helen dinner
- Oct 9 Thanksgiving/Pre Xmas dinner (Family)
- Oct 14 Party/Roast for Jim and Gus Horton (Operator going to Sadaf)
- Oct 15 Banquet at SGCC.

All of this plus a list of other lunches and dinners for Doreen with her personal friends.

Thursday Sept 28th, Panic stations setting in, "what if" regards our house usage being abused and impacting on our family members in our 794 Pineview house while we are away, e.g., Mike, Elaine, and possibly Jeff. Doreen is feeling the stress now and a bit down due to flue, late nights, fear, excitement and all the rest, “hang in there Jim and Doreen”.

Received final details of BCIU Orientation course in Washington, looks like 6 very busy long and demanding days, hope we can still leave for Scotland as scheduled on Friday Oct 28th.

Packing continues on, “good God” how much do we really need for day to day living in Saudi. Oops I forgot we would be gone for at least 2 years. Doreen attended her “last” Ladies monthly meeting for a while at her sister Aileen’s house, apparently there was lots of emotion that night.

Thursday Oct 6th Dixon Van Lines came to the house, packed and removed for storage our Air and Sea freight shipments, a significant step we were close to being on our way. We received a cheque for approx. $5K USA dollars from Saudi Petrochemicals Co to cover our Relocation and Shipping Allowances.

Our new address was going to be c/o Saudi Petrochemicals, PO Box 363, Madinat, Al Jubail, Al Sinaiyah, Kingdom of Saudi Arabia.

Asked our kids to be available for our “final” Family meeting midOctober regarding arrangements/issues when we were away, some items we discussed.

- FOOD, assume $zo person/week.
- BILLS, paid out of our account (Elaine to be the accountant)
- MAINTENANCE, Jeff/Mike or call Uncle Alan or Uncle Ron
- HOUSE, $zoo Monthly if working to account.
- WASH, shared responsibility
- VISITORS, use discretion and control, call Uncle Alan if needed
- TRANSPORT, help each other.

- DISHES, shared responsibilities
- We are just a phone call away in emergencies 03 341 5490.

The transition at Petrosar continued during all of these activities, Bob Harwood a very capable English chap had been chosen to assume my position as Olefins Production Superintendent when I moved on, I felt a strange sense of relief growing as the end of my career at Petrosar was imminent.

A Poster went up at work announcing a Farewell Party/Roast for Gus Horton and Jim Currie at the Legion Hall on Front Street on Oct 14th, promised to be a fun night.

On Oct 11th we received Confirmation of Non-Residency status from Revenue Canada, this was a significant milestone as now we would not have to pay Canada Income Tax on earnings while overseas but would have to severe all ties to Canada temporarily. Arranged to meet Bob Hussey a Chartered Accountant on Oct 17th to conclude other important business, including the non-residence issue implications, bank accounts, RRSP's property taxes and any other business.

Received a phone call from Mary-Ann Rogers at the Sadaf Office in Houston confirming dates Oct 19th and 20th to fly to Houston and finally "sign on". Accommodation had been arranged at the Downtown Sheraton and to report to Shell Plaza Sadaf Office by 7:15am on the 20th. The return flight would leave Houston at 16.00hrs on the 20th and arrive in Sarnia at 23:30hrs with stops at Pittsburg and Toronto, promised to be a busy 2 days.

Things were really starting to happen now, a phone call from Mr. Nashwa also in Houston office that all flight arrangements from Sarnia to Washington (via Toronto), Washington to Edinburgh (via Heathrow), then Edinburgh back to London and on to Dhahran had been booked and confirmed. Mr. Nashwa mentioned that excess baggage should not exceed 110 pounds and we were allowed 2 bags each, and to keep all receipts.

My last workday at Petrosar was October 14th, a very emotional experience since it had been a wonderful life experience for me, but I guess I was ready to move on to other challenges, goodness me the growth of experience during this tumultuous seven years was tremendous but my knees had buckled with the workload. The Plant Management Team took me out for lunch at the Sarnia Golf and Curling Club (SGCC) where I received some nice momento's and compliments for my contribution to the Organization during my time there.

Later that same day around 7pm the employees had arranged what turned out to be a Fabulous Farewell party/roast for Gus and I at the Sarnia Legion Hall, we both received some nice gifts and some meaning full "trophies" of our successes and failures all meant in good fun. I will treasure my replica of a Rhefla valve from Furnace # 2 commemorating one of the incidents that I had been involved with early during the construction phase. It was a great and memorable night for Doreen and I and all our Petrosar friends.

Tuesday Oct 18th, we sold the K-Car to Jessie and Alex Mackay, had some minor problems but got that sorted out and they let us keep the car till the day we were departing. Played golf with my brother Alan, Brian Spowart and another friend at Huron Oakes, then we went to a pub called the Snowbirds on London Road for farewell drinks, met some other friends of Alan's there and we had a really good time.

Wednesday Oct 19th all flight arrangements were good for the trip to Houston, Samia to Toronto to Chicago and then on to Houston arriving at 13:40 pm local time, had a beer and went shopping. Dinner had been arranged for 18:30 pm, good meal and then off to bed for an early rise in the morning at 6:30am.

- Thursday Oct 20th up at 6:30am and off to Shell Plaza Sadaf office to "sign on" Doris Shoemaker went through comprehensive list for new employees.
- Company Benefits Salary Administration
- Work hours (Fri and Sat weekends?) Savings Plan
- Medical and Health plan Sick Benefits
- Disability
- Severance awards
- Expense Allowances Relocation Allowances
- Practices and Pre-Requisites

She then gave us an expense allowance cheque of $1137 USA dollars for Washington and another cheque for $1000 USA for arrival in Al Jubail, generous or what but again make sure you get receipts.

A guy by the name of Joe Carsiola gave us a short Shell Oil (Sadaf) Orientation session mostly to do with Bechtel Construction who had the main contracts for building the major Petrochemical complex with support from a sub-contractor Fluor Construction. Afterwards he made some comments about "Wealth belongs to God, therefore each person should share", then he said, "equal pay for equal work" (women?) strange comment considering where we were going. Then he said, "don't allow family disruption" followed by "change is inevitable" and then finally "be careful taking photos, very restrictive in this culture".

He then touched on Safety and Health Issues and discussed the equipment available at the construction site, pretty standard stuff. Shortly afterwards we had a short break, signed the Contracts and soon it was time to head back home to Sarnia as we were leaving soon "maybe" for Washington DC.

If all went well the following day we would leave soon after for the BCIU Institute, part of The American University, 3301, New Mexico, Ave NW, in Washington DC, but only if our Passports, Visas and all the other paperwork had arrived in Sarnia.

Friday Oct 21st, Doreen's birthday! Panic stations no Visa and no Passports, took care of some bills and banking instead of just hanging around waiting, we were all packed ready to go but had this feeling of running out of time. We had a drink at the house with the twins "Doreen and Aileen" who had been out with sister Moira, Elaine, and Karen celebrating their 23rd Birthday. We still had no Visa or Passports by 4pm so I contacted Micky Reeves in Houston, and she claims that TNT Sky Packs Inc should deliver the packages later today and gave me their phone #, "no problem, sir" they said it will be there soon. "Inshallah" or "God willing" in English I found out.

We had a beautiful supper that night prepared by Elaine, Jeff, and Paula plus we had lots of phone calls and visitors during the evening, received the "packages" with all our documentation at 11"30pm that night, all the travel arrangements had now been confirmed and we were "ready to go".

The flight from Sarnia departed at 6:50am on Sat Oct 22nd, we flew to Toronto and then to Buffalo before arriving in Washington DC at 13:50pm. It was the most beautiful, day, sunny and warm, we had a wee cry after reading Elaine's farewell note to us, last night had been a very emotional experience for all of us, now we were on our way to who knows what. The last 3 months finally caught up with us later in the afternoon, so we had a nap before going for dinner in the hotel, watched a movie on TV and then crashed again.

Sunday Oct 23rd. We woke up about gam after a great sleep and it was pouring rain outside, Hmm ominous! Today we start at BCIU

Institute with Arabic Instruction, basic language 4hrs a day, culture shock, middle east traditions, what to expect on arrival and how to behave sort of "when in Rome do as the Romans do" philosophy.

Plan to call Elaine later tonight, she will be anxious and worried about how the flights and our day went. She will be heading to Brock University soon; how will she manage changes?

We had a very busy and demanding schedule during the week at BCIU, some nice meals in very exotic restaurants but our days were very long and tiring, 4 hours Arabic Language each day plus another 6 to 8 hours "Traditions and Cultural Orientation" was a bit much for all of us attending even although we did have many breaks during the workday. We finished up pretty well wiped out at BCIU by Friday Oct 28th, had farewell drinks with Instructors and participants then off to Dulles International Airport for a flight to Heathrow Airport in London at 9:45pm and then a connection on to Turnhouse Airport in Edinburgh where we arrived at 10:40am on Oct 29th Betty Low Doreen's sister picked us up at Turnhouse Airport, dropped me off at Ma and Dad's house at 61 Stevenson Drive and took Doreen home to her house in Barnton. After a good blether Dad and I went to Tynecastle to see the Hearts play St Johnstone (Ma not too happy), had a pie and a pint at the football match and then went home to spend the night till midnight chatting, now I am really knackered. On Sunday we were all invited over to Betty Low's house for a bang-up dinner and met all Doreen's Family, got home by 9:30pm, weary but happy and recovering slowly from the BCIU week. Was great to see and be with Ma and Dad and some of the McFarlane family.

The few days we had in Edinburgh Scotland were short and sweet and soon we were heading for the Airport again, tearful emotional cheerios, just rips your heart out and soon we were on our way on Saturday November 5th to London and then on to Dhahran

Airport where we arrived at 22:10 hrs., flight time from London was about 6 hours. The flight on Saudi Airlines was very good (but obviously no booze) and we went through customs relatively fast. We had had a very busy week in Scotland but when we left this morning although Ma and Dad had a wee greet, they were happy for us and the fact we could possibly see them twice a year now when we went home on leave from Saudi. Our luggage happened to be overweight in London and we had to pay 281 British pounds for excess baggage, thank goodness Sadaf was picking up the tab. The temperature when we arrived in Dhahran was 23C hot and humid.

The Airport was very busy and soon we were feeling the effects of the warm humid atmosphere, a wee bit tired and grumpy and being herded like cattle towards Customs and Security by lots of Saudi soldiers with rifles about the same size as they were. Most of us had to open up our luggage for fairly intensive scrutiny and anything that they found as questionable to their culture was immediately confiscated not to be seen again, no arguments. We had to repack all the cases which were left in complete disarray scattered all over the long counters.

Outside the airport there was a row of Mercedes Benz taxies waiting to transfer some of us from the airport to the very exotic Dhahran International Hotel, truly a thing of majestic beauty where we were to stay overnight before being transferred in the morning to Al Jubail. We were met by some new Sadaf staff employees including a couple of people who had worked at Petrosar in Sarnia, and we had known quite well who would look after us for a couple of days.

Had a wonderful evening in the hotel, fantastic room, great meal, nice breakfast and lots of "soft" drinks! (No more alcohol for months) And then off to bed for a good night's sleep before heading north to our destination in the morning, what will this bring?

Sunday November 6th, we had a good night's sleep (basically exhausted) and a really nice breakfast in the Hotel and before you know it an old yellow school bus showed up and 2 older looking trucks for all our luggage and some scruffy looking locals who started loading the luggage, my immediate thought was "wonder if we will ever see our luggage again". So off went just after 11:00am on our way to Al Jubail about 90 kms up the road. It was a hot bumpy ride and some interesting sights with males squatting on the road relieving themselves (customary) and car wrecks almost every mile up the road, just pushed to the side (customary) and mostly Mercedes Benz cars flying up what they called a highway at 120kms/hr. We really began to wonder again "what have we done?"

We were met at the Al Jubail Hotel by a Walter Harbuck (Superintendent from Shell Oil) and Tom Hughes who had been my boss at Petrosar for several years. Doreen spent the afternoon at the Hotel, and I was taken to the Plant for a quick visit. The Al Jubail Hotel was small but comfortable and because our houses were not quite ready, yet we would end up spending longer than they thought in what was a downtown hotel near the market place (souk) in what used to be a fishing village. A car would pick us up at the hotel daily, take us to the Plant site and bring us back at night for several weeks was the plan, the Plant was still in the construction phase.

We met Roger Sullivan also from Shell Oil in Houston who would be the Ethylene (Olefins) Manager at the new Plant during commissioning and start up and he said we would be provided with a Company car for a month till we could arrange to buy our own car with the company benefits allowance, we were also told again that housing had been delayed and it could be several weeks till our house was ready to occupy. Basically, Sadaf had built a village with all the roads /utilities/ shopping and recreation facilities for all the incoming employees. Al Jubail had been an old fishing village which had been converted into a modern commercial Port to accommodate the very large Crude Oil Tankers and other shipping that was going to be associated with the Petrochemical Project, not the least was all the "modular pre constructed components" for the Petrochemical Complexes coming in from Japan and Korea. Roger asked us to report to the Saudi Petrochemical Plant (Sadaf) where we would work by 7am the next morning and go see a gentleman by the name of "Saud" in the Employee Relations Dept.

Doreen was managing "ok" at the Al Jubail Hotel but probably still wondering what had hit her, she had met some of the other ladies who had arrived and was making the most of staying at the Hotel. All our expenses were covered at the Hotel, just keep track of all your receipts. We found out that although Ex-pats normally would stay in a compound "we would not", we would live in the village that had been built with all the Saudi Employees, this apparently was a first for this area, the village we would live in was called Al Fanateer, a beautiful subdivision, a strange mix of western and local cultural designs.

On Tuesday Nov 8th. Would you believe Sadaf gave us 5000 Riyals (about $1700 USA dollars) to "help us out" till our first pay day with no questions asked! At work we were going through all the necessary steps with Employee Relations, Government Relations, Housing, Shipping, Safety and Medical but all at a very leisurely pace then out of nowhere we received a phone call saying our house was going to be available earlier than expected. Early on Thursday we drove about 10kms from the Hotel to Al Fanateer subdivision to our assigned Apartment #11001-1A and we were "absolutely astounded" when we arrived at the beautiful 3-bedroom, 3 bathroom, 3 balconies, large living room, family room fully furnished and the most modern kitchen and appliances that one could imagine "Fantastic".

We checked out all the gadgets, including our air conditioning, domestic appliances and admired the quality of all the furnishings, drapes, and flooring, "we can't believe this".

Called the Shipping Agent and he said he could deliver our Air Freight Thursday between 11:00am and 12.00 noon, hard to believe we were actually in Saudi Arabia. Doreen has been getting involved with all the ladies, swimming, coffee, lunches, and sharing info with her new friends, some of it good some not so good. Personally, I was going through some major mood swings almost daily not really realizing what we had done?

The bachelor status chaps who had just arrived about the same time as we had been very unhappy with their accommodation, 8 operators to a trailer! What will they think when they see "our house", apparently status is huge over here. Tomorrow night we have invited Tom Hughes (Management), Grant Dawson, Dave Coppard, and Gus Horton (Process Operators all from Petrosar) to a Barbeque to be held at the Al Jubail Hotel.

It is now November 11th, 33 years ago to the day my Family had moved from the Lawnmarket area in Edinburgh out to Broomhouse near Sighthill and eventually that is where I had met Doreen some 5 years later. Now here we are in a new house (apartment) in Al Fanateer just north of Al Jubail in Saudi Arabia, really hard to believe?

We had left the Hotel this am after paying 3301 Riyals (about $1000 USA) for our time there, again thank goodness we are on expenses. On our way to Al Fanateer, we stopped at another housing area called Al Huwaylat where we did some shopping at the commissary and spent another 500 Riyals ($180 USA dollars) on groceries. Earlier in the day I had an interesting experience while bargaining for a Radio in the marketplace (souk) with a local, he had asked for 300 riyals and I offered him 260 riyals and we had almost reached a deal when it was suddenly Prayer Time, so we had to close up shop so "no deal", everything closes down for prayer time 5 times a day.

It is now 9pm and we have put all the groceries away, Doreen has done a wash and unpacked some stuff, we went for a jog (not appropriate here) on a beautiful night so all things considered a reasonable start to the next step in our "adventure", now go to work in am and try to adjust to this different lifestyle.

Things to do:

- Look for a car fill in expenses/ check sea shipment, due date Dec 16th.
- Open bank account.
- Prepare a budget and look at finances
- Plan next 3, 6, 9 and 12 Months
- Telephone/Television
- Get interested in new job/letters to friends and Family.

Friday November 18th, Doreen had spent a few days in our apartment and was almost going bananas, on Tuesday she went shopping in Al Jubail with some of her new friends. On Wednesday she took the Newcomers tour and had coffee with a Women's Group and then on Thursday we spent 2 hours on Camp 9A beach (later found out it was a single man's beach), 5kms of beach and only 4 people on it? That night we went to Gus Horton's place to watch a film called Dinner with Andre with Tom Hughes and a Charlie Carradine from Shell Oil who we had got to know. On Friday I went to the swimming pool for men only for a couple of hours with the guys, this is going to take some getting used to especially for the women.

At work I went through a week of Orientation, Industrial Relations, Safety, Health, Environment, Policies, Work Permits, Firefighting etc, etc, etc, and "qualified" or so they said. I expect soon they will want us to go to work. Made a contact with a Saudi who had a car for sale, if I decide to buy it then I would have to do all the complicated paperwork and try to find an insurance company now.

On Sunday November 20th I met Abdul Nasser who had a 1982 Mazda Sports car for sale and arranged to talk to an insurance guy about it, was advised not to buy the car as it had a history, opportunity missed. Later this day I made contact with 2 soccer enthusiasts who had heard about my coaching of kids in Canada so decided to get involved with local kids' soccer.

Thursday November 24th, another quick week went in between work, sports and we were slowly settling in it seems. We had enjoyed a beautiful dinner at the Al Jubail Hotel on the 21st to celebrate our 24th wedding anniversary "Saudi Champagne and all" (non-alcoholic) but a nice evening, nevertheless. On the night of the 22nd we had some friends over for a dinner and invited Joan and Jerry our American neighbors over for the evening, Grant Dawson one of our Petrosar guys was a great guitar player and he played a few songs for us, was a really nice night.

The Thursday was the first day of the weekend as is the custom in Saudi Arabia, so we decided to drive to Abu-Ali beach (where all the Ex Pat Brits usually hang out on the weekend), not much security (Muttawa Religious Police) out and about at this remote beach. We got through a local check point ok but about 2 miles into the desert trail we got stuck in very soft sand, "oh boy" Boc temperature, blistering sun still 2 miles from the beach area and at least 2 miles back to the highway access road and here we are up to the axles in sand. After digging for about an hour in the hot sun we gave up and started walking back to the highway, we had thought that there might be at least some traffic going to and from the beach but not on this day, just as we were within sight of the highway access road a car came up behind us from the beach area, A Korean lady was driving (this is a definite no no) but anyway she had a cell phone so we were able to contact some friends in Al Fanateer who arranged to come and rescue us and brought some shovels and nice cold bottles of water, so much for our quiet day on the beach.

Shortly after this incident in the desert we had to return the company car that we had used since arriving, so we decided to buy a new Mazda 626 at $19K Riyals, the company car allowance would see us paying it off in 12 months, really nice arrangement. We now had our own transport, we had settled in at the house, Doreen was slowly adjusting to our new way of life? and my job was going very well, The Plant was still in the construction stage so we were busy doing extensive training, field and classroom with the young Saudi Technicians who were expected to be trained to Operate the plant on their own within 5 years. The Plant once completed would have what is called a "Punch Out" prior to the "Commissioning Phase" and would eventually be started up with Ex Pats from all over the world who had extensive Ethylene Plant experience (each would have a Saudi Technician working with them on shift).

Friday November 25th, Doreen and I discussed specific objectives for the next 12 months to help us through this period, WORK/SOCIAL, Low key, don't get too involved, will be working 12hr shifts during start up, be active. FINANCES, Target optimistically $25K USA in the bank. TRAVEL PLANS, Doreen to Canada July to September, Jim to Canada around August September time, consider trip for Elaine to Scotland and Saudi (boys were not interested in Saudi Arabia). PERSONAL, Lose at least 10 lbs. should be easy "no booze", relax, learn to play the guitar, be reasonably active, do lots of walking morning and night. Take some day trips and enjoy the sights.

Thursday December 2nd, I am reading a great book at the moment called the Drifters written by James Michener, read most of it at Abu Ali beach after shopping today. did not get stuck in sand this time. The book is very interesting and provides some of the history of the Middle East and the problems after the Second World War. I have also recently read The Arabian Development Book and will soon be starting anther book called The Arab Mind.

I continue to be impressed by the Basic Fundamentals of Life here, the simple laws and attitudes about, Religion, Crime, and Family Life in general, maybe there is something about Islam and the Koran?

Some wonderful one liner from the Drifters Book

- The daughter of a Lion is also a Lion.
- For God's sake give me the young man who has brains enough to make a fool of himself.
- Your old men shall dream dreams; your young men will see visions.
- The blunders of youth are preferable to the success of old age.
- A man who changes his country is like a dog who changes his bark, not to be trusted.
- I took my girlfriend home to meet my Parents, they liked her but couldn't stand me.
- The best way to change society is to replace it one man at a time
- Our Country is wherever we are well off.
- Never was a Patriot yet, but was a fool.
- I travel not to go anywhere but to go, travel for travels sake, the great affair is to move.
- The fool wanders, the wise man travels.

- Don't put off till tomorrow what can be done today, if you enjoy it do it again tomorrow.
- Crabby old age and youth cannot live life together (Shakespeare Quote by Michener).

Friday December 9th, another relaxing week, what a transition from Petrosar, I could get used to this pace, I am starting to think clearly again, and some thoughts are crystallizing in my mind. One of our (Doreen and I) specific objectives back in April of this year was to "enjoy life while we can now", it seems ironic, but I do believe that is exactly what today's young people do, it has just taken us much longer to get there. Another wee gem from the Drifters Book "We are really cutting out from society", seems our values are different, and motivation isn't a need to demonstrate to someone else. We can use our life experience for education plus I have the confidence that I can do a good job and will obtain a job doing something without climbing the social structure ladder. I am slowly feeling better and better about the decision to walk away from my very demanding Petrosar job now. I know I gave all the positions I held in that organization everything I was capable of and achieved some very good results along the way.

Doreen and I are both quite competent people who don't want to be part of the rat race, we seem to have found our own "contentment" and we have no need to fight or elbow our way through life, we do not have aggressive "traits". Maybe our kids seem to have demanded a much better life from society than we had.

It also seems as if instinctively I have decided to eliminate career gratification (is this possible?) From my thinking, how long will this last? We should no longer take promotions, large incomes or big fancy houses seriously, sort of an "Awakening".

Wednesday December 21st, I wonder where the last 3 weeks went? We are settling in pretty well, relaxing, exercising daily and doing lots of reading and listening to music. The situation at the Plant is becoming familiar again with many unhappy people regards contracts, vacation allowance, living conditions and of course the almighty dollar is always an issue. It seems we have as many as 4 or 5 different types of contracts which are subject to interpretation depending on the market value of the country you were hired in. Big issue was some of us Brits who had emigrated to other countries e.g., USA or Canada were hired at much higher rates than our fellow Brits, really will be fun supervising Americans, Canadians, British, Indians, Sri Lankans, and of course the Saudi. s all with different contracts. Interesting dilemma as "all" employees had been told "not" to discuss salaries or benefits with anyone.

I had been assigned along with many other responsibilities to mentor Trainee Supervisors from Britain, Canada, and 3 high potential Saudis all of them with different contracts and lots to complain about but otherwise good people. One of the Saudis informed me that he been sneaking past the guards/security people at the gates to "get into the plant", a multimillion-dollar Project, claimed he did not have an Identity card, go figure, this was just the beginning. During construction we had been training the Saudi Fire Crew when a fire broke out at the top of the Ethylene (C2H4) Splitter unfortunately it was just at prayer time (everything stops) plus we found out that the firewater system did not have enough water power to reach the fire, fortunately it was just wooden scaffold and it burnt out, obviously we did have some significant learning's from this incident.

That evening, I got a call saying that I had a soccer coaching job, 5-, 6-, and 7-year-olds playing in the newly developed minor soccer league in Al Jubail, the interesting news that surprised me was those boys and girl would be playing together, not really expected in this culture.

Friday December 23rd, Doreen hasn't been feeling very well these past few days, could be a sore throat that is going around, or it could be its Xmas time and we are separated from our Family and friends. I have 4 days off work, so we went on an organized Plant Tour this morning. It was the first time that Doreen had realized the scope of the Total Project. At this moment in time, it was the World's Largest Single Train Ethylene (C2H4) Construction Project and looks very impressive on film. The Engineering, Planning, Construction, Management, and Execution of a Modular Built Plant is really something to behold. We realized going home to Al Fanateer in the bus that we have now been involved in 2 Major Projects.

PETROSAR First World Scale Ethylene Plant in Canada and now SAUDI PETROCHEMICALS CO (SADAF) Largest single Train Ethylene Complex in the World.

On the human relations side of things, I think we were now both suffering a bit, we are getting lots of rest, enjoying our food, enjoying our quiet time, trying to get involved socially "but" there is something missing? (Xmas)

LIKUL MUSHKILLA LA HA HALL (Arabic for every problem there is a solution) so we started planning 1984 Vacations and that brightened things up. Elaine is going to visit us in June then Elaine and Doreen will head home to Canada, and I will follow a few weeks later. In November all going well at work Doreen and I will plan a nice trip for our 25th wedding anniversary.

December 29th, Christmas 1983 is behind us now and it probably was our biggest challenge to date, how can you enjoy Xmas in a strange country away from your Family and friends? Xmas eve was Doreen's lowest point to date but somehow, we survived and got through it with a few tears along the way. A party we had attended at neighbors Joan and Jerry's house on the 24th and having Gus and Sue Horton over for Xmas day dinner really helped and then Elaine came through with flying colors phoning and getting through to us on Xmas Day.

We have been fortunate enough to have been included in several social events along the way with some new friends too, we were at Jonathan and Carolyn Rogers (from UK) last night, tonight we visited Sue and Gus and on Saturday we go to a New Years Eve party at Sue and Andy Hart's house. We were really enjoying our new car, Silver Mazda GLX 626, 4 gear stick shift (chosen by me because you see Doreen can, t drive in this country), we had a few problems with insurance and financing but got that sorted out. Can you believe we will own this car in 12 months "great stuff".

Most of the paperwork and bureaucracy related to the job is behind us now, Xmas is over, the job is going well, Doreen is slowly settling into this different way of life, and we now have quite a few "bob" in the bank both here in Saudi and back home. Roll on 1984 (In shaala kwayyis). "If God wills it will be good".

The three high potential Saudi Operators I had been assigned to groom/train/and developed to be Shift Supervisors were Bazzam Al-Ruwaily, Abdulla Al-Omani and Ahmed Al-Ghatany, they all seemed to be nice young men and eager to learn. It will have to be "Shwayya Bas" or as we say in Scotland "a wee bit at a time".

On Thursday Dec 30th, we had a nice trip on the Sadaf bus to Al Khobar, about gokms south of Al Jubail, the markets/souks were full of TCN's (Third Country Nationals) mostly single status men on contract from the Philippines and very interested in all the females who were there with their husbands. The shops closed early afternoon for prayer time, so the bus headed back to Al Fanateer, the ladies laiden with brass, gold, and silver "stuff". Introduced Doreen to Chess that night, very boring she said but we will see as time goes by.

On Monday January 4th, 1984 our sea shipment had finally arrived, but we owed 588 riyals for customs and duty tax that had to be paid before they would unload, by now we had realized that we could have bought everything we needed here and still had money left over from the relocation allowance, but one lives and learns.

Today I had my first soccer game on artificial turf at Camp Huwaylot with a group of Saudi employees and friends and tonight I have my first minor soccer meeting to set up the kid's leagues. Doreen spent today at Dammam another small town south of Al Fanateer with a bus load of ladies including Sue Horton and her young son Scott, found more brass, gold, silver and "stuff" but no purchases today.

Wednesday February 8th our mail is starting to come in regularly now and the weather has been good for the beach and evening walks, some concerns at work that Expense Claims are being audited and investigated, apparently some discrepancies had shown up and all employees were a bit apprehensive about the interpretation of what was actually eligible. Turns out that several expat employees had already been investigated/terminated and sent home for alleged cheating on what had been generous allowance expense claims. The next few weeks were a nightmare as each person second guessed what they thought they could have claimed. The number of people who had to leave was staggering but the Saudi management dealt with the problem swiftly and efficiently and the message was loud and clear we pay generously and provide excellent benefits "but" don't screw with us. Wednesday February 15th, the morale at work has dropped to zero, many experienced and skilled people have been sent packing for expense violations, can't believe what is happening. We were told today that all the British and Americans have now been audited and they are now checking our fellow Canadian's. Sure, hope my guardian angel looks out for me as you just never know! Anyway "just in case" we established a contingency plan. Now we aren't sure after a couple of months here whether or not we really want to stay on, maybe a month or two in Scotland sounds good then head back to Canada and look for a job "In shaa Allah?".

Thursday Feb 23rd, still a very gloomy atmosphere at work, uncertainty eats away at you. Can't remember ever being in a vulnerable situation like this during my work career, the moral of the story is clear but then so was my conscience.

On Saturday February 25th. The President of SADAF Mr. Carpenter said the Audit was now complete, can't believe the emotions Doreen and I experienced, we were ok, no surprise there but you just never know do you? 20 to 40 Families have now been sent home for expense violations, how sad after giving up all kinds of careers throughout the world to come here in the first place.

We reviewed the status of our Goals, relaxed and sane again (except for the last few weeks), I have now lost 14 lbs. and feeling the better for it, we have doubled our savings accounts in 4 months and are making good progress with my guitar lessons.

Thursday March 1st, we decided to buy a TV, zo-inch Sharp7 system remote control with antenna, booster, rotor, cables, and all connections for the grand price of 2000 riyals, a steal back in Canada. Later in the day we visited Alf Lightfoot, an old friend from Petrosa in Ab-Quag near Dhahran we also met several other old friends who were working there. They were all working for Aramco Petrochemicals and living in a compound just like being in the USA, certainly a more relaxed atmosphere and would you believe it they made a type of homemade juice that was absolutely forbidden outside the compound. Needless to say, we had a few drinks and felt terrible afterwards yugh, tasted awful.

We took a bus trip to Al Qataf on Thursday March 8th, it is about 60kms north of Al Jubail, we enjoyed the bus ride and scenery and walking around the many souks but just another sandy town. The big attractions were the Fish Market and a fenced in compound where all the Saudi women were expected to stay while the men did the shopping. Strange it seemed that although a fairly restrictive society here some of the young women were feeding their babies out in the open.

At work I had started to compile a list of excuses received from Trainees for missing work, Government Relations said we have to accommodate any requests from the locals.

- Too tired to work
- My sister's wedding
- Family problems
- Personal problems
- Car troubles
- Negotiating marriage
- Too hot to work today
- Engagement
- Mother is sick
- Father is sick
- Mother-in-Law sick
- Wife to hospital
- Have a headache
- Have to go home to my village, out of town
- Passport problems
- Housing issues
- Salary problems, can't find my safety boots or coveralls.

We planned a weekend group trip on March 14th to Al Hofuf a villagenear to Al Dhahran famous for its date production and other commodities, the weekend package included an overnight stay in the Al Ghazal Hotel. We had a tour of the facilities which were fairly modest by our standards, rooms were ok then a trip through the date processing area before having a swim in the hotel pool and then the most fantastic dinner/barbeque you could possibly imagine. The food was excellent with 5 courses of Arabic food highlighted by several locals either dancing to music "or" swatting the hundreds of flies that really wanted to share our dinner, as we squatted around the eating area. The other tradition we were asked to respect was "not" to use our left hands while eating as that was not acceptable here, of course we had no utensils just our right hands to eat with. Had a really enjoyable time, amazing how by now alcohol was just a pleasant memory and not required to have an enjoyable time "but".

Saudization was the word often used to try and describe where Saudi Arabia was trying to get to; a country that is so rich in natural resources was trying to manufacture responsible people who don't seem to understand yet what is expected of them. The local males are trying to maintain their basic values, culture and traditions that in my opinion are admirable during sweeping changes all around them that are causing frustration and confusion. The role of the women here for example must be very difficult as they watch the expat wives influence their society, the changes are interesting and obviously challenging especially to the elders in this community.

On April 2nd, I received a memo that all employees would be starting shift work on May 1st, as the Plant Construction neared completion, Punch out and Commissioning work would begin at that time. I started processing Elaine's Visa for her June visit with us and decided we would finalize plans for a Bahrain weekend April 25th, to April 27th. I also applied for an expat bank account on the

Jersey Islands as we were starting to accumulate several thousand dollars. Saturday April 7th, Doreen still feeling a bit "down", enjoying her activities but something is missing for her, she hasn't been too healthy for several weeks now so I will have to keep an eye on her as I am very busy at work. I have my good days and some not so good days, don't have a lot of energy yet but certainly more relaxed, but also something missing, kids, friends, freedom to act?

Reading a good book called "Space" by James Michener, two quotes worth noting,

1. Like many successful men he believed that what was required of him at that moment represented the "happiest experience" of his life.
2. Ablative Fortitude, The Ablative absolute is used by men of action who don't want to waste words (solve it and get on with it regardless of who does it or how much it costs). "Ponte Facto Caesar Transit" Julius Caesar a no nonsense engineer once said "build the bridge and I will cross it".

On April 14th, we received Elaine's Visa permit #M/D/Z/5178, this brightened up our sagging spirits, Grant Dawson (Operator from Petrosar) had resigned and would take the Visa home with him to Canada, Grant had decided this way of life (single status) wasn't for him after just 6 months.

We are now into our 7th month April 30th on this adventure, and we have just had 3 fantastic days in Bahrain, crossing over the recently completed bridge (approx. 15kms) from Saudi Arabia and staying at the Sheraton Hotel, first class all the way. We had been to Bahrain one time before but had to fly, took just 15 minutes, this time quite a difference. The biggest difference in Bahrain was in the culture and attitude and some acceptance of western habits, the

Bahrain people still believe in Islam, but they have accepted the fact that there has been some progress and habits have changed and have allowed for this, night club entertainment seems to be ok.

We toured the North portion of the Island and saw much of the local industries (e.g., fishing, basket weaving, dhow boat building, clothes weaving, and bakeries. Visited an old Portuguese Fort and Palace built before 1000BC. Had a great weekend, great food and several parties, we went to a Leo Sayer concert in our hotel and certainly had lots of what is forbidden in Saudi. Also went to the old town of Manama to see some Ottoman relics and the famous Dilmun diggings.

Several days later we picked up Elaine's tickets for her trip to Saudi which leaves Sarnia on June 12th, Doreen had phoned Mike on his birthday April 27thLooks like my "holiday" will be over soon as I start shift work on May 1st on line #4. Oh well can't complain now, been on days for over 6 months. However, Elaine will arrive here in 6 weeks, Doreen and Elaine will leave 4 weeks later then I head home for my first leave Aug 9th, for 5 weeks yippee. Still have to send a letter of references and Flight Information # to the Saudi Consulate after Elaine's call on May 6th. The paperwork is unreal but has to be done.

May 26th, we seemed to have achieved our financial goals for the first year in Saudi early, we are both healthy and making the most of the situation. I am really enjoying my job and feel 100% better and have now lost about 15lbs weight, keeping busy socially and work wise.

The situation in "The Gulf" has become worse due to eight ships being attacked and the escalation of the war between Iraq and Iran. We will watch this situation very closely since Elaine is arriving in 2 weeks and she and Doreen are scheduled to leave in July, guess we will have to reevaluate our position at that time.

What would cause us to leave, what would we do?

If the situation in the Gulf continues to deteriorate and Doreen becomes concerned, I would not hesitate in sending her home early. We have to develop a contingency plan to travel in a hurry and decide what we would take if travelling light, also when? to take action.

- WHEN, attack on Saudi Territory
- Saudi becomes involved in war
- Western involvement unrequested
- United Nations unable to deal with situation
- WHAT, if time to pack, most possessions
- If little time, valuables, money and I bag each
- Need Passports, Visa, Transport
- HOW, drive to Dhahran if possible and leave our car
- Take bus to Dhahran
- Head west to Riyadh or go northwest (need Passports/visas/Iqama) and supplies

On May 31st, the Canadians working at SADAF were informed that we should contact the Canadian Embassy in Jeddah 02-643-4900 and ask them to Register us and send any advice to us just in case we had to evacuate, exciting times coming up it seems.

Ramadan Holy Month will be starting Juneist, thanks to my fellow Saudi workers I now have a slightly different perspective and better understanding on this regard when to fast, abstinence from food, drink, and sex as originally set out by the Prophet Mohammed. It was intended to remind one of the poor, under privileged, the deprived and to encourage selfdiscipline and make personal sacrifices during the fasting periods but it seems that "some" followers actually gain weight and become very tired during the Holy Month due to eating, drinking and enjoying fun time with their families during the long night hours when they don't have to fast. Needless to say, some of our Saudi employees had a difficult time putting in their day shifts at work but allowances were to be made for this tradition and all expats were expected to refrain from making life difficult for the Saudis during Ramadan. Management gave us the authority to be compassionate, considerate and allow long rest periods during the day at work if they showed up.

Elaine arrived in Dhahran on June 14th at 7pm 15 minutes early, looking great and bubbling over with excitement but was quickly whisked away by the local Muttawa (religious police) as she was not dressed appropriately, we had asked her to be sure and "cover" up all her female bits with a long dress (abaya) with sleeves when she arrived but don't think she believed us. Anyhow after much discussion and several phone calls to SADAF Government Relations we cleared the situation up and were on our way to Al Jubail with Elaine in disbelief, "are you kidding me" she kept saying "this is the 20th Century". She looked absolutely great and very "spirited", it was great to see her after nearly 9 months since we had left Canada.

The weather had been averaging about 105c, hot and windy when she arrived but it would take a few days for her to believe that going to the lovely beaches might be difficult due to the many restrictions but since I had 3 days off work, we would go one of the Family beaches and do lots of chatting and catching up "but" no bikinis. One Friday we went to one of the remote Family beaches for a picnic and Elaine decided to not swim covered in the abaya and whipped it off and in she went bikini and all, we had a risky but nice time for about an hour, I was very concerned just in case the Muttawa showed up, but they didn't, who knows what might have happened.

On June 22nd, Elaine was enjoying her time with us but still struggling with all the rules and regulations of this country where her parents were now living. Elaine and I had a chance to go out on an old fishing Dhow boat but since we would be out in the hot sun for about 10 hours Doreen decided not to go. We would travel out to Jurayd Island about 27kms NE of Al Jubail where there were the most beautiful coral reefs and exotic fish, snorkeling was terrific for 2 hours before we had a picnic lunch on the small island before heading back, fantastic day.

The time Elaine was with us just flew in and we had lots of interesting times at the souks and shopping malls with exotic meals at a variety of restaurants in the local marketplace. She was totally amazed at some of the cultural differences and was really amazed when we were invited to Abdulla Alomani's house for dinner one night. Abdulla had become a very good friend of mine through work who shared some very personal stuff with me, his bride had been selected for him by his parents and he wasn't too pleased. He had asked me for some advice on the matter, but I told him I couldn't get involved so he ended up getting married, wouldn't you know it but after several months he ended up falling in love with his young bride and they soon had a beautiful young daughter. He approached me again at work several months later and said he had a "big mush-kalla" (problem). Seems his parents had decided they didn't approve of his wife now and he should get rid of her? "What should I do he asked?" Once again, I told him I couldn't get involved. I did offer the thought that now that he had his own family, he should tell his parents how much he loved them but that he also loved his wife and baby girl and see how they reacted. Over time his parents began to accept Abdulla and his family who eventually moved in with them and they all seemed to be happy "living together" now, so a happy ending.

On the night we went to dinner at Abdulla and his family's house we arrived early and went in the front door, there was a door to the right in the hallway and a door to the left, Doreen and Elaine and some other ladies went left and me and some other men went to the right where we settled in 2 different rooms, had great meals and didn't see the women again until it was time to leave. Elaine could not believe what she had experienced, out to dinner with Mum and Dad but didn't see Dad for 3 hours. Strange customs indeed but another great learning experience as she had had the opportunity to listen and try to understand some of the Saudi ladies explaining their point of view without any males around.

Soon on Saturday July 4th Elaine's vacation was over and on reflection the 4 weeks was probably too long for her and a bit of a cultural shock, but she had enjoyed her time with her parents. It had been great seeing our daughter as we have always had a fantastic relationship with her, and she had made the most of our time together. Doreen was ready to go home after being away for so long, was really happy to be travelling with Elaine, I hope she enjoys herself, but I will miss her very much, we do need each other it seems.

I had given some thought as to how I would answer the question, "What do you think of Saudi Arabia?" It is a very complex question really that that sounds so simple and there should be a simple answer. I have no regrets regarding our decision to come here, we will move forward with no regrets.

It has been an interesting life experience that I would not have missed. So far, we have achieved most of our objectives, we are more relaxed and enjoying life, we will appreciate our life when we do go home for good, it has certainly put a different perspective on "what is important" We have benefitted financially, we will certainly see lots of the World. "But" are we enjoying life?

Work was very busy during the weeks that Doreen was back in Sarnia but the time for me seemed to go very slowly at first as I experienced the single status expat life, not a lot of fun, especially on weekends, don't know how they do it, after a few weeks I was anxious to "go home" so time started dragging but we had lots of problems to solve as the Plant was being commissioned and I actually enjoyed dealing with them.

Left Dhahran August 1st heading for Schipol Airport/Amsterdam and then home to Canada what a great feeling that was, first leave home so after we left Saudi airspace it was two Heineken beers and two small brandies, now we are on our way. Lots of excitement as you can imagine when I got home but it was "so very busy" wow was it always like this? The time went in quickly and although it was nice to be home, I missed the "sedentary" way of life we had found in Al Jubail, time for walking, time for reading, time for listening to music and time for actually having a conversation and listening. However, I am almost certain that Doreen was more than delighted to be back "home" in familiar territory with her family and friends but soon our vacation was over, and we headed back to the "middle east" with very mixed feelings.

We quickly settled back in at Al Jubail "not quite "home" but we had both agreed we would not be over here forever, plus we had another wonderful trip planned in November for our 25th. Wedding Anniversary. The Plant was up and running now in what was called Run and Maintain mode after several months of challenging problems, long hours, little sleep but it all came together, and we were now producing record numbers of Ethylene Product so everyone including the Saudi Management and of course Shell Oil who had made a huge investment in the Project were delighted. As a result, getting time off for special occasions was being allowed so going to Cyprus for our Anniversary so soon after our annual trip home was granted without issue. Sri Lanka had been our first choice for this trip, but a civil war had broken out there so that got canned.

THE CYPRUS 25TH ANNIVERSARY TRIP, NOVEMBER 1984

WE ENDED UP CHOOSING CYPRUS, THE ISLAND OF APHRODITE (GODDESS OF LOVE) FOR OUR TRIP BECAUSE IT WAS ONLY 3 HOURS FLYING TIME AWAY, IT WAS IN THE MEDITERRANEAN SEA AND HAD ALL THE INGREDIENTS WE ENJOY INCLUDING, SUN, BEACHES, HISTORY, MOUNTAINS AND IT HAD BEEN STRONGLY RECOMMENDED BY MANY FRIENDS.

We left Dhahran on Flight CY408 at 19.30 hours on Friday November 16th, and enjoyed our first drinks within an hour having moved out of Saudi air space, it turned out to be a very rough flight as we hit a storm, so we were given extra free drinks and soon were very tiddly and even worse when we eventually arrived at Larnaca Airport in Cyprus about two hours later. We enjoyed a 45-minute taxi (Mercedes Benz) ride to the Miramar Hotel in the town of Limassol. Room service at the Hotel had been advised to treat us well because of our rough flight so soon we were checked in enjoying sandwiches, beer, wine and coffee overlooking the beach and the Mediterranean Sea.

Saturday November 17th, we had a nice British style breakfast before setting out on foot to explore the surrounding area and have a pint at one of the local Taverna's.

We spent some time reviewing brochures and checking all the items of interest to try and decide what we actually wanted to see and do. Later on, this day we ended up having a fantastic Greek dinner with some local wine and brandy at the "Paliospito Taverna", we had a good time.

On Sunday we had breakfast delivered to the room and ate it on the balcony in the morning sun before leaving on a half day bus tour where we visited Kollossi Castle built in 1210ad, Curium Theatre a superb Greco-Roman amphitheater, then on to the Kouriun Area to see the Apollo Stadium the Cyprus Tree Tunnels and some mosaics from the area.

After the bus tour we had arranged to visit Jean Hope a friend of Doreen who actually lived here in Cyprus and then in the evening we all went back to our hotel for a lovely candlelight dinner with local wine.

Monday 17th, we decided to rent a car and do some touring, "went daft" and picked a Suzuki Jeep (the kid in me I guess) our kids will never believe this. Left Limassol at gam and headed east along picturesque coast road to toward Nicosia, on the way we took a 6-mile trip through the mountains to Lefkara to visit the quaint village where world famous "lace" is made. On the way up the mountains, we gave a ride to Andreos whose car had broken down, he said, and he would take us to a friend's house where we could have some coffee and guess what, they sell "Lace". Doreen did buy some beautiful Lace and some knives and forks too, we found out later in the day that this is all part of a "Scam", and we may have been subject to a game they play to get customers to go to their relatives to buy stuff, oh well we had a goodtime anyways and had some souvenirs to boot.

We drove on to Nicosia through several small villages and then on up the Troodos Mountains where the choice of a Jeep appears to have been justified on some very scary but beautiful mountain roads going up and back down, the scenery was spectacular.

On Tuesday 18th after a nice breakfast, we took off from our hotel heading west this time along a fantastic scenic coast road past the reported birthplace of Aphrodite (Goddess of Love) and on to Paphos passing a British Forces Base on the way. Paphos is a quaint old fishing village surrounded by lots of historic sites which we visited before stopping in the harbor area. On our way back to the hotel we stopped at the Temple of Apollo took lots of pictures, along the way we picked up a bottle of wine, some bread and cheese to have at some secluded "Romantic Spot" on Aphrodite's beach to fulfill a childhood fantasy but it didn't happen, too many people but the cheese and wine were great though.

Wednesday November 21st, 25th Wedding Anniversary Day, picked up some carnations and wine for pre breakfast celebration of 25 years marriage, spent the day sunbathing and enjoying a relaxing time with a few drinks along the way. We were heading out at night to a Night Fiesta and Bouzouki Folk Show. Unfortunately, things started to go wrong, the hotel had fouled up the booking and we didn't find out till 9:

30 at night, undaunted we headed out for the Paliospita Taverna another favorite spot of ours but would you believe it was closed.

We ended up in the Klima Taverna the third-choice restaurant, but it did have excellent food we thought and very good entertainment with a Greek girl dancing and doing the "Dancing of the glasses" to really good Bouzaka music that is so popular here. Doreen ordered Scalloped Veal Cutlets, I had Alfelia (Cyprus food like pork) with a superb local medium dry red wine followed by complimentary after dinner drinks including local Brandy. Unfortunately, on the way home after a really good time I felt very sick all of a sudden (food poisoning we think) and I was violently sick as a dog for

4 hours (vomiting, diarrhea, and the chills). I lost my body heat and had hyperthermia for about 2 hours, fortunately Doreen who knows about such things just wrapped her warm cuddly body around me and to this day I think she actually "saved my life".

Thursday, needless to say was a fairly quiet day but we did go shopping in the morning and then had lunch with Jean Hope and her son David at Paliospito's. In the evening although I was still a bit fragile, we had dinner and danced at our hotel since it was to be our last night.

Did some last-minute shopping on Friday November 23Rd after a wonderful breakfast, then a Mercedes Benz taxi picked us up and whisked us off to the Airport at Larnaca for our 3 pm flight back to Dhahran. We were back in Al Jubail (home?) About 10 pm tired and weary but happy, I think. It would have been nice to be "really going home" to Sarnia to share our wonderful anniversary trip with Family and Friends!

The next few months were quite busy at work and Doreen was trying to make the most of her time exercising, oil painting, quilting, playing bridge, shopping and socializing with the other expat wives. I was fairly busy at work and play, coaching the kid's soccer team was fun, playing soccer and softball for SADAF in the local Industrial Leagues was enjoyable so with all this and trips into the desert for picnics the odd weekend the time was passing fairly quickly. We had evolved to the expat "trap" it seems already, putting in time between vacations, must be a message here me thinks?

Our next trip was going to be a major project and would take lots of planning, the plan would be to tour some countries in Europe in June/July 1985, have Elaine and Doreen who would be home in Sarnia at this time meet me in Schipol Airport in Amsterdam, tour parts of Europe in a rented car then fly to London England and head north via the Cotswold's, Stratford on Avon, York where Doreen and

I had our honeymoon, visit my sister and Family in Thornaby north east England then on to Scotland where we planned to celebrate my Ma and Dads 50th Wedding Anniversary in Edinburgh. Among the wonderful countries we toured with the car after picking Elaine up were Holland, Switzerland, Austria, Belgium, Germany (where we visited Phyllis and Gerhard's family in Rommelhousen) and France, Paris and all with some spectacular scenery everywhere we turned, and the weather was very favorable for us during this time.

The most challenging part of this trip was to arrange the 50th Anniversary party in Edinburgh on July 12th, at the "Chesser Inn" on Dalry Road and make sure all Ma and Dads Family and friends were able to attend, they were scattered all over West Lothian and Edinburgh, but they all attended, and we had the most wonderful night, lots of fun, food, booze, music, and a sing-along. Ma had insisted that Dad be "careful" this evening and he was till about 9:30.

We had really enjoyed our European tour with Elaine and the trip through England was first class all the way, to finish up in Edinburgh for Ma and Dads 50th Wedding Anniversary was just the icing on the cake. Soon however it was time to go, Elaine heading for Sarnia and Doreen and I on our way back to Saudi, lots of tears and emotions as we said our goodbyes but the way my work schedule was evolving at SADAF (Plant was running well) we would have lots of visits going through Edinburgh on our way home to Canada much to my parents' delight. This expat type of life isn't too bad after all, or is it? Doreen and I were able to arrange a visit home to Sarnia for Xmas and New Year December 1985. The kids were asked to put together a few days holiday for our Family to go Skiing at Blue Mountain Lodge near Collingwood, they picked a nice package with a lovely Lodge that could have accommodated 12 people it seems. Jeff and Paula, Elaine had a boyfriend but chose not to invite him and Mike was flying solo at the time too so just 6 of us. The trip up to Collingwood in 2 cars turned out to be a nightmare, wind, snow, ice on the roads, basically a blizzard. We were about halfway there when I decided I can't see any more so Mike who had actually been outside in the blizzard leading our car trying to keep us on the road took over the driving and we made slow progress but finally got there safe and sound and it was soon to be time for a very long "Happy Hour". The next day was ski day, I reminded the kids to be careful and safe on the downhill runs, Mum and I were going to go on the crosscountry ski trails, wouldn't you know it I tripped and fell, damaged my right thumb and took lots of flak for "not being careful". Had a fabulous couple of days not only skiing but also enjoying life at some of the spas, hot tubs, swimming and oh yeah, the Bars. The meals were not too shabby either, good Family times together.

We enjoyed Xmas dinner at 794 Pineview and later on December 315 we attended and had a really good time at Eric and Jan Ritchie's New Year Party, with lots of our family and mutual friends dancing the night away.

Back at work, we were making good progress with the Saudi Training Program and also introducing "efficiency" into our work habits, because of the abundance of feedstock that was basically the tonnes of light hydrocarbons left over after trying to process the Crude Oil, efficiency had not been a priority during start up time now it was. The Saudi Trainees were adapting to the realities of actually having to work by now and some of the high potential employees were doing very well much to the delight of our Saudi Managers.

Social life was fairly routine now, shopping, picnics in the desert and house parties were commonplace every weekend and somehow or another there was always some type of homemade juice or drinks available, and we found that even with the threat of dismissal if caught the risk was something you had to come to grips with or "abstain". Some folks did in fact get caught and paid the price, jail or heading home one way.

Doreen and I had decided that we would seriously consider a "Round the World" trip for our next vacation in the summer of 1986, our finances were in very good order and things were looking bright for the future even with all the exotic trips we were considering.

The following itinerary we developed for June 1986 without going into a lot of specific details will give you an idea of what we were able to even consider doing. Start off in Dhahran with stops in, Bangkok Thailand, Hong Kong, Taiwan, Osaka Japan, Tokyo Japan, Oahu Hawaii, San Francisco USA, Sarnia Canada, Boston USA, London UK, Frankfurt Germany then back to Dhahran. Highlights "everywhere" we went obviously but the Floating Market on the Chao Phaya River in Bangkok, Aberdeen Harbor with all the floating restaurants and the Kai Tak Airport in Hong Kong were right up there with the most memorable sights, phenomenal trip.

Somehow or other we were then able to go to Scotland in August this same year and managed to catch the Edinburgh Military Tattoo, The Edinburgh Festival, and the McEwans Jazz Festival while visiting our families. We also embarked on a slightly ambitious car tour of Scotland while on this visit, jumped in a rented car and headed north to Royal Deeside, Balmoral Castle, Braemar, the Spittal of Glenshee (Dad went up on the ski lift to the top of the mountain scared to death), Pitlochry, the Schiehallion (a mountain near Pitlochry where we had cycled many years ago). The Queens View at Strathtummel with a spectacular view of Loch Rannoch and Loch Tummel called the road to the Isles, on to Crianlarach, Killin Falls, Loch Lomond, Helensburgh Castle, Rothesay, and Wemyss Bay. It was a busy few days but we all had a good time.

It may seem that all we did was plan and go on vacation while in Saudi and the truth is that although we had to "produce at work" our minds were always either at home with the family or planning the next trip and accumulating money at a healthy rate, we realized that this was only temporary, and we (the expats) were all making the most of it. There seems to be a wearing down process that takes place and you have to deal with it while in this environment, even although all this sounds wonderful to those on the outside, "there is always something missing".

It was about this time I was approached at work to see if I might be interested in becoming the Department Training Manager and try to develop a "formal" Training Program for Ethylene Operations personnel with electronic data recording information. I accepted the position with the condition I would need some fast-track computer training myself, I had been fortunate enough to have been involved with Frank Van Delft helping to develop the Petrosar Modular Training Program years ago, so it was a good fit for me. Really enjoyed the assignment and time went by very quickly and no Operations responsibility now unless the Plant was down for some reason.

1987 promised to be another "good" busy work period so we had to make sure our travels were not neglected, April 1-3 weekend we had a great trip driving over the fairly new "Bahrain Causeway" joining Saudi and Bahrain, (built at a cost of $546 million USA dollars) with some very good friends, John and Sheila Vincent, Neil and Mary Bark, Dick and Dorothy Travis. This little island was fast becoming our favorite weekend get away with the mixed cultures and lots of night clubs and the stuff we weren't supposed to drink, restaurants were spectacular in the Hilton Hotel, Sheraton Hotel, and the Holiday Inn in Manama to name a few, sometimes you just pinch yourself, the little fridge "bars" in our rooms certainly got big licks over the weekend too.

Jeff and his longtime girlfriend Paula Ziller had decided that they were going to get married on July 8th 1987 and at first, they thought they wanted a big grand event but as time went by, they had reconsidered and now decided that maybe that wasn't such a good idea so the wedding was to be held at Paula's parents' house on Lombardy Ave in Sarnia which had a nice big garden and a swimming pool. So, the invitations were sent out and we had that event to plan and look forward to in July. My parents in Scotland immediately made plans to be in Sarnia for their grandson's wedding and as it happened Elaine had to attend the Graduating Ceremony from Brock University around that same time. Doreen planned on going home from Saudi ahead of my vacation time, meeting Elaine in Toronto where she was living now then driving to Brock University in St Catharine's for the ceremony. Seems in the rush Elaine forgot her shoes and had to borrow a pair of Mums which were several sizes too small but did the job.

All the plans went well and when I got home, we had lots of social events, BBQs, parties etc. and of course we had to arrange a Stag night for Jeff and all his male friends and family. Unfortunately, poor Mike recently had a slight disagreement with the local Police about why he was sleeping in his pickup truck at the curb with the keys in the ignition and wasn't able to make the Stag, but we did manage to get compassionate "leave" for him from his temporary "home" with certain conditions on the day of the wedding. We had the Stag night at the Ups and Downs Pub on Front Street in Samia and boy did we have a great night, how we managed to get home "nobody knows".

The wedding was a smashing success at the Ziller's house, after the brief ceremony, a few toasts to the Bride and Groom, some food, good music and lots of drinks most of the guests including the Bride and Groom, my parents and "almost" everyone else in attendance ended up fully clothed in the swimming pool Everyone had a really good a time soaking wet or not, a wedding to remember indeed.

Shortly after the event Doreen headed for Germany to visit Phyllis on her way back to Saudi, Ma and Dad headed back to Scotland and I went rather reluctantly I recall back to the Desert which was sort of losing its attraction to both Doreen and I by now. Job was great, house was great, car was great, life was quiet and relaxing but we were wearing down a bit. Yet there was so much to be thankful for over the few years we had been there, meeting most of our objectives, SADAF was providing excellent Health care including operations for Doreen (a scare about a lump in her breast) Jim (with a damaged cartilage playing soccer) and good Dental work for both of us as it was required, really generous salary and expense allowances but somehow it just didn't feel like we were here for the long haul.

Training Managers job was going well back at work, and I was really enjoying getting involved with creating electronic record keeping for all employees, quite a change from 24/7 Operations and responding to any incidents that could occur at any time. The weekends continued to be most enjoyable and in October we headed for Bahrain once again with Tom and Adrienne Hughes for another weekend package deal that included a dinner show at the Diplomat Hotel with a popular English Band and a French Cabaret and then the Dorlan Show at the Café Royale before finishing up at the Sheraton for a night cap.

Due to minor attrition from our expat Process Operators staff who had successfully commissioned and started up the Plant, the SADAF Management had decided it would be prudent to send a recruitment Team to London England in December 1987. I was asked to go and accepted if I could incorporate a visit to our Families in Edinburgh. To our delight they accepted and away Doreen and I went again, Doreen would stay in Edinburgh while I was down in London involved in the Interviewing Process for several days. On the way to Scotland, we had arranged a stopover in Paris and did some sightseeing including the Eiffel Tower, River Rhine and some really interesting Café. s along the way. We had a memorable time staying at Ma and Dads house on Stevenson Drive sharing our first Xmas in 27 years with them along with a small Xmas tree in the window (Dad was quite chuffed with this) and a nice dinner. Managed to see a Hibernian and Rangers football match at Easter Road plus we met an old Hibs player called Alex Linwood in the local Pub, he had played for them 20 years ago. We were also lucky to get 4 tickets for the annual Xmas Pantomime show Jack and the Beanstock in the Kings Theatre and made a night out of that, Ma and Dad really enjoying us being around even for a short time.

Soon I was off to London to do some recruiting at the Richmond Hill Hotel where the Interviews had been scheduled over 3 days coordinated by Surrey ATS Recruiting Company. The initial interviewing went well with some prime candidates who were interested in working in the middle east and had lots of Ethylene Processing experience. One of the many candidates that I was scheduled to interview was an English chap who had worked with me at Petrosar in Canada before moving back to England with his homesick wife and Family. This was a "no brainer" so we ended up going to the Hotel Pub for a few pints and a good blether before the day was over and SADAF had another excellent candidate to offer a 2-year contract to which they did. We were lucky enough to offer jobs to 4 other very good candidates who were ready, willing and able to report for work once all the paperwork was arranged.

One night while in London a couple of us from SADAF went to a show at the Piccadilly Theatre called "The Blues in the Night" starring one Carol Wood, several memorable moments occurred that night, I was approached by a beggar on the way to the theatre for some money which I refused and moved on but he came after me and I offered a small amount of money and then he threatened to beat me up so I ran like hell and managed to escape unharmed. So, we are now safely standing at the bar in the Theatre before the show and lo and behold who is standing beside me? Dustin Hoffman, the movie star, can you believe this?

We stayed at the Cumberland Hotel downtown London although our Interviews were conducted at The Richmond Hill Hotel, the price per night for our individual rooms was 77 British pounds at that time, of course all our expenses were covered by SADAF.

Flew back to Edinburgh after interviews and had a few days R&R before Doreen and I headed back to Al Jubail with another overnight in Paris staying at the Central Park Hotel near the Champ de Lyses, what a wonderful city and nice way to end a very successful 3 weeks.

When we arrived back in Al Jubail and settled down a bit, we had a long discussion about our future and decided that we had had enough of the expat life, and it was maybe time to go "home", so we began the exit process and planned an exotic trip on our way home to Sarnia.

Exit Saudi first time March 13 1988, went back to Saudi (1989-1992), Exited Saudi a second time, Then, "Around the World" contract work.

We had made our decision it was time to go, processed the resignation paperwork, applied for exit only Visa and made arrangements to sell of all our "stuff" and planned for a March 1st Exit, some mixed feelings but excited about going back to a way of life we seemed to be more familiar with. It had been an exciting adventure and now we were moving on with the knowledge we were well placed now financially for the future. Needless to say, there were lots of farewell parties as it seems expat people come and go on a regular basis.

The trip home was a fantastic adventure on its own with just too many details to get into but we left Dhahran on March 1st as planned and from then on it was just a whirlwind of flights, exotic stops to name a few along the way, Bangkok, the Zoo and Temples, Singapore (Raffles Hotel famous for the Singapore sling drink and Santoza Island a WW2 Prison Camp), Australia, Perth where we visited Helen Currie's sister Christine and her partner Elsie, Sydney, with all its beautiful sights including The Opera Cenre, Goulbourn, Breadalbane where we stayed with one of Doreen's cousins Helen Lee and her husband Robert in an old railway station building that was now being used as a house right beside the main railway track that went on through to Canberra, visited Tidbinbilla Space Centre while in the area. Doreen also had another cousin Pat Busby who came in a bus from somewhere up near the Great Barrier Reef to Helens house, took 12 hrs. but she was anxious to see us, apparently not too many people visit Australia from Canada or the UK. On to New Zealand, Auckland where we had a 4 hour city tour, spent a few days sightseeing there before heading north and visiting Abbey Coves Road in a place called Whangarei where Doreen's other cousin Harry Bunt lived, it turns out he had waited for us to arrive so we could be Best Man and Best Maid at his wedding to Jackie his long time girl friend to be celebrated on the top of a nearby mountain. After a short Church ceremony, we drove up the mountain in a large fancy car, chauffeur and all, music, chairs, folding table and a large hamper with Champagne, beer, liquor and all kinds of fancy food including caviar in the trunk. We drove down the mountain after this "magnificent reception" with the spectacular view to where Harry and Jackie lived in a small farm and stayed with them for 3 days. We then headed south on the north island for an overnight at Rotorua Hot Springs then on to see some old friends from Petrosar in New Plymouth who were originally from Petrosar Sarnia, then Fiji overnight in Nada, Hawaii Oahu, Los Angeles, Hollywood, San Francisco where we developed a problem with the plane on the runway and stayed overnight in the airport, on to St Louis, Detroit then home to Sarnia via Port Huron by March 27th.

Along the way I had dropped off a resume in the office of a brand-new company being formed called Petrochemicals Industry Company Limited (PICL) in Perth Australia as we had heard there was a group of investors trying to obtain finances in order to build a new Ethylene plant in Freemantle just south of Perth using readily available Ethane Feedstock never thinking for a moment, I would hear from them. The Australian Government apparently was willing to put up 50% of the estimated $500M Aussie pounds cost of this Project in a joint venture if the private sector could find investors for the other 50%. An Englishman by the name of Allan Bond who had emigrated years ago and had made his fortune here in Australia apparently had shown interest in the Project.

We enjoyed a relaxing summer in Sarnia becoming familiar again with old friends and Family after almost 5 years of globe-trotting. Just having picnics in the parks with the open areas and the trees, flowers etc. that we had really missed in the desert was great. Having BBQs, socializing and really enjoying the "freedom" we have here in Canada especially on the beaches. However, I was still pursuing work options with a different frame of mind, much too young to retire. During the summer of 1988, we reflected on the many cultural differences between the middle east and the western hemisphere, looked at the pros and cons and concluded that a nice mix of both would be ideal but unfortunately that doesn't seem possible. Family seems to be one of the main common denominators and a sedentary life as we had lived in Saudi might be an objective but here in the west sedentary life is well-nigh impossible it seems, very high paced living and materialistic.

So, the summer slips away and I have pursued work here in Sarnia but nothing doing, got a call from MW Kellogg in Houston to see if I might be interested in a small contract job working in Chiba Japan teaching Korean Trainee Process Operators. George Milne an old Petrosar Collegue had heard I might be available, called me so I decided to have a chat with them.

They offered me a short-term contract as a Technical Advisor/ Consultant, a fancy name that would get me through all the bureaucracy as they needed someone readily available and the paperwork for a Scotsman living in Canada getting hired by an American Engineering Co "could" be tricky I was told, reported to Houston M W Kellogg Plant Services on Aug 8th, 1988. Doreen stayed home till I got the lay of the land, really didn't want to go overseas again "but?". Stayed in the Residence Inn for a while, Doreen visited for a few days, but it was looking more and more like I would be heading for Japan soon, we had a nice time together in Houston, visited Galveston, The Astrodome, The Galleria where we bumped into George Bush Senior at a political rally, and our favorite spot "Angelo's Fisherman Wharf" restaurant.

Soon after the fun was over and Doreen headed back to Sarnia, I was off to Tokyo Japan on September 16th, where I spent a night at the New Otani Hotel before heading on the train to Chiba Prefecture where the Idemitzu Petrochemical Plant was located. Checked into the Goi Grand Hotel where I would stay while involved with Training the Korean Operators. Should be interesting I thought, Scotsman, Koreans, Japanese and some American Engineers, yes, we would need a translator asap, called Houston and they said quote "well get one" so we did, and it worked out reasonably well after some difficult moments.

After a few days it was obvious we were all going to get on well and each night we would go to a local bar where we would have something to eat and a few drinks and sing to a karaoke machine and we all had to sing a song from the country we were from, unfortunately I had to sing for both Scotland and Canada. The Operator Training was going very well, and it seemed like most of us working together had an interest in the OLYMPIC games that were taking place at this time sad moment for us Canadian Citizens though as Ben Johnson had won the Gold Medal for the 100 yard sprint which we had celebrated well into the night but unfortunately we found out the following morning that he had been disqualified after a drug test proved positive, our hangovers suddenly became worse, it was very big news all over the world.

We were in the middle of an interesting discussion in the classroom at the Plant on September 29th at 3pm when I got called to go to the main office, the Secretary had received a call from Doreen in Canada that my Dad had passed away and she had contacted the Plant Manager who got the message to me right away, needless to say I was stunned but immediately started thinking about how I was going to get home from Japan. Houston said pack your bags and instruct Idemitzu Travel Dept to make all the necessary arrangements to get me flights to Scotland as soon as humanly possible and send M W Kellogg's the bill.

Houston would arrange for someone to fly out and take over my job as quickly as possible. I was checked out the hotel in a Taxi and on my way to Narita Airport within 3 hours of the call and booked on a KLM Flight flying out that night to Edinburgh via Alaska and Amsterdam at 9:30pm. Now we are on our way, I have ordered two brandies and two beers, will try to relax and have a wee greet to myself when it struck me "why am I going to Alaska?" Panic stations, did they book me on the wrong flight? Called the stewardess and she could see I was upset. It's ok she patted my shoulder going via Alaska to Amsterdam is the fastest route for you to get a connection to Edinburgh. Would you believe I arrived in Edinburgh 29 hours after receiving the phone call much to my Ma's delight as she needed all the support she could get; sister Betty had already arrived in Edinburgh and we knew our brother Alan was already on his way to Scotland from Canada.

The next few days were very busy and emotional making the Funeral arrangements and looking after all the paperwork, Ma had said that Dads wishes were to be cremated, the Service was to be held at Warriston Crematorium. On Monday Oct 3rd, 1988, we had the service and the reception was back at Ma and Dads house on Stevenson Drive. Most of the invited relatives showed up along with many old friends and neighbors, we had a really terrific "wake" if you can call it that, fabulous going away party/sing along for Dad that went on for hours, he would have loved it even although there was many a tear shed.

We were able to stay with Ma till Oct 10th as I was supposed to report back in Houston on Oct 16th for status update on the Japan job, it was very difficult leaving Ma behind on her own without Dad there so we suggested she may want to look at coming to Canada soon and stay in Sarnia for a while. I was only back in Houston a few days when I realized I really did not want to go back to Japan and since I had an offer for another wee job back in Samia I handed in my notice and flew home.

On Oct 21st Doreen's 48th Birthday I started work at a struggling company called Partek Insulations, Stewart Lyall who had been a Senior Manager at Petrosar had retired and was asked as a consultant to try and rejuvenate this company, he in turn asked me if I would like to join him as a Maintenance Superintendent (5 man Dept) and help him try to turn things around, of course I couldn't refuse it was work and it was in Sarnia. It really was a mess, but we gave it a good shot using our Petrosar Participative Management Style, met with hostility by the employees, but we did make progress.

The employees at Partek Insulations were slowly coming around as we tried to ensure they were involved in any changes that were discussed for improvement, the place was now tidy and becoming better organized and even social events were being set up to get to know each other a wee bit better not just at work. Suddenly out of the blue I received a phone call on November 15th from one Dave Macey that turned everything on its head. Dave explained he was the Project Manager for the PICL job In Perth Australia and he would be in London Ontario soon to discuss positions available as the Project was now a "go" and was I still interested in the Ethylene Unit Managers job what? After doing several hands stands, I calmly said yes, I would.

On November 19th we met Dave for dinner in London Ontario at "Michael on the Thames" a rather fancy upscale restaurant, we had a wonderful dinner and chat, not much to do with work stuff. When we finished our meal and were enjoying an after-dinner drink he said, "what do you think?" My response was I am not an Engineer but I do have lots of Ethylene experience and could really be of value during the construction, punch out, commissioning and run and maintain phases. His reply was I was told by Dick Self the Project Director to offer you this job if you want it, he does not care if you are an Engineer or not. If you are interested in the job, go to Perth Australia and discuss it with him, take a week to look around and all expenses Travel and accommodation will be taken care off for you by PICL How could we refuse an offer like this? Partek might have to find someone else if this works out and Doreen seems to be on board after some discussion for the moment.

Arranged a week off work from Partek in December and off I went on December 12th for a very long trip (25hrs actual flying time) from Sarnia, to Toronto, to Los Angeles, to Sydney and on to Perth. The Company, as it was at the time, had arranged transport for me from the Airport to Observation City Hotel in downtown Perth.

On December 15th I met with Dick Self, right to the point, he said the job is yours if you want it, once again I reminded him that I was not an Engineer, "we want someone who knows the practical side of the Ethylene business to sit in at meetings with the Engineers and tell us if what they propose makes sense based on your experience". He said "we want Ethylene by December 1991, 38 months from now can it be done? Yes, I said. Japanese Gasoline Corporation (JGC) will be the main contractors. He said I needed a Visa to work in Australia but if he hired me as a consultant in the meantime would that be ok, about now I am a wee bit overwhelmed by his perception of what I had to offer. At 10 am we had a short meeting to discuss Process Design, simple questions I thought, capacity of the Plant, how many furnaces, how many compressors, what do we use for cooling, rough idea of costs, schedule of activities, how many Operators and what type of Advanced Control Systems. We then had a very brief discussion on Operability, Efficiency, Flexibility, Maintenance and the Effects of losing the operating unit.

On December 16th apparently, I have a job, paperwork will be processed asap, meeting with PICL and JGC personnel about feedstock and what type of furnaces and options, at times I have to pinch myself, this could be a lot of fun and well paid and I don't feel out of my depth, Dick Self is obviously another practical person and respects humility. At 2pm on day two Dick runs by me a list of

Relocation benefits and tax implications plus lots of other compensation options and a generous salary to boot.

On December 17th Dick asked me to layout a staffing plan based on my Dow Chemical, Petrosar and SADAF experience, basically Operations Staff including Supervisors and Operators per shift, Day Staff including Maintenance, Training Coordinator and Engineering Support. He said give me this later today and then you can head home and start looking for staff with Ethylene Production experience while we draw up your contract. He formally offered me the job and gave me a copy of the "draft for assessment" then took me for a drive to look at some houses that could be available when and if we decide to come. Earlier in the day we had gone to a very large "field" located down near Freemantle close to a BP Refinery where the proposed facility would be built.

December, I headed home still having to pinch myself at this wonderful opportunity that has come my way, flew out from Perth, to Sydney, to Los Angeles, to Toronto and then home to Sarnia enjoying a few beverages along the way "was all of this a dream or what". Made up a long list of what we had to do if Doreen and I decided to accept this offer, here we go again I thought so much to think about. On January 3rd I received a copy of the minutes from meetings in Perth, some interesting stuff to review regarding Process Design Proposals.

January 22nd received a call from a Dave Dickson who had been asked to put together a draft budget for the PICL Project, he needed to know how many Supervisors and Operators we might need, when would we start Training them, so I explained about a staggered start hiring some very early in 1990 and then adding more in 1991 as the Plant Construction progressed. He also needed to develop some all the Operating Staff which can be very expensive.

In the meantime, I received some positive responses with updated resumes from at least 9 people with years of experience in the Ethylene business. All of them had worked with me at Petrosar in Sarnia who were very interested in joining the Company if the plans went ahead, lots of interest spreading around it seemed at the time.

On February 16th I received a copy of an advertisement in an Australian Newspaper with a carefully worded list of requirements for an "Ethylene Specialist" with responses to a box office in South Perth (Reference # 949), "what is this"? I called Dave Self and he explained that although he had asked me to be the Manager of the Ethylene Unit, he had been informed by Government Agencies that Australians have to be considered first and foremost for any new jobs. He had worded it in such a way that basically nobody had "all" these qualifications so he could pick who he wanted and not to worry but continue to travel to wherever meetings were scheduled, observe and listen then keep him well informed of progress.

Due to some unclear reasons at the time, I was offered and signed a Consulting Agreement that would allow me to travel for PICL to California, Japan and the UK to review proposals by companies like MW KELLOGG, LUMMUS, STONE & WEBSTER and CF BRAUN. I would travel with a new Engineer Peter Beatty who was recently hired.

The Plan called for us to go to Los Angeles for about a week to review the CF Braun package on February 27th, 1989 (had an opportunity to visit Ron Phillip's parents vacationing in Pasadena over the weekend while there). Return to Sarnia then head a few days later to Scotland (some personal time) for about 2 weeks to meet an Operating Team down in London then proceed to JGC in Yokohama for 4 or 5 days. Expenses once again were very generous on a per day rate calculated in American dollars, cheques were automatically deposited in our CIBC Bank. After Japan we were supposed to head to Houston to check out what progress Stone & Webster had made. Just before we left on this trip, we were asked to cancel the Japan portion of the trip and it would be rescheduled for April/May ("if necessary?").

- A VERY BRIEF SUMMARY THAT WAS PRESENTED MARCH 2ND, 1989, AFTER EXTENSIVE MEETINGS DURING THIS TRIP WHICH HAD VERY LONG EXHAUSTING DAYS, LOOKING AT ALL THE AVAILABLE OPTIONS/ INFORMATION/ STRATEGIES/ BUDGETS/TIMING/ OBJECTIVES WAS AS FOLLOWS.
- PLANT DESIGN TO PRODUCE 180,000 MTA ETHYLENE LOW CAPITAL, ENERGY EFFICIENT, RELIABLE, PROVEN TECHNOLOGY AND SAFE
- 4 LATEST TECHNOLOGY CRACKING FURNACES, 3 CAPABLE OF 100% PRODUCTION
- 8200 HRS./YEAR STREAM FACTOR
- 4 STAGE CHARGE GAS COMPRESSOR (CF BRAUN TECHNOLOGY)
- FRONT END DE-ETH AND ACETYLENE REMOVAL WITH CAUSTIC REMOVAL AND DE-PROP
- PROPANE REFRIGERATION SYSTEM
- COOLING WATER PHILOSOPHY WITH SOME CONSIDERATION TO AIR COOLING POTENTIAL

We had received Process Flow Diagrams (PFDs) of a "similar design" for reference only but were awaiting updated PFDs or Piping and Instrument Diagrams (P&IDs) to review.

After a flurry of activity, it seemed things started to slow down a bit so I had time at home with Doreen and family "waiting" to see what would develop. On April 14th Letter regarding Australian Residency Visa arrived from a P Friedlander I was to contact the Aussie Consulate; not open many hours it turned out. Finally contacted Mrs. Ross at the Consulate and she said paperwork was now being processed, Doreen and I had to arrange to have full medicals and x-rays, contact RCMP re history, provide fingerprints and send them plus photographs.

May 8th Talked to Gord Grocott a Senior Project Engineer for Stone and Webster he informs me that there was to be a meeting in Houston on May 16th. This didn't happen, what is going on I began to wonder.

May 29th Received clearance from the RCMP "No Record", sent our immigration package to Toronto Australian Consulate General Office, informed Dave Macey at PICL of our status but we were starting to hear some ugly rumors that the Project had had run into financial problems. Dick Self called several days later and said that the Project was indeed in trouble, on hold because private investors had backed out and that a Lawyer would contact me and discuss any compensation and expenses owed to me would be forwarded in the near future.

Barry Ryan Tecsar Engineering had heard I was back home and "on hold" so offered me some work back in Petrosar working as an Inspector th in the Ethylene Unit during a Major Shutdown between August 28" and September 26th, 1989, which I gladly accepted and enjoyed.

We had decided to invest in a new home, Doreen felt that "bricks and mortar" her father's philosophy would be a better alternative to other investment opportunities at this time, less risk so we went with it and found a beautiful house at 536 Cathcart Boulevard that we had admired for years not knowing that someday we could even consider buying it. We negotiated with the 2 young married Engineers who were selling the house for a reasonable price, they were being transferred out of town. Unfortunately for Mike Farmer (good friend of Jeff) and his wife they had really wanted this same house but apparently, we had a better down payment thanks to our Saudi Adventure. We were delighted with the purchase and set in motion a plan with Jim Pumple a Real Estate agent to rent both this new house if we had to travel again and continue to rent 794 Pineview Ave which was currently being rented.

It was September 27th when I had a Telex delivered from a Tracy Collinson in Canberra updating me on the PICL Project status on behalf of their Lawyer and it was not looking good and to feel free to explore other employment opportunities, seems like the "dream" had ended, the irony was we received our Australian Personal Documents, Visa, Passports and other important papers on Oct 1st. The Visa had been issued to us with 3 conditions, we would Require a Security Interview, to be checked out on arrival, approval will be issued "only" if Project is given the go ahead.

Really had mixed feelings about the whole situation but soon I began to explore a few other employment opportunities, obviously PICL was on hold and might never happen now "too bad" I thought but I did get an offer to go back to Partek Insulations in Sarnia, there was the possibility of going back to work at MW KELLOGG in Houston and low and behold I received a call from my former boss at SADAF in Saudi Arabia, Mohammed Al Rabi that got my attention, was I interested in a 2 year contract back in Saudi updating their Training Program and Operating Procedures.

ACTION. I made the assumption that PICL would go ahead sometime in the future but didn't want to wait for that, reject the Partek offer but be available to them for MTS Training purposes if required. Proceed with processing Saudi offer but continue to pursue other options. If "no" other options develop, go to Saudi till either PICL is a go, or we want to come home.

Did a quick "Situation Appraisal" regarding life balance assessment, The balance is between Self/Family/and Work. Normally when one of these is out of synch one looks at the other two for cause and effect, seems like all three are out of synch for me at the moment, serious dysfunction! SELF is Restless, Bored, Dissatisfied, Unhappy. Family has some serious issues, poor inter relationships, little respect and no group discussions taking place. WORK, left a good job in Saudi wrong time, PICL Job collapsed, a major disappointment, didn't fancy Partek or Houston options, no other work in Sarnia. DECISION, accept the Saudi offer and try again, Doreen agreed.

About the same time as we bought our 536 Cathcart Blvd house "BALKYMOR" to us now, Jeff and Paula had moved from a house they had shared for a few years on Savoy Street to a bigger, nicer house on Bedford Crescent. Jeff had originally bought the Savoy house with a good friend of his Doug Cunningham, Doug had decided to move on at some stage, so Paula moved in with Jeff after some "interesting discussions" with both sets of parents, it seemed to work out ok for them. Elaine was now living and working in Little Italy in Toronto experiencing life in the big city, working a couple of jobs to make ends meet, had a boyfriend but was looking for better employment elsewhere, Toronto was brutally expensive to live in.

Mike had worked at Holmes Foundry in Sarnia for a while till it closed down, moved to Ethyl Corporation in Corunna and worked 5 years there before it also closed down, he was on Unemployment Insurance for a while before going back to Lambton College and taking the Process Operators course and managed to get a job down in Windsor working for BP which used to be Amoco which used to be Dome Petroleum and found steady work

Once we had accepted the offer to go back to Saudi for the second contract, we had some time to enjoy here at home in Sarnia while all the paperwork was being processed again in Houston. We went away for a few days with Aileen and Ron to Ridgetown on September 30th where Ron's construction company "Tollbooth Homes" had a small housing project going. While there we stayed at the Silver M Ranch near Rondeau Park, enjoyed some nice meals and played golf at the Ridgetown Golf & Country Club, we had a great time, and the weather was warm and sunny.

When we arrived home from our trip to Ridgetown there was a package waiting for us that included some paperwork and forms to be filled in "plus" a relocation cheque for $5K USA dollars and another cheque for $1.3K USA dollars for shipping allowance. This time however we would travel "light", no shipments and buy what we needed when we got there, should have done this the first time.

By October 24th all the necessary paperwork was complete and sent back to Houston, mailed Doreen's medical information and the signed contract, I had completed my medical a few weeks ago as I had to leave earlier and go to Saudi on my own for a few weeks as the entry Visa rules had changed since our last contract. A close friend of ours, Norm Benoit who I worked with at Petrosar and his wife were also going to Al Jubail about the same time we were so we planned to meet in Amsterdam Airport.

November 29th, I left Sarnia for Toronto and on to Edinburgh for a few days, stayed with Ma a couple of days and then we both went down to Thornaby for her first great grandchild, Betty's daughter Fiona's child (Rachel) christening and then I had to leave on December 5th to catch a flight to Amsterdam and meet Norm Benoit (who had upgraded his ticket to 1st Class from Toronto and topped out his credit card) so I went on to Dhahran where I was picked up at the Airport by Mike Evans and driven to Al Jubail. Norm unfortunately was delayed because he couldn't pay 1st Class from Amsterdam to Dhahran so had to borrow some dollars from another friend at the Airport before flying out the next day.

December 6th Reported to Ken Leslie SADAF Employee relations, my salary and benefits would start as of December 5th, was assigned a really nice 3-bedroom house in Al Huwaylot and then found out Doreen's Visa would take at least 6 more weeks to process and get approval, not good news for me.

The Plant was in good shape, the Saudi Operators were doing well, there were some new expats on site and some "veterans", and it was actually nice to be back here in a different role and "not" be too involved in day-to-day operations. It was obvious that "efficiency" had crept into the daily Operations dialogue now that budgets had to be considered and maintenance costs were being monitored. So, I settled in my new office and was briefed by Mohammed Al Rabi as to what was expected in the next few months, and I sensed a reasonable challenge ahead as I reviewed the Training Records.

The house we were assigned in Al Huwaylot was very well maintained and well-furnished and had all the mod cons that one could expect so Doreen would not be disappointed when she did arrive. I shopped around for a reasonably priced used car (found a two-year-old Mazda 323) as we didn't expect to be here more than 2 years this time or as Doreen had clearly put it "till we know our first grand-child is on the way, then I am out of here".

I had kind of a down day on Deember14th so I wrote down some of my thoughts, missing Doreen, don't want to be by myself, don't want to be with crowds, want to work, don't really know what kind of work, material gains in life seem meaningless at the moment, will work on a 30 day philosophy, this job assignment may not provide satisfaction, looking forward to life back at "BALKYMOR", struggling with Optimistic Philosophy, When does this "life phase end" NO! Not life itself, there will be good times ahead. I need to learn to like the everyday little things in life again "The Lonesome Dove".

Doreen and Janet Benoit planned on heading for Saudi as soon as all the paperwork, Visas, passports etc. were cleared, in the meantime I did a lot of thinking about "why do I enjoy being here?" In Al Jubail, climate, slower life, enjoy job, financially rewarding, away from pressures of life, Only Doreen to consider. Norm and I headed home at the company's expense to pick up our wives January 25th 1990 and we had to be back by February 2nd 1990, I had a huge list of gifts to take home for family and friends plus a list of "things to do" while there, so the time home went fast and soon we were on the plane on our way back to Saudi via Amsterdam.

February 25th general feeling of wellbeing, Doreen was here with me and in good spirits it seemed with all the activities she shared with the other wives. We seem reasonably happy and content at the moment, together again, our social life had picked up and we were now entertaining some of the UK and USA Troops who were in the area for War exercises at rotating locations. Susan and Elmer Beach from Saskatoon coordinated this effort. By now I had settled into my new job, and all was going well at the Plant for the moment. There were a couple of things we were hoping would happen soon these were to get our "BALKYMOR" house leased back in Sarnia,

Mike to find employment, Elaine to find a good job suitable with her credentials, Would like for Ma to make it to Canada for Scott Currie's upcoming Wedding and of course Doreen would love to have a grandchild soon from Jeff and Paula and for Jeff to start feeling better as he had been dealing with anxiety attacks for some time now.

About this time Saddam Hussein current Leader of Iraq was making noise about taking back Kuwait a small country to the south which apparently at one time in history had actually belonged to Iraq, the Kuwait border was only about go KMS north of Al Jubail so we were watching the developments carefully as was the rest of the world. USA and UK Troops had started to arrive by Troop ships for "exercises" as the threat was becoming serious, a threat to the northern border was of concern to both Saudi Arabia and the USA who had large investments in the area.

During the month of March Doreen hadn't been feeling too well when we got some shocking news from Sarnia that didn't help either one of us, Peggy Turners husband Phil a really good friend of ours had taken his life and on top of that we got word that my Ma back in Scotland had a very bad virus and wasn't very well. These are the moments when one wonders "what in hell are we doing here", you feel so absolutely useless, it was a very difficult week or two to get through.

In spite of all this bad news our daily life went on, Doreen had been settling in quickly and got involved again with some of her older friends who were still there and some new ones. We all decided we needed a break in April and went to visit our favorite Island "Bahrain" again from April 24 to April 28th during the religious holiday "Eid al Fitr" where we stayed at the Holiday Inn and enjoyed visiting all the historic sites again, went to some shows, wined and dined, shopped at the local souks and generally had a good time all things considered. Unfortunately, during one shopping trip Doreen fell and twisted her ankle on the sidewalk and couldn't really move very well so we had to have a few more beverages along the way then we had to visit the hospital to have it checked out. Highlight of the weekend was in the Sheraton Hotel with the Manila Band called "Car Park Show", it was great.

After 4 great days in Bahrain, we did get some good news, Ma had recovered from the virus and was feeling much better and then Jeff called to tell us our house "**BALKYMOR**" had been leased to a young family and the real estate guy would fax us all the details and paperwork, a good day.

At work we were making good progress with updating the SADAF Operator Training Program, Norm Benoit was rewriting all the Training Manuals and we had converted most of the Employee Records on to Computer Files thanks to a couple of very good Saudi Technicians, no thanks to me really, I just had good resources. Doreen headed home for the summer in Sarnia, and I planned a short trip to Scotland in June to see how my Ma was doing, the short answer was not very well, she was really missing Dad and hadn't enjoyed her long stay in Canada recently where we had thought she might want to live after Dad died with Alan and I. She really missed her own house and lifestyle in Edinburgh and felt more comfortable and at home there, she said, even on her own.

While in Scotland for that short visit with Ma we drove to Bo'ness through Queensferry to the Annual Fair, also had another nice drive to Musselburgh, Port Seton and Gullane with Pub Lunch stops along the way. Ma just loved being with any one of her boys, loved to have a wee "Scotch" and reminisce about the past and talk about Dad but I realized during this time that she wasn't long for this world as she seemed to have lost the will to live. Managed to arrange home help for her and install a phone for her but leaving her after these few days still brings chills to my spine, there she was hanging out the front window crying her eyes out and waving cheerio, was this the last time I would see her?

August 2nd, 1990, Middle East crisis, received a phone call from Doreen that Iraq had finally invaded Kuwait and the BBC and CNN had raised concerns about the Saudi borders. SADAF and all the other Plants in the Al Jubail area started developing contingency plans. We were advised to have food, water, and fuel available and to stay indoors "if" an event happened.

August 6th It was business as usual, but the World condemns the invasion of Kuwait, Saudi moved some troops to a neutral zone as a precaution.

August 7th sanctions were being imposed by the United Nations on Iraq who now had troops at the Saudi border and refused to withdraw.

August 8th SADAF started reducing inventories, we are now developing Shut Down plans, and started evacuating dependents (women and children) in a large bus convoy during the night through the desert heading west to Riyahd where they would be flown home. USA were now activating their troops as Iraq had now annexed Kuwait. I was assigned as a Block Captain with responsibilities for keeping remaining employees informed of all activities including any SCUD attacks. King Fahad condemns Iraq, the USA, UK and other UN countries were sending in troops, Saddam Hussein calls for a Holy War, so evacuation plans were put into place.

On August 13th Iraq links withdrawal from Kuwait to Israel out of occupied territories and Syria out of Lebanon, first British soldier shot.

August 15th an uneasy sense of calm, some Brits and Yanks interned in Kuwait, Naval blockade was now in place, two Iraqi ships were intercepted in the Persian Gulf. Iraq threatens to starve foreigners, UN condemns this action, Saddam Hussein offers to free "guests" if the USA pulls out of the area, King Fahad orders recruitment for the Saudi Forces. "THE DESERT SHIELD" was being implemented, seek peace or there could be a Global disaster between Iraq and USA, SCUD Missiles were now in place in Kuwait, USA has Patriot Missiles in place in Saudi. UN agrees to enforce more sanctions; Iraq troops have surrounded Embassies in Kuwait.

August 28th Commander in Chief claims Iraq did intend to invade Saudi.

August 29th UN Secretary gets involved with peace bid but Embassies are still isolated, peace bid gains momentum, Iraq names Kuwait as a Province, all women and kids to be released.

August 30th USA Troop buildup continues, Bahrain says to use force.

September 6th, The Gulf crisis continues, sanctions against Iraq are being enforced, 100,000 coalition troops are deployed in north Saudi at Al Khafgi near the Kuwait southern border. USA General Norman Schwarzkopf had been appointed to lead the UN coalition forces for the Persian Gulf War and asked to draw up plans to eject Iraqi forces from Kuwait.

We continued to Operate the Plant with limited resources (some expats and some Saudis left for home during this time), the threat of SCUD missiles which had been passing overhead on their way to Dhahran south of us was constant "but" we could not be seen to be yielding to Saddam Hussein's threats and our products were seen as an important source of fuels if there was a to be a War, those of us who were daft enough to stay after our dependents had left were told we would be compensated for our loyalty.

Doreen had left for Canada in June and was still there, my Ma was not well and going into hospital soon so no Canada for her. KLM Flights out of Saudi were drastically reduced so I was looking for alternative flights to get home to Canada for my leave, the next couple of weeks could be long.

Just managed to get on a Saudi Airline flight on Sept 24th from Dhahran to Amsterdam with a good connection to Toronto and then on to Samia, some obvious anxious moments before we left Saudi airspace with all the activity in that area There were lots of things to take care of while home and then decide if going back to Al Jubail during the crisis made any sense. Attended Scott Curries Wedding on Oct 6th had a goodtime although we missed Ma. Celebrated Doreen and Aileen's so birthday treating all the Family and some friends to fine food and drinks at a nice st of Restaurant (converted Heritage House) on Christina Street on the 215 Oct before heading back to Scotland to see Ma, then on to Saudi our decision had been made. Needless to say, everyone thought we were nuts with the threat of war very real in the Middle East.

On our way back to Saudi Doreen and I spent some time in Edinburgh with Ma, she wasn't well at all, we arranged to go see her GP a Dr. Tunney who basically said she was missing Geordie, having difficulty living on her own, didn't want any help and seemed to have lost the will to live. We rented a car for a few days and took her to many of her favorite places, visited Auntie Jean and Uncle Davie Gibb along the way, had a few Pub Lunches and some good chats but she appeared to be just putting in time. Sadly, we had to leave on October 27th, but my brother Alan was arriving soon and would stay with her for a few weeks, Mrs. Roy my Ma's long time good neighbor would look in on her and make sure she was ok till he arrived. Two major concerns I have to deal with, leaving Ma and taking Doreen back to Saudi? hope I do not regret this.

December 20nd received a phone call Ma had been admitted to hospital and we should try to get there as soon as possible, applied for emergency leave and an exit Visa through Government Relations which normally takes 21 days but was approved almost immediately, Ma passed away on December 21st her 76th Birthday and we didn't arrive in Edinburgh till December 23. My sister Betty and Alan were both there but waited for me to arrive to discuss Funeral Arrangements. It would be arranged the same as Dad, Warrington Cemetery, Cloisters Chapel on December 27th "Goodbye Ma say hi to Dad". We sang Amazing Grace and Abide with Me as the tears fell from our eyes and then we had a nice reception back at her "house at 61 Stevenson Drive". Doreen would be staying on in Edinburgh for about 3 months to look after the house and settle any other business affairs, possibly fix the house up to sell or rent if Ann Roy the neighbor's daughter would be interested in looking after it for us. As it happened Doreen staying in Edinburgh was a blessing in disguise for her as the Persian Gulf War looked like it was about to start 14 Days to what they were now calling "K" Day as peace appeared to be failing.

Now I am back in Al Jubail without Doreen, a Block Captain in Al Huwaylot, trying to keep busy at the Training Managers job, the Plant jugging along with all kinds of procedures in place "just in case" the Iraqis decide to invade Saudi, seriously? Yes. Anyhow now we were "drinking" the forbidden stuff, more than usual and anxiously waiting to see what might develop.

January 14th, 1991, 24 hours now to "K" day, it is wet/cold and windy, why am I here? no answer, SADAF Evacuation Plan now in place, expat communications set up, gas masks being issued, Diplomatic options have gone, several of our managers gone, tense atmosphere at work, Revolutionary Council supports Saddam, Civil Defense Systems in place. "GOOD BYE" to Peaceful tranquility, but we have an uncanny sense of wellbeing? enjoyed a short chat with Doreen at noon.

Thursday January 17th, 1991, at 00:50 am "Operation Desert Storm" begins, USA F15 Bombers are bombing Iraq in the first step to try and liberate Kuwait. Civil Alert was announced from Dhahran, Red Alert at 5 am, Iraq has launched SCUD missiles at Israel. January 20th 4 Red Alerts, January 21st 3 3 more Red Alerts but the good news is that the USA Patriot Missiles are intercepting most of the SCUDS heading for Israel and several SCUDS that were intended for Dhahran and blowing them out of the sky. So far as the Canadian Block Captain I have received over 200 calls and tried to calm down the concerned parties. By the way I used to joke about being under the kitchen table as I was dealing with the phone calls, some employees apparently failed to see the humor in this.

On January 22nd Saddam Hussein Iraqi troops started to systematically blow up the Oil Well heads in Kuwait just north of Saudi border causing major environmental problems in the sea, in the air and general havoc in the area. Several more Red Alerts over the next few days as the United Nations fought a brilliant ground attack against the Invaders.

January 26th Iraq continues to dump oil to the sea in spite of major losses with the ground forces.

January 30th Iraq attacked Al Khafji in Saudi territory but paid a huge price for this as they were quickly demolished and forced back to the border.

February 1st The past 2 weeks have been exciting, depressing, anxious, frustrating, and apprehensive. In spite of all the activity in the north of the Eastern Province SADAF Management continues to take the position of "Business as Usual". I am a wee bit frustrated because I have no control, no authority to make things happen in our Dept. (Situation is deteriorating) I am just a pain. Norm Benoit then reminded me I had been there before, "do what you can do and forget the rest", very good advice.

Going home to Scotland for a brief break, the most important person in the world is there and waiting again for me (what a fortunate person I am) and yet I am going to put myself in a position of making another decision, do I go back? SADAF management gives me no confidence at the moment, employees are nervous and tense, Plant is very shaky, a major oil slick is getting closer to Al Jubail, major environmental issues and of course SCUD missile attacks continue. Anyway, God only knows why I went back, leaving Doreen still working on Ma's house at 61 Stevenson Drive. Cleaning and renovating as required.

February 23rd Just got out the Al Fanateer Hospital shortly after returning from two great weeks in Scotland with Doreen. We had rented a car and headed south to England through Jedburgh over the Carter Bar to Newcastle, on to Thornaby, then Redcar to visit my sister and her Family. From there we went on to Leeds and Manchester to visit some retired friends from SADAF who lived in this area, we had lunch at the Kilton Inn in a wee village called Lyme, before heading back to Edinburgh up through the Borders. Regarding the hospital visit, I had returned to Al Jubail with a badly swollen right leg, a Dr. Kadekar suspected DVT (Deep Vein Thrombosis) so I was admitted through the emergency dept, and an anti-coagulant IV was started right away. There was no blood clot, so the doctors concluded that it probably had been a ruptured muscle and I was released that day.

On the way back to Saudi from Scotland our flight had been diverted to Muscat Airport in Oman and I found myself sitting in the Airport with the badly swollen right leg, surrounded by what seems to be thousands of refugees heading places like India, Pakistan, Sri Lanka, the Philippines and the noise was deafening, children are scurrying around, men and women are doing their best to fill in the 5 hours or so till their next flight. My flight coming from Bahrain had been delayed another 2 hours, but somehow, I felt calm and relaxed but weary. Why go back? keeps popping up I can't seem to enjoy the current day without thinking of tomorrow. Finish the current contract? 10 more months, try to pay off the balance of what we owe on "**BALKYMOR**" (neither really necessary, we have very healthy bank accounts by now) have another beer, Jim.

February 24th a massive ground attack begins in the Northern Province Saudi as the United Nations Coalition Forces plans were being executed and the Iraqi forces were systematically routed and on February 27th midnight the Iraqi forces who were suffering huge losses surrendered and a "Cease Fire" was declared.

February 25th Returned to the hospital to follow up on the swollen leg issue, had a Venogram X ray to check for blood clots and had a moderate reaction to lodine but no clots. The following day I had to see Dr. Kumars (Orthopedic Surgeon) who checked out leg joints and he found slight arthritis developing and the inside right knee cartilage was slightly collapsed but not a problem at the moment, got all clear.

Now that Saddam Hussein had been sent packing and Kuwait had been liberated, we could expect things to return to some semblance of order in Al Jubail and all the chemical Plants, there had been some damage to Dhahran and many casualties along the way. Soon Doreen was on her way back here having done a bang-up job renovating the house at 61 Stevenson, it was great having her back with me again but we both sensed the end for this second adventure in the middle east might be near. In the meantime, we went about providing entertainment and providing support to the Coalition Troops up North. A support group was formed to provide rotating scheduled visits to all the casualties in a huge field hospital "Fleet Field Hospital #15" 10kms just west of Al Jubail, this really was "a moving experience", this is where we experienced that there really had been a war.

We visited this huge, tented complex approximately half a mile long on a poured cement base just west of the industrial area of Al Jubail on Tareeg 130.85 people had volunteered and we were in the first group of 6 on the first night.

We had a tour of the facilities which included 12 wards (burns, trauma, elective surgery, dental and casualty etc. One young lady marine from USA severely burned. Young man burned in his tank explosion, his Officer was killed, and others were injured, all from New Jersey. Shrapnel wounds to marines from Idaho, Connecticut and Florida. Broken leg and abrasions from a truck accident during offensive near Kuwait, smoke and road damage caused the crash. Two real tragedies, Marine Commander lost his left foot on a land mine shortly after the "cease fire" and one UAE Arab lost an arm a leg and had serious internal injuries. We were overwhelmed with all of this but to a "person" they all said they had served their country and it was a good cause, unbelievably dedicated people.

The Al Jubail Support Group was formed by the expat community around March 4th, 1991, and arranged house visits, showers, baths, phone calls home to loved ones and dinners for many of the USA and UK Troops from the nearby camps, it seemed to be the least we could do, and they certainly appreciated our efforts. Many of the Troops were not even regular soldiers but Army Reservists or "Weekend Warriors" as they were sometimes called, never really expecting to see action, among them young Mothers and Fathers who got training every few months, got a small payment to be ready when and if needed and were prepared to respond on demand for any crisis, home or away. Can't imagine the shock they got when they were called up for the Persian Gulf War and had to go.

Doreen as always just tried to fit in, we took our turn at entertaining the Troops, had some of the SADAF staff over several times for dinner. She had continued with her oil painting hobby along with quilting, tea parties, and exercising the thing I admired the most though was when she volunteered to assist an Environmental group who were trying to save the "wildlife" from the Persian Gulf which had been polluted with oil from the Kuwait wells that had been bombed. Thousands of different types of birds were coated with oily substances, couldn't fly and got trapped on the beaches just north of Al Jubail. This group obtained permission to use "all" the available swimming pools to be used as a cleanup centre for the birds. Truckloads of men would catch and bring all the birds to the pools and the volunteers would scrub and clean each bird tenderly and then put them in a recovery area where they were kept warm and fed, was wonderful to see with a really impressive successful survival rate, it was very hard and demanding but rewarding work for those involved.

We had many long discussions in the evenings about where we going in the near future as the time was getting near for a decision whether to move on or not, I was ok doing the Training Managers job I thought, Doreen seemed to be busy enough but sensed she was putting in time waiting for the call about our first Grandkid coming but maybe another weekend in Bahrain would help us decide.

The Eid al-Fitr Holiday (April 16th-19th) 1991 came along so off we went once again over the spectacular new causeway to the Holiday Inn in Manama, Bahrain where we have had so many wonderful times, signed in then headed for the Saddle Club Bar then on to the Dilmun Night Club (hard to believe we were in the middle east). The following day we visited Jim and Olive Crossman from Sarnia who were working and living in Manama at the time. Decided to do some sightseeing and walked through some old "souks" in the

Mina Salman Area in the next 2 days before heading back to Al Jubail after having a great meal at "The Peak Restaurant".

The roads coming from the Northern Province in Saudi seemed to full of Military Vehicles as they headed back from the "Road to Hell" in Iraq to the large docks near Al Jubail to be loaded and shipped home on USA and UK Fleet Ships, Mission Accomplished, Kuwait Liberated, Saddam Hussein being hunted down for War Crimes and Iraq in complete disarray.

For some reason on May 13th, I woke up irritable and angry, didn't get any better at work and it was just "not a good day" even after I got home from work and spent some time with Doreen. Later that night Doreen suggested I look at the "Self-Assessment" notes I had written some time ago while down in the dumps then.

- CONSIDER SEEING A COUNSELOR
- DON'T REALLY LIKE WHO I AM
- OVERREACT TO THINGS.
- WANT TO HAVE CONTROL
- LESS HAPPY NOW, MORE ANNOYED
- EMOTIONAL IN DISCUSSIONS
- LOTS OF ANGER WITHIN
- VERY DEFENSIVE, NEGATIVE
- DON'T LISTEN TO PEOPLE ANYMORE, 10-MINUTE ATTENTION SPAN
- ILLUSION OF RESENTMENT
- TIRED, SORENESS, FRUSTRATION AT CONSTANT PAIN, MOODY
- IRRITABLE A LOT AND THINK "TOO MUCH"

This Dude sure has some issues it seems, Doreen and I had just had a good spell recently I thought she could not have been any more supportive so, give yourself a shake Jim.

Three days later on May 16th Doreen discovered she had a small lump (actually it was me!) on her right breast, we were both shocked and went to the Al Fanateer Clinic the following morning to talk to a doctor. He immediately arranged for X-rays, an ECG, and a Mammogram then scheduled for us to see an Anesthetist. Doreen was then scheduled as an Outpatient on May 30th to have the Lump removed and tested for cancer. We were delighted to hear later all tests were negative, it was a testing couple of weeks for Doreen but thankfully the news had been good.

The next few months were quite uneventful, the War cleanup was progressing well, we were enjoying our Al Huwalot house and doing some entertaining, the job was going ok at the moment, and I seemed to have emerged from what Winston Churchill used to call "The Black Dog Days" and Doreen was looking forward to the summer in Canada. She left for Sarnia on June 13th, and I joined her a couple of weeks later, unfortunately Jeff had been having a very difficult time and wasn't too well.

Jeff had been seeing Dr. Gannon who was treating him for anxiety/ nerve problems and trying to help him with prescriptions that had become addictive and complicating his life even more, somehow or other Jeff hadn't been able to reduce the dosage on his own and the medication could cause some problems in the future so it was suggested that he could consider going to a Rehab or Health Centre. Homewood Health Centre near Guelph was recommended, and Jeff agreed to give it a try. It was a tremendous challenge for Jeff to see this Rehab course through to a finish but despite many ups and downs over the 6 weeks he came home "clean", and we were all very proud of him.

It came as a huge surprise when I was home on vacation that summer, but I got a call from the Canadian Ambassador for Saudi Arabia who was in Canada at the time and I was asked if I could be at The Oberoi Hotel in Toronto on a certain date to receive a "Certificate of Appreciation" for being a "Block Captain" during the Persian Gulf War. Thought it was a joke really but no it was real. As it happened, I didn't go but they sent me the Certificate anyway.

Before I left Sarnia to go back to Saudi when my vacation was just about finished, we took the Family for a Golf weekend at the Oakwood Golf and Country Club where we had a great time wining, dining, and of course playing Golf, good times.

Since arriving back in Saudi, I had a small growth removed from my left temple, turned out to be basal cell carcinoma, Malignant, good decision by Dr. Ugoji to remove it.

Some things that I have come to grips with in spite of Doreen still being in Canada I am feeling more relaxed, and the anger seems to have gone! Some other Factors:

- LEFT SAUDI IN 1988, SHOULD NOT HAVE
- AUSTRALIA TRIP WENT BAD HEALTH WISE
- COULDN'T ADJUST TO "DOING NOTHING"
- AUSTRALIA PROJECT COLLAPSED.
- DID NOT LIKE MW KELLOGGS IN HOUSTON
- DAD DIED WHILE IN JAPAN.
- PARTEK INSULATIONS DID NOT WORK OUT
- NO WORK IN SARNIA THAT I WANTED.
- PROBLEMS DEALING WITH FAMILY AND FRIENDS
- PHIL TURNERS SUDDEN DEATH IMPACT.
- TAKING DOREEN OVERSEAS "AGAIN"
- MUM'S ILLNESS AND SUBSEQUENT DEATH

Can't do much about any of these factors now, however:

- I LOVE DOREEN MORE NOW THAN EVER.
- I DO ENJOY INTIMACY AND BEING AROUND DOREEN.
- I ENJOY A BEER OR TWO.
- THOUGHT I HAD A "SPECIAL ROLE IN LIFE BUT PROBABLY EVERYONE DOES.
- DID THE VERY BEST I COULD FOR MY PARENTS/
- DOREEN AND OUR KIDS.
- NOT IN CONTROL OF EVERYTHING AND THAT'S OK.
- WE ARE WELL OFF AND SHOULD ENJOY LIFE AT "BALKYMOR".
- MORE POSITIVE THAN NEGATIVE NOW.
- REASONABLY CONTENT WITH LIFE, ALL I REALLY NEED IS DOREEN.
- LIFE IS OK AGAIN, SO LET'S ENJOY IT.

On September 26th, 1991, I received a phone call from a Mr. Ray Growell who was representing a company called ACEC out of Kuala Lumpur and he said they were Interviewing in Al Khobar about 60kms south of Al Jubail the following day for experienced Ethylene Personnel (all positions) a new Plant was going to be built. Decided to go for the interview the following day and talked to Mr. Tom Blythe, the opportunities were there but the benefits and compensation packages they were offering couldn't compete with what we were already getting at SADAF, besides we were hoping to head west soon to try and find work nearer to home after this current contract was up, not move to what sounded like the "jungle".

October 2nd, 1991, during a meeting in Al Jubail with some personnel from SADAF and an Engineering firm called Stone and Webster out of Houston who were soliciting work at our Plant, it sounded during our social moments that "they" were always looking for experienced Ethylene Manufacturing personnel. Had a good chat with the Lead of this team, he said sometime in the future there could be something in Houston if I was ever interested, this could be a "way home" I thought so I passed on my resume with the comment "maybe" down the road.

Doreen and I once again had a chat about this possibility, we do want to return to Sarnia at some time soon, would like to live and work there, if possible, our finances are ok whatever we decide to do. We looked at 3 options (1) Stay with SADAF and finish the current contract in November 1992. (2) Go home now, this was a "no". (3) Pursue the Stone & Webster option. It must be said that at this time I wasn't sure if I had the energy/ enthusiasm for a new Job/Projects.

Decision was responded to Stone and Webster, yes interested but might not be available till early 1992, they were ok with that and soon I had a firm job offer working out of Houston as a Consultant. Doreen may consider staying in Sarnia and visiting Houston periodically if it all works out.

Now that all that seemed settled?? We could concentrate on our extensive travel plans for the next few months and oh yes continue to update the SADAF Training programs and develop electronic records for personnel. Bahrain was planned for November 27-29, India was planned for January 14-24, Canada and the Barbados proposed Family trip March 9-April 10. Unfortunately, we had to cancel a return trip to Cyprus to visit a friend Geoff Fennah because we may have left Saudi one way by then.

October 24 Call from Jeff the Barbados Family trip was booked March15-22, 6 people @ approximately $1200 each plus we would need insurance etc., "was this, okay?" he asked nervously as this was a good chunk of money "but" yes it was ok, our Family deserved and would have an exotic vacation together at the KINGS BEACH HOTEL, so that was arranged and booked.

The Bahrain weekend in November came and went, time was flying in now with lots going on and to think about including our next "big" trip in January 1992 which was to India and to realize a childhood dream to see the Taj Mahal among all the other attractions there. However, the news that probably changed our lives forever was from Jeff and Paula on January 3rd, 1992, they were "expecting" a baby sometime around August/ September. Doreen was especially delighted "love you to death Jim "but" I will be heading home one way soon", she was so excited, and I was too, we are going to be Grand Parents "WOW".

While we were really enjoying the exciting news, we had received about expecting a baby our trip to India had been planned and we decided that it was still a go and we would start processing what happens next after that. It was pretty clear what Doreen was going to do and that I had some decisions to make and soon. I had thought all along that when Doreen decided to go back and settle in Sarnia as she so much deserved after years of "wandering" the world with me that I would possibly stay on for a year or two on my own and shuttle back and forth every couple of months. Suddenly I realized this wasn't a very attractive option being here without her.

Early January after some debate my decision was made, confirm and accept the Stone and Webster Houston offer, draught a resignation letter for SADAF when we return from the India trip and target for a March 1992 departure from Saudi with some stops on the way home.

Vimal Kapila was the Thomas Cook Travel Representative in Al Jubail who put together the India trip after several good discussions on "what to do and see" while there. On January 14th we left Dhahran Airport at 19:45 on an Indian Airways flight packed with Indians and Pakistani people heading home for their "annual" vacation from Saudi, you have never seen so many cardboard boxes all taped together going on the plane as "carry on" items, gifts for Families and Friends, the excitement was unreal as you can imagine. The plane would make stops at Doha, Muscat, before landing in New Delhi where we were to experience as Doreen called it "SEETHING HUMANITY" thousands of people at the Airport, little or no Air Conditioning and a strong smell of very hot uncomfortable people, there were beggars, cripples, handicapped people and moochers everywhere you turned, "Rupees, Rupees", was the call we became very familiar with, we had been warned to be careful about handing out any kind of money as riots were commonplace.

We didn't know it at the time but a clean small tidy man was standing with a placard for Mr. Jim and Mrs. Currie in the arrivals area and we thought it was the driver of a tour bus to take us to the rather fancy Kanishka Hotel, but he was "our" driver with his own car and unknown to us he had been prepaid back in Al Jubail and would escort us during our time there. He introduced himself as Pieer Chandi and explained it was his duty to look after us during our tours, he said he had been prepaid but it was ok to pay extra if we wished after he returned us to the Airport "but" please Mr. Jim do not hand out any money rupees or American dollars to the beggars who are everywhere or it could be very dangerous for all of us. On the way to the Hotel, it became obvious that we would be dealing with crowds constantly and trying to get inside the gate at the Hotel was quite a challenge for him. When you are settled in your hotel each day, he said I will disappear but will be available early every morning for our planned tours.

We slept well that night but wondered what had we got ourselves into, Day one was a tour of both the Old and New Delhi cities, too many sights to list, high lights for us was the Raj Ghat memorial to Mahatma Ghandi, the nearby Shakti Sthal memorial to Indira Ghandi and the Veer Bhumi memorial to her son Rajiv Ghandi. Each memorial marks the place (Samadhi) where they were cremated The Red Fort with Delhi and Lahore Gates, the India Gate and the largest Mosque in India "Jama Massid", the Presidents house, and a famous business/tourist area called Connaught Place. It was a great day but very tiring so a nice cold beer and cocktails before dinner and then an early night. Pieer Chandi, our driver was waiting patiently for us after breakfast, said we were going on a long trip today called the Golden Triangle that included New Delhi/Agra/and Jaipur on very very busy roads and to "please not distract me". The highways were a nightmare, but Pieer was a good driver and soon after some stops along the way we came to "THE TAJ MAHAL" built by Mughal Emperor Shah Jahan between 1631-1653 in memory of Queen Mumtaz Mahal. One of the wonders of the world and the tour of the Taj with tour guides named Mohan and Vinod was simply fantastic, what an experience, definitely worth the trip. Beggars were everywhere but as time went on you couldn't help but feel "some" sort of sympathy for them, we were told that it was not unusual to maim yourself in some way to appeal to the tourists. We stayed in Hotel Ashoka that night in Agra and had another wonderful meal, can't help but think of the masses outside the gates to the Hotels who were looking for a few Rupees. Rather stupidly I went for a walk outside the gates and soon became engulfed by locals, one little girl who could not have been more than 10 years old grabbed my pant leg and said, "I can take you to a good time mister". The following day we drove 4 frantic hours from Agra to Jaipur, on the way we witnessed lots of women dressed in bright colored dresses working on the roads with picks, shovels and rakes, the few men who were there watched and supervised, different culture.

Jaipur is known as the "Pink City" because of the color of the "Palace of the Winds", we visited the local Museum/Gallery and the Royal Observatory built by Maharaja Singh then stopped at the road up to the Amber Fort where we were loaded onto an Elephant for the half mile ride up the side of the mountain to the actual Fort where we had a Rajasthan lunch and did a bit of extortionate shopping while constantly being pursued for "rupees" but Pieer reminded us not to. We did talk to one 13 year old girl sitting by herself for a few moments who was breast feeding her baby, skinny but lovely girl and as we were leaving, I handed her some American money, well WW3 almost started as we were quickly surrounded by a crowd of beggars who also wanted money, we were rescued by Pieer who managed to get us in the car and slowly pulled away. Needless to say, I got my blessing and told very clearly "not" to do that again. We drove back to New Delhi having had a wonderful few days but weary of the poverty and begging but recognizing if your country has a population of gooM people it certainly would provide some significant challenges. We said our goodbyes to our driver the following morning when he dropped us off at the Airport, he seemed pleased with the USA dollars we gave him. Now walking through the seething humanity once again at the Airport we had to find our plane to Goa, a Portuguese enclave on the east side of India south of Mumbai formerly Bombay that we were told was a nice quiet holiday resort to relax for a few days on the beach before heading back to Saudi.

We arrived at Dabolim Airport in Goa, a car was waiting to take us to the Majorda Beach Resort and the contrast was instant. Peaceful, quiet, beautiful little spot, as we were unloading our luggage at the resort this nice-looking young kid who was just hanging about came up to me and said, "you like beer man", love it I said, don't buy it here I will get it for you. Sure, enough the knock comes to the room door later and he held out a 12 pack of cold local beer, so I gave him a Szo USA, he says with a smile "nay man" ten is more than enough, think we were friends for life after that and I had a cold supply of beer for the duration of our stay. We ate at the Aquarius Beach Restaurant that night and the following night we were at a BBQ in the hotel and listened to local Goan folk music, really good times.

The following day we did the grand Tour, old Goa churches, the local marketplace, visited the Basilica of Bom, Jesus, incorrupt remains of St. Francis Xavier. Se, Cathedral (largest in Asia), the St Augustine Tower and then went on the Mendoza River Cruise before having dinner at Dr. Hugo Menses restaurant. The few days in Goa were very enjoyable, had some fun time at Colua Beach and Magoa Market especially at the Lounghouni Bar before heading out for Bombay (Mumbai now) stayed one night there at the John Centaur Hotel and we actually managed to get a horse and cart ride on Jehu Beach where I had to negotiate the price "again" before he would let us off the cart or he was going to call the local police, such is life in India.

After this wonderful once in a life time trip to India we are back in Saudi and on January 27th 1992 I sent in my letter of resignation to SADAF with no real regrets, booked our ticket back to Sarnia one way leaving March 2nd on BA 128 at 2:40am. Long list of items that needed to be taken care of but we were excited and ready to go asap, sold most of our "stuff" including the car to new arriving expats. On March 2nd we were on our way, Dhahran/London/Montreal/Detroit/Sarnia and home over the imposing Bluewater Bridge, was a great feeling, Doreen was home, and we had a grandkid on the way, I was home but with a job in Houston to look forward to in the near future. Plus, we had a family trip to the Barbados to look forward to soon; life seems good at the moment.

Our "**BALKYMOR**" house in Sarnia had been rented during our absence but fortunately it wasn't when we arrived back in Sarnia. Since our 794 Pineview Ave home was currently rented we decided we would move into Balkymor for a while and see what the future brings. We had the kids help us with painting and general clean up and Doreen picked out some fine furniture at Goudy's Store in Strathroy. In the meantime, we had all kinds of paperwork regarding our reentry to Canada, contacted Stone and Webster in Houston, agreed on a start date with them then finalized plans for the Barbados Family Vacation.

On March 14th Jeff, Paula, Mike, Elaine, Doreen and I left Sarnia headed to Toronto for an overnight in Howard Johnsons Hotel before departing for Barbados at 7am, we had a wonderful evening wining and dining before settling in for the night, Jeff and Mike burned the midnight oil and were slow moving in the morning. The sun was shining, and the bands were playing calypso as we arrived in Barbados Airport before being whisked away to The Kings Beach Hotel for a week of sun and fun. Day 1 we visited Speightstown (Mangos Cave) among other tourist attractions, Jeff and Mike were really enjoying the local beverages along the way. We had a whole day island Tour with stops along the way visiting Bridgetown, Crane Beach, Sam Lord Castle, St John's Church, Farley Hill Park with Lunch at Atlantis then on to Bathsheba. In the evenings we were at a Plantation Dinner Show, The Calypso Festival where Elaine met a young man who really fancied her, we called him Wayne "the Animal" but he was a nice chap. The highlight of the trip was "The Jolly Roger Cruise" where we all got dressed up as Pirates and went off to sea, had great fun, walking the plank, sword fights and even a mock wedding and of course buckets of "booze", what a fabulous day that was. Our last night was spent at the Coco Banana Night Club, Paula was being careful as she was pregnant "but" the rest of us just let it hang out and enjoyed every moment. The Resort had a beer drinking contest one night to see who could drink a pint of beer the fastest, after several rounds I was declared the Champion, "yahoo" sign of an ill spent youth me thinks. Then suddenly it was all over, and we were on our way home to Sarnia.

The Stone and Webster Consulting job working out of Houston had suddenly become a problem for me, they hadn't been able to acquire a visa for me to work in Houston "yet", needless to say, I was disappointed. However, they sent a representative to Toronto, and I went down and signed a contract. The deal was I would work out of a Toronto office reviewing work packages until such time as they could obtain a work visa for me to work in the States. So, I had to drive to Toronto and work Monday till Friday each week and then head back to Sarnia for weekends. This became very boring after some time, so I was offered work in several places overseas again to which I said no. Go to Turkey, go to Malaysia, go to Korea but I steadfastly refused as this had not been the deal that I had signed. While working in Toronto Doreen had some nice weekends there with me and we went to some great stage shows including Miss Saigon and Les Miserables on May 6th her personal favorite show, we stayed at the Delta Chelsea Hotel on most of these occasions and enjoyed food at Ed's Warehouse and the Hop and Grape Restaurant, this was a pretty decent set up for us but this couldn't really last much longer as I was not being fully utilized reviewing work packages.

On June 1st 1992 it was decided that I would be "sent" to Houston to prepare for an assignment in Han Yang Korea, not happy about this but I accepted anyway so Doreen and I left for Korea on June 4th on NW 029 Flight that would take 14hrs flying time, really was very apprehensive about this whole deal because we didn't come back home from Saudi to go back to Korea to work. We arrived in the Seoul Airport, (Seoul population is approximately 10M people) and were taken downtown to the Plaza Hotel for the night. We visited the Doeksugung Palace of Virtue (home of King Sejong the Great in 1397) had a meal and off to bed very tired and "not sure what to expect tomorrow". In the morning a company car picked us up and drove south to Yosu, Yochun, Tulsan Bridge and to the Han Yang Chemical Corporation to see the plant and then on to Peondong Apartment Complex where we had been assigned a very modest flat with 2 bedrooms and minimal furniture. This was a sign of what was to come for us, Doreen and I both felt "quite disappointed" these were like the tenements in the old part of Edinburgh.

We were told to take a few days to settle in and make a list of what we felt we might need to make the flat more livable. After going for a walk, the following morning, we realized that this was not a very nice part of town and listed all our concerns which we were told would be dealt with in time. I left Doreen with some trepidation on Day 2 and headed to work and suddenly I felt "what am I doing here". The Plant itself was fairly modern and was undergoing some Major Process changes to improve the Efficiency and Productivity "but" the resources seemed limited in knowledge on what was going on. After 2 weeks of no action on our apartment conditions and a sense of disaster at work we agreed that this was not going to work for us.

On June 20th we decided let's get out of here, informed the Houston Office, booked our flights and left on June 26th for home very disappointed with Stone and Webster. Called the office when we got home to Sarnia and informed them, I had no desire to work for them now at all since I had returned from Saudi to work in the Houston office which they had offered and not fulfilled. We had several weeks of haggling about who was paying for what but finally agreed that due to a series of misunderstandings and the fact they could not obtain a visa for me to work in Houston most of my expenses would be covered, this chapter was now closed.

When we got back to Sarnia, disappointed about how the Korean episode had finished I bumped into an old friend Barry Ryan who was now a partner/ shareholder in a local Company called Tecsar Engineering, he knew my background and asked if I might be interested in doing some Project work for them. Barry arranged for me to have an interview with Pierce Mc Sweeney, the owner of the company, the interview went well and I was offered a job as a Project Co-Ordinator to be available when and if required for certain jobs which I gladly accepted. This was the beginning of a very good relationship with this Company and provided a nice transition for me toward retirement (not a word I liked) or having a choice not to work.

One of the first jobs I was assigned to was at Nanticoke Refinery where we were contracted to change out a very old 230 foot De methaniser tower for a brand new one that had been prefabricated off site and was to be "dressed" on site before being lifted into place in the Plant. A giant Crane had been ordered and delivered from somewhere in the USA by a convoy of six trucks, assembled on site by smaller cranes, approved by the Government Authorities and readied for "lifting" out the old Tower and "lifting" in the new one. I spent 9 weeks in Port Dover commuting from Sarnia every Monday to Friday, staying in a local Motel during the week and driving home in a company car every weekend. Doreen came down to visit me occasionally on the weekends and the Project went well, can't tell you how much I was impressed by the Crane Driver, lifted the old Tower out and new one in on a dime, this was a sight to behold, a no-nonsense elder gentleman but not much for paperwork.

On September 9th, 1992, Jake Aaron Currie was born, a healthy 7lbs 13Ozs, son of Jeff and Paula our first Grandchild, we were all delighted but my immediate concern was "how are his feet?" I had been worried all during the pregnancy that since I had been born with a club left foot, was there even the slightest chance a grandchild of ours could be born also with this handicap? All research that I had done to date suggested "no" it was not hereditary and as it happens Jake had normal feet much to my relief.

Interesting to note that our daughter Elaine some years later had done a "Thesis" as part of her Graduation Package at Brock University on this very interesting subject, club feet in the 1950s and club feet in the 1990's (see attachment dated October 29, 1998).

Doreen was settling in nicely back in Sarnia, she had a beautiful wellfurnished house at 536 Cathcart Blvd we named "BALKYMOR", a lovely wee grandson, Elaine and Mike were doing well, Jim was working for Tecsar Engineering on lots of nice little jobs that occasionally he had to go out of town for but also doing some work in town at places like Imperial Oil, Union Carbide, St Clair Chemicals and of course some nice trips to Windsor to work at Dome Petroleum and eventually going back to work for what used to be Petrosar but now Nova Chemicals in all their Samia Plants for a variety of Projects.

January 23rd, 1994, Doreen and I went to Jamaica for a short vacation, stayed at the Fantasy Resort Hotel, we caught the Monday night Carnival at the Zulu Bar then on Tuesday we went to Ochios Rios and climbed the Dunn's River Falls. The rest of the week was spent touring, parties, a lively Jamaica party during Happy Hour at the Hemingway's Pub then spending a day at Montego Bay. Weather was brilliant 28c and sunny most of the time "and" if you were interested lots of "stuff" to smoke.

One of the areas we both really enjoyed the most in Jamaica was the Cornwall Beach (topless bathing, wow) great margaritas with our dinners, but Doreen wasn't too interested in the topless stuff but really enjoyed the margaritas.

The job at Tecsar Engineering probably was one of the best I ever had in my working career, they assigned you a Project to manage, scope was clearly identified, budget clearly spelled out which you were expected to reconcile, resources assigned and just let you get on with it, terrific to work for but you had to keep them fully informed as to progress or any issues that had to be dealt with. They included every employee and all contract people in all social activities, just a really nice "Family of People".

The next few years were a dream for us being back in Sarnia, working for Tecsar, integrating with all our old friends and of course spending time with our Family and Friends which Doreen had missed so much while overseas following her "Nomadic" hubby. We were still able to enjoy periodic vacations to places like Panama City Florida in January 1995, visiting Nashville, Memphis Tennessee (Elvis Presley and Graceland), Montgomery Alabama and then fabulous New Orleans on the way down.

Visited Tropicoco Resort in Havana Cuba in January 1996 visiting both the old and new Havana Cities, Revolution Square, Ernest Hemingway's house where he wrote for "Whom the Bells Toll" and the Cojimar Fishing Village where he wrote "The Old Man and the Sea", had a few drinks at the nearby Terraso Bar overlooking the small harbor before enjoying The Tropicana Cabaret Show in old Havana in the evening where you just have to drink either a Moquito Cocktail or a Mint Julip.

Had a great few months starting in May 1996 at a place called Kitimat 309 miles north of Vancouver in British Columbia on a job updating Process Manuals at the Methanex Plant working with a good friend Malcolm Lamb who had moved there from Saudi with his wife Elaine. Doreen was able to join me there for a couple of weekends and we had a nice weekend in Prince Rupert (where Doreen had the experience of a lifetime on a small 4 seater plane delivering mail to some nearby islands, we had to pay the pilot a reasonable "stipend" but it was worth it). My heart was in my mouth as this small plane took off from the water skipped over the nearby mountains and then was on its way. We also had a chance to visit Vancouver with all its wonderful sights including Grouse Mountain and spent one day on Vancouver Island, we had been told you have to have "High Tea" at the Empress Hotel on the Island, what we had "not" been told it was by appointment only and it would cost $so a head boohoo!! We somehow managed to get an appointment and the tea and biscuits were "just lovely" thank you.

Our very good friends Malcolm and Elaine were gracious hosts here as they had been in Saudi Arabia, showed us around Kitimat and we wined and dined in several favorite local watering holes, was a fun time and a nice manageable Project to complete and head home. One small issue I encountered caused some concern at the Methanex Plant, I have always gone for a walk during lunch hour wherever I work, so I had walked the half mile to the main road and back when I was stopped by Security, "do you know we have "Bears in this Area" sir. I said no, they then took me to a small office where a young man worked and he had "gone for a walk" at lunch time years ago, he had been attacked by a large Bear and severely mauled while walking. One side of his head and face was disfigured and he shared his horrible experience with me. I admired him for his attitude and recovery but didn't go for a lunch walk again.

During this time period I had been having some difficulties with my right knee which seemed to be deteriorating by the day, my hips were bad, and I had a sore ankle but one just soldier on. On Monday

June 10th I was home in Sarnia for a short period and had Dr. Uppal set up an X-Ray for my right knee, results were severe decay and Arthritis, not good news at all. Dr. Uppal gave me a reference to Dr. Duncan McKinlay a well-known Orthopedic Surgeon who I had actually used in previous years. Doreen went off to Scotland for a short visit, during this time Lainie and I had lunch, she told me she was really proud of her Mum because she was "incredibly unselfish" and would do whatever it takes to "see me happy again". On Sunday June 16th (Father's Day) Lainie drove me to Sarnia Airport and I left for Kitimat once again with some interesting thoughts to digest. Are there reconcilable differences to consider back in Sarnia?? Jeff and Paula seem distant, Mike is occasionally inconsiderate, Elaine is trying very hard to hold our Family unit together and Doreen deserves commitment from all of us.

July 9th Doreen is at Stobo Castle Spa with her sisters back in Scotland and I am winding down here in Kitimat soon we will be home together back in Sarnia. I got home to Sarnia on July 10 and Lainie picked me up, so we went to the Brittany Arms for a pint, I had a strange hollow feeling, going home and no Doreen, she arrived much to my delight on July 12th in Toronto where I picked her up. On Saturday July 13th we went to Kelsey's to celebrate my brother Alan, s 50th Birthday.

On July 23rd I started Volunteer work for the VON as a friendly visitor for 4 hours a week, then out of the blue on July 31st we heard from Paula that she might be pregnant again, great news.

On August 13th we had almost exhausted the options for saving my right knee joint when Dr. McKinlay suggested something called Synvisc and Naproxen to relieve the pain, the Synvisc would be an injection into the knee joint once a week for 4 weeks but not covered by OHIP (approximately $400), so we agreed to try it. In the meantime, I had several job offers from an Ed Robinson in Houston

Stone and Webster job in India for 12 weeks that I declined and another small job in Houston that I also declined, need to get my knee fixed first.

Another call for work back at Kitimat through Tecsar Engineering for a shutdown October and November but unfortunately had to decline due to knee issue. Spending some time painting and decorating the house but knee is limiting mobility now.

On November 4th, 1996, the second Bluewater Bridge was connected in the middle above the St Clair and there was an impressive ceremony in Point Edward for this Historic occasion, managed to get a great picture up close with a telescopic lens in my camera as the last piece was bolted together.

Had a bone scan for my knee, sharp pains and seems like bone on bone, I was getting really grumpy and unhappy almost daily, Doreen keeps asking me "where is the optimist" you seem to show more gloom and doom than ever before" tough times all around. Lots of social and Family stuff going on during Xmas and New Year, not all enjoyable from my point of view, Dr. McKinlay had finally yielded to consider a Knee replacement, but he had to go through all kinds of "justification" because technically at 58 years old I was too young to qualify. Apparently, what swung it was I had endured a "club foot" issue for many years and the right knee/leg had carried the load during that time so to speak and he got approval to proceed, now we need a date.

On January 1st, 1997, New Years Day we walked over to Jessie and Alex Mackay's for the annual Traditional soup and Chili and a drink they always generously provided for "Our Gang", had a nice time and walked home with some discomfort, yes, we could have walked but you know, "these stubborn Scots Guys" they don't listen to anyone do they. On January 3rd we were at Eric Fairbairn's Funeral (brother of Norm Fairbairn), we also found out that a very close friend of ours May Tracy passed away what a way to start a year. We did have a Family dinner at Jeff and Paula's house for his 36th birthday.

The following day as we were preparing to leave Sarnia for Atlanta we received more bad news, Doreen's palliative care client through the VON Archie Strangway had passed away. Great start to 1997 it seems but off we went heading for Atlanta anyway on our way to visit my cousin Liz Gibb, her husband David and her parents who were over visiting from Scotland (my Auntie Jean and Uncle Davie) in Marietta Georgia. We stayed overnight in Korbin Kentucky on the way down then on to Marrieta by noon the following day, made a good time. Had several wonderful days with them and headed for Myrtle Beach for a couple of golf days (played at Azalea Sands GC and Quail Creek GC) staying at the Sea Mist Resort before heading back to Sarnia via Carolina, West Virginia, Sandusky Ohio. We drove a total of around 4000kms but the one major disappointment we had we were not allowed into the home of the "Masters Golf Championship" in Augusta Georgia, apparently one needs a sponsor to even get in the front gate.

We were settling back in Sarnia with the cold weather and all, Elaine was planning a long stay trip to Australia, Jeff and Paula were preparing for the arrival of baby #2 sometime in March, Mike came and went on occasion, quite a busy young man. We had decided that since I was going to be laid up for several months after the knee replacement maybe a trip to Scotland might be in order, after much debate we adopted the new Nike logo "Just Do It", so we did. Booked a trip from February 18th to March 12th, that would give us 12 days after returning to deal with any issues before the Operation on March 24th.

Doreen had joined a Recovery Group she had been involved with some years ago when our kids were younger and felt the need at this time to re visit for several reasons. Our Family was just like any other Family and had its good times and some "moments" of conflict. We had many emotional discussions about a variety of subjects, got tense at times but somehow, we managed to persevere.

We were making some progress on our list of priorities for "BALKYMOR" home improvements but to me it seemed endless to Doreen it needed to be done so we picked away at the list and the end results were very satisfying even for me. We loved this house, and I will always be grateful to Doreen for encouraging us to buy it, a great investment and we actually "owned" it by now.

A nice wee quote I remember during this time "complaining is our enemy, humor is our goal "I must try to remember that, even went to a Recovery Group Session at St Lukes Church as a visitor which I rather enjoyed and helped to put things in perspective for me. Doreen was involved and really enjoying Scottish Country dancing, I had become involved with Canada Mental Health as well as the VON as a volunteer, but we were also busy preparing for our upcoming Scottish trip.

On February 16th we had an "Aussie Farewell" dinner at Balkymor for Elaine, we all had a comfortable, happy time with all our direct Family members in attendance, lots of tears and emotions as we said goodbye later that night, she would be gone for several months travelling all around Australia what a wonderful adventure for her.

Wednesday February 18th, we left for Scotland where we had lots to do with the flat at 61 Stevenson Drive as we had decided we might sell it if we couldn't rent it and many people to visit and of course try to enjoy our holiday at the same time. The first 4 days were just a whirlwind of activities in "Auld Reekie", visiting, lunches, dinners and the odd pint along the way. On the 25th we headed to Redcar to visit my sister Betty for a couple of days then drove to Lyme near Manchester to visit John and Sheila Vincent from our Saudi Arabia days. On the 28th, we headed north via Penrith, Kendal, Carlisle, Gretna Green, Glasgow, Dumbarton, up to Crianlarich, to Oban where we stopped at Lagganbeg B&B for the night, had a lovely meal at the Rowan Tree Restaurant. The following morning, we left for Ballachulish, Glencoe, Fort William, Ben Nevis, Spean Bridge, Kyle of Lochailsh, over the new Skye Road Bridge to the Isle of Skye where we found another nice B&B (Coolin View) in Portree. Had a great evening at a "Caeleigh", in the Royal Hotel Pub that night. Headed home to Edinburgh from Skye back through Blair Athol, Pitlochry, Perth, Glenrothes and Leven then over the Forth Road Bridge and on to Barnton where Betty and Ernie live. Finished that day with fish/white pudding/ and chips/wine and beer.

The rest of the trip was dealing with all kinds of business issues and "dinners" with good friends including Betty and Ernie, George and Jessie Lee, Dave and Maureen Bold, Moira and John Roy in Linlithgow that turned into a marathon/overnighter but a great time with "big heads" in the morning.

We did manage to go see the show "Riverdance" at the Playhouse, did lots of shopping in the Royal Mile and I also managed to attend several Scottish Football matches on the weekends. By now my knee was a constant pain but the "end was in sight". On Wednesday March 12th, in foggy cool weather we left Turnhouse Airport for Amsterdam where we would pick up the connecting flight to Toronto.

The Robert Q Airport bus was waiting for us and off we went heading back to Sarnia kind of weary but having had a memorable trip in Scotland and England. We were in bed at 10pm Canada Time but 3 am UK time not likely to move for at least 12 hours, isn't travelling wonderful.

Morning came fast and before you knew it, we were unpacking and getting reorganized, made several phone calls, reviewed mail/

bills and called the hospital about Pre-Admission procedures for March 24 Operation, doesn't take long to lose the "glow" of the vacation. We had a wonderful call from Elaine in Australia she was having a great time.

On Saturday our gang celebrated Dick Fletchers 60th Birthday at May and Bill Riddell's house what a wonderful night we had, Ron Phillips came dressed as a "Hooker" and was all over Dick for most of the night much to Dicks delight he laughed and giggled most of the night, a good time was had by all.

March 17th, St Patrick's Day for some reason I had a "wonderful feeling of peace and content" this day but couldn't understand why, had a pint at the Brittany Arms with brother Alan took care of some tax issues had a long walk in the park with Doreen and felt good. Doreen had ordered a Tiffany Marble sink for upstairs bathroom, and I went to donate blood then did 4 hours VON stuff with my client Jim Ward a nice old English Chap.

Soon it was March 23rd, walked to Point Edward in the snow and had coffee with Doreen, Helen and Alan we all were trying to avoid talking about tomorrow's operation, guess I was a wee bit nervous but I do not know why, this Operation was going to fix the knee problem, wasn't it? No food or drink now for 24 hrs.

Monday March 24th, be at St Joseph's hospital for 6:00am, at 8:00am they started the IV and shortly afterwards they gave me the anesthetic, goodbye world. Somewhere around noon I could hear my name being called Jim, Jim, Jim, I was in the recovery room after what they called a smooth morning. Dr. McKinlay came in and asked me how I was, I had an antibiotic drip, oxygen/morphine drip/vacuum on the wound and taking an anti-coagulant shot, I smiled and said "oh I am just fine" as he walked away. Doreen was right there, and I was glad. We watched the Oscars on TV that night, would you believe it?

Tuesday March 25th, reasonable sleep, lots of pain woke at sam, the outside of the right knee was very painful, more morphine. Would you believe this? At 11am the physiotherapist showed up to ask me to get up on a chair and try to move the leg, I felt sick to the stomach. Lots of pain, need more morphine then they brought food "had to be a joke!". Jake came to visit me with Doreen, but I was feeling really bad it had been a long day. The following morning the 26th, after a very long night in excruciating pain, I developed a rash, but all my other signs were positive. Little did I know that in the maternity ward around 9:30am this very day Paula was being induced, around 10:30am I am now on a knee machine that moves your knee back and forth to get it moving, then they get me a "walker" and I am asked to try walking.

At 12:00 noon on March 26th, 1996, Kelly Lynn Currie, our first granddaughter at 8lbs 3ozs was born while I was attempting to walk in the hospital hallway with my new right knee, what a moment. The rest of the day was just a blur because Doreen had told me about the birth an hour later around 1pm and that the baby had been born with 2 club feet which was devastating to all of us as you can imagine. Doreen was a bit disappointed shortly after the birth, Diane was now in with Paula and the baby when an intern came out to the waiting room and said, "ok Grandpa you can go in now". Paul immediately stepped forward as you would expect him to do but when Doreen stepped forward, she was told by the intern "you will have to wait a bit, only two visitors at a time".

One of the first questions we had asked when Jake was born was about the club feet issue as it was a major concern with him being the first Grandchild but for some reason with Kelly our second Grandchild, we had made a really bad assumption that all would be well and totally stunned when we got the news.

Later in the day I was still struggling with the news about Kelly/ the morphine/the pain and discomfort. Doreen/ Jeff/ Dr. Uppal/ Dr. McKinlay/ Jimmy Mac/ Alan and Helen/ Alex and Jessie/Dick Fletcher all made multiple visits/Aileen phoned later in the day while I was on the knee machine.

That night I had a terrible nightmare and even had heart palpitations, so the nurse gave me Tylenol 3 Codeine to try and help me get back to sleep. This was one of the longest nights of my life. The following morning after another uncomfortable night they put me on the knee machine for another 3 hours, so I had 2 Tylenol 3 with codeine, toast and fried egg for breakfast. Had a visit from my Dr. Duncan McKinlay and then Dr. Southcote who had been called in regarding Kelly's Club Feet situation understood my personal concerns about Club Feet, and he said you need to "go see the baby".

The nurses got me in a wheelchair with all the necessary tubes and connecting fluids and with Doreen beside me we went to the Maternity Ward.

March 27th, 1997, Years of positive confidence in dealing with what life had to offer evaporated in a few minutes as I sat in a wheelchair with tubes supplying vital fluids to my recovering body from a full knee joint replacement while holding my first granddaughter Kelly in my arms. The tears began to flow with a mixture of absolute joy and despair as my hands caressed her tiny malformed feet and my own discomfort was quickly forgotten as I thought of what the coming weeks, months and possibly years would bring to this beautiful child and her parents.

It seemed like just yesterday when our first Grandchild (Jake) was born and the first question on all of our minds was "are his feet ok", "yes" replied the Doctor and we were overcome with relief. Somehow with Kelly this question hadn't seemed necessary, genetics maybe after all hadn't been a real concern "we thought", this was not to be the case as we discovered some time later.

After the initial outburst of emotion for some reason I felt peaceful and calm as I looked into her puffy little eyes, and she cried for her Mum. The nurses wheeled me back down the hospital corridor to the elevator still with some tears in my eyes where I would return to the recovery room floor with my own thoughts of "**WHERE THIS ALL STARTED ALMOST 60 YEARS AGO**".

ADDENDUM 1

OCTOBER 29, 1998

"Clubfoot Report: Prepared by Elaine Currie at the Chaminade University of Honolulu

When a child is born with "clubfeet," what is the effect on the child's family and on the child's development in the first two years of life?

In September of 1992, my brother and his wife, Paula, were blessed with a very healthy, happy (cranky at times) baby boy. Jake Aaron went through all the normal stages of development that a healthy baby experiences, bringing to his parents vast amounts of joy as well as the regular minor frustrations (the odd temper tantrum and fussy eating).

I watched in wonder as Jake's body grew strong and fast, changing in some small or large way almost every week I saw him. He was walking before he turned one; by the time he was two he was running around the backyard with a soccer ball, shuffling along on ice in tiny hockey skates, making fabulous attempts at climbing trees and basically using his body and limbs in every possible way. His parents, grandparents, uncles and aunts (including me) were filled with that miraculous delight that accompanies the excitement of a human being of our own blood beginning his life journey in a healthy, happy manner.

In March of 1997, when Jake was 4 years old, his mom gave birth to a second child, this time a girl. How perfect to have one of each! She was gorgeous, with fluffy blond hair, mesmerizing blue-blue eyes and the cutest tiny female facial features. Her smile lit up the nurse's station and her attitude were, "The world is awesome, and I am excited to be here!"

In the first few delighted weeks of her life, and for many months before the beginning of her treatments, Kelly Currie was totally oblivious to the fact that she had been born with a deformity which would challenge her physical and psychological strength in ways undeformed babies would never have to endure. She had been born with Talipes (clubfoot) in both feet.

The definition of this condition according to Mosby's Medical, Nursing and Allied Health Dictionary (1994) is as follows:

A congenital deformity of the foot, sometimes resulting from intrauterine constriction and characterized by unilateral or bilateral deviation of the metatarsal bones of the forefoot.

In other words, one or both feet are turned inward and downward (Kelly's case) or outward and upward. In some cases, the extremely mild ones, the feet correct themselves after birth before walking begins. In more severe cases, such as Kelly's, surgery, casts and splints are required, without which the child would find it extremely difficult, if not impossible, to walk. Since the ankle is twisted in place, the foot can't move up or down as it normally would in walking. When both feet are affected, the child walks on the balls and sides and even on the tops of the feet instead of the soles. The entire leg is often unable to grow as it should. Kelly's doctor informed us that "clubfoot" is one of the most common of all birth defects, affecting 1 in 400 in the USA, and has been one of the major orthopedic problems in children since doctors began to specialize in that field more than 200 years ago.

As not only an observer of this sad situation, but also an emotionally involved family member, I was very upset for my brother's family and for Kelly, not only because of the special treatment and challenges she would be facing in the first years of her life, but also because of the long-term effects she might have to endure her entire life, such as scarred and strangelooking feet, underdeveloped calves and unproportioned legs in general.

On top of that, being a very athletic family, we worried about what limitations in physical activity would result from this. All we really knew at this point was that treatment depended on the extent and rigidity of the deformation. We knew Kelly's feet were a severe case and that casts, surgery and braces were going to be part of her early years. But how long would she have to be under special care? There was no concrete, definite time period or result we could count on except that she should be able to walk eventually. but how normally? And when? Would she be able to run, jump, climb and play like other kids? We were in a frustrated fog for now.

My parents, Kelly's grandparents, were obviously upset, but my father in particular felt really bad. He himself had been born with one clubfoot and I think he wondered if perhaps there was some connection. As it turns out, according to Kelly's doctor, most cases are acquired during development in the uterus and not through heredity (congenital).

However, during a quick bout of research I did, I found some information in a periodical entitled PEDIATRICS FOR PARENTS

(November 1994) which claimed that "clubfoot" can be caused by a combination of heredity and external factors (e.g., teratogens such as drugs, disease, infection etc.).

I also discovered a study in MCLEANS (Feb 2, 1998) that had been done by some specialists in British Columbia which revealed that amniocentesis performed before the 15th week of pregnancy caused clubfoot in 29 of 4374 babies (tests were given earlier, as older women sought reassurance about their pregnancies). Paula had not gone through early amniocentesis, so that was ruled out in Kelly's case.

Neither the doctor's comments nor my research seemed to resolve my father's angst as he knew well the devastating limitations his childhood had suffered because of his clubfoot. These included being stuck in the hospital for long periods of time; painful physical therapy his mother had to put him through daily, and restricting, uncomfortable braces he had to wear until he was 12 years old. He couldn't even take "normal" steps to walk or run until he was 6 years old.

"So much has changed since then, Dad," we told him. We all knew the treatment would be more advanced today and secretly hoped it would not cause Kelly the suffering our father had endured. The leg of his clubfoot was underdeveloped shorter and skinnier than the other. His left foot was smaller, without an arch, much scarring on the ankle and a misaligned toe. Although he had risen above this difficulty to become a long-distance racing cyclist in Scotland, and by some definition, a star soccer player in Ontario, as well as a regular runner, the appearance of his leg, his limp and its effect on his hips certainly caused him grief.

As I observed the various reactions of my family members over the first few weeks of Kelly's life, I realized how amazing a perfectly healthy baby really is and felt deeply grateful that Jake was not facing any health limitations. I also recognized the strength our family had, especially Kelly's mom and dad. The two of them have a relationship that has blossomed over the years and just keeps getting better.

Not only are Jeff & Paula loving and supportive of each other and their children, but they have a unique and wonderful way of seeing the humorous side of life and keeping things light. Their house is full of laughter and kidding, as well as warmth and acceptance. Both Kelly and Jake definitely have an awesome home support system. This love, support and humor were crucial elements to survival in the challenging months which began the treatment to "fix" Kelly's feet.

In the interview that follows, Kelly's parents answer specific questions concerning the treatment of Kelly's feet and her development progress:

Q At what age did treatment start and what did it involve?

A Kelly was 2 weeks old when Dr. Southcott put her in her first bilateral foot casts, after he manipulated her feet. It was heart-wrenching to watch him twist her feet in ways which seemed horribly painful. Supposedly, she was not in pain, but my little girl was screaming bloody murder and at that point I felt like the doctor was a heartless torturer. He continued to manipulate her feet every 2 weeks, changing casts each time until she was 4 months old at which time, he referred us to another specialist in London who told us she would require surgery within 3 to 4 months, and we would have to go to Montreal (a 10-hour car ride, 14-20-hour train ride) to receive treatment from now on.

Q What happened next?

A On September 7th, we took Kelly for her first train ride all the way to Montreal. The specialist, Dr. Hamdy, checked her over and casted her. After that we had to return every 2 weeks for recasting until she was ready for surgery, which was supposed to be in December.

Q Didn't it happen in December?

A No, her surgery was rescheduled and cancelled 4 times over three months. One time there was a blizzard in Montreal, then Kelly had a bad cold, then she had a yeast infection 2 times. We wondered if it would ever happen, but it finally did when she was almost one year old on March 4th. She actually went through two 4-hour operations to insert metal rods in her feet to straighten them. These stayed in and she had cast again for another 6 weeks. She then had 2 more operations to remove the rods and again wore casts for another 6 weeks.

Q How did Kelly handle this?

A All I can say is she is a real trooper! She's too determined to let anything get her down and despite yeast infections, colds, painful twisting of her feet, vast amounts of drugs and a severe and persistent case of eczema under her casts, she always had a smile and giggle for us. There was one night that really me concerned, after her first operation. As I held her in my arms, I felt her reacting strangely to the morphine, acting like a junkie coming through withdrawal. Her eyes were rolling around, her arms and legs were flapping around uncontrollably. I was afraid I wouldn't be able to hold her. For 2 hours she went through hell. By midnight, she was totally exhausted and passed out. I will never forget that night.

Q What was the next step after surgery?

A We continued our trips to Montreal for cast changes until May 14th when she got her first set of braces. These will have to be adjusted as she grows, and her feet and legs become stronger and more agile.

Q Were your medical expenses covered by a health plan?

A A lot of the expenses for casting and doctor visits were covered, but when we found out how much travelling we were going to be doing to get Kelly to and from her specialists, we began to get concerned. As it turned out, the Shriners paid us a visit and decided to "sponsor" Kelly at their Montreal Shriner's Hospital. They would pay for her train tickets plus one adult train ticket each time she had to go. They would also cover hotel expenses and meals for our many overnighters. This turned out to be a real lifesaver. Even though we would never make up for all the lost wages for workdays that we needed to take off to take Kelly for her treatment, we felt pretty lucky.

EPILOGUE

Kelly has progressed amazingly well with her braces and took her first steps with the aid of an adult hand on June 1st, 1998. On September 14th, she started walking on her own with at least as much energy and enthusiasm as her brother Jake had at that age. What she accomplished in a year and a half took my father 6 years to accomplish, with only one affected foot. Her future looks optimistic according to the "experts." She will walk, run, climb and do whatever she wants just like other kids do. The only differences will be reg-ular progress checks (if the feet begin to move back inwards, she will need minor corrective treatment again), her calves and feet will be slightly smaller in proportion to her upper leg, and her feet will have some extra skin folds and mild scarring.

It is evident that the condition of "clubfoot" (one or both) can have an emotionally and financially draining effect on the family of a clubfoot baby, and as well slow down the physical movement of the child in the first couple of years of life. Unfortunately for Kelly, once she begins to gain a sense of self-consciousness, the slightly different appearance of her feet and legs may affect her self-esteem and confidence. However, with the love and support she has at home, her feelings of self-worth should be very healthy, and, if her "trooper" trait and positive attitude continue, she will lead a happy, healthy and successful life.

ADDENDUM 2

Written in appreciation to
The Sarnia Lambton Shriners Program, June 2003
KELLY LYNN CURRIE

Born:
St Joseph's Hospital, Sarnia March 26th, 1997.
Brother:
Jake Aaron, born September 9th, 1992.
Parents:
Paula & Jeff Currie.
Grandparents:
Paul & Diane Ziller, Jim & Doreen Currie.

Doctor Blunt approached us shortly after delivery to inform us that our daughter had club feet, she told us that 1 out of 750 babies are born with club feet, usually just one foot. She also said that this type of deformity could be corrected by surgery and/or casting.

Doctors are not sure why children are born with club feet. Some feel it is genetic, others believe it happens in the womb where the foot or feet get stuck in one spot and can't grow properly, Kelly's Grandpa Currie was born with one club foot.

A Doctor in Sarnia put casts on her feet every two weeks beginning when she was only a week old. Her feet were manipulated before each set of casts were applied above her knee. After 3 months the Doctor in Sarnia had done as much as he could and sent us to London to see a Doctor there.

The Doctor in London told us Kelly would probably need surgery to correct her feet, but we were not entirely comfortable with this Doctor and felt uneasy about what we should do. Hugh McDougal of the Lambton Shriners knew both sets of Kelly's Grandparents and another mutual friend Bob Gabriel, during a conversation with them it was mentioned that the Shriner's Organization takes care of children with these types of Medical/Physical problems. Al Jaques and George Dunsworth also of the Lambton Shriner's came to our house in June and we had no idea what they could do for Kelly. They assured us that wearing funny hats and driving miniature cars in the parades was only part of their duties as Shriner's. They informed us that there was a Hospital in Montreal that specialized in helping children with problems like Kelly's. They also said if Kelly was accepted as a Shriner's Kid, her medical expenses, travelling, accommodation and food would all be paid for. We could hardly believe what these men were telling us, but we agreed to go through the application process.

We received a call from the Montreal Shriner's Hospital in July. They asked us to come to Montreal in September so they could assess Kelly's case. We called Al Jaques who is the Committee Chairman for Children's Welfare and proceeded to arrange our first of many trips to Montreal. We boarded the early morning train out of Sarnia on September 7 and arrived in Montreal around supper time. We were picked up by Taxi and we were taken to a beautiful place called "Le Riche Bourg Hotel" near the Forum. All of this was arranged by the Shriner's organization, relieving us of the stress involved with Travelling.

On September 8 we took Kelly to the Hospital by Taxi. The Hospital looked like a Spanish Villa built on the side of a hill, it was beautiful, and we had never seen a hospital quite like this one. Walking in the front door, the lobby was filled with large stuffed animals and children's paintings. The building was designed for handicapped children, ramps, low toilets, sinks etc. We were taken to see Dr. Hamby who explained to us that Kelly's feet would require surgery but that he preferred to wait until she was one year old. Dr. Hamby applied new casts to Kelly's legs and asked us to return for new ones in 2 weeks. Over the next 8 months we travelled to the Shriner's Hospital in Montreal 23 times. Dr. Hamby performed the surgery on each foot separately during the Month of March 1998.

She was kept in casts right up to the surgeries and then for 6 weeks afterwards. The Shriner's fitted Kelly with custom-made braces that she wore for the next 6 months.

Kelly took her first steps with the braces on when she was one and a half years old. She is now 6 years old and runs, jumps and plays the same way any other 6-year-old would. Kelly will require yearly visits to the Shriner's Hospital in Montreal just to make sure her feet are growing properly. The Shriner's will take care of Kelly's medical needs until her bones stop growing.

Since the day we met Al Jaques and George Dunsworth of the Lambton Shrine Club, we have not paid one cent for Kelly's medical expenses, travelling or food. We cannot imagine what this has all cost, but more than that, we cannot imagine having the quality-of-care Kelly has been given. The Doctors, Nurses and Staff of the Montreal Shriner's Hospital come from all over the World.

The Shriner's provided the children and their Families a Christmas party, complete with clowns blowing balloons and twisting them into animals or hats for all the kids, along with magic tricks. Santa then came in to deliver to the kids and their Families some early Christmas surprises. Each year we are also treated to attend the Annual Shrine Circus, which is enjoyable to all.

We will always be grateful to the Lambton Shrine Club, Allan Jaques and the Montreal Shriner's Hospital for what they have done and continue to do for "KELLY".

PAULA, JEFF, and JAKE (2003)

KELLY LYNN CURRIE

Kelly Lynne Currie age 17 years old visiting #1 Upper Bow in Edinburgh, Scotland where I lived as a wee boy about 67 years ago. Last spring Kelly travelled for a month throughout the UK visiting several Universities including Edinburgh University with an educational group called "Global Journeys".

Kelly currently attends St Clair Secondary School in Sarnia Ontario where she maintains a 96% Average for all subjects and placed first in Grade 11 winning several awards and is looking forward to going to University somewhere in Ontario in 2015.

ABOUT JIM CURRIE

Jim Currie was born in Bo'ness a small town just west of Edinburgh, Scotland. He has been married to the love of his life Doreen for over fifty-five years. Together, they have three children and four grandchildren. Now retired to Sarnia, Ontario, Canada, they enjoy walking, exercising, reading, listening to music and visiting with friends.

www.ingramcontent.com/pod-product-compliance
Lightning Source LLC
Chambersburg PA
CBHW051004140626
46546CB00016B/290

* 9 7 8 1 9 6 4 1 0 0 6 9 2 *